MICHIGAN COPPER AND BOSTON DOLLARS

STUDIES IN ECONOMIC HISTORY

PUBLISHED IN COÖPERATION WITH THE COMMITTEE
ON RESEARCH IN ECONOMIC HISTORY

WILLIAM B. GATES, JR.

Michigan Copper
and Boston Dollars

AN ECONOMIC HISTORY OF THE MICHIGAN
COPPER MINING INDUSTRY

HARVARD UNIVERSITY PRESS
CAMBRIDGE, MASSACHUSETTS
· 1951 ·

COPYRIGHT, 1951
BY THE PRESIDENT AND FELLOWS OF HARVARD COLLEGE

DISTRIBUTED IN GREAT BRITAIN BY
GEOFFREY CUMBERLEGE
OXFORD UNIVERSITY PRESS
LONDON

PRINTED IN THE UNITED STATES OF AMERICA

TO MARGARET D. GATES

WITHOUT WHOSE COURAGE AND DEVOTION THIS BOOK — AND THE LONG YEARS OF INTELLECTUAL APPRENTICESHIP OUT OF WHICH IT GREW — MIGHT NOT HAVE BEEN POSSIBLE.

Preface

During the century following 1845 copper evolved from a metal of secondary importance — mainly useful for household utensils, sheathing material for ships, some lines of the engineering trade, and the fine arts — to become a requisite of the expanding electrical industries and a basic material of modern warfare. World production of new copper rose from an annual total of 50,000 short tons in the 1840's to more than 500,000 around the turn of the century when the electrical industries began to hit their stride, and finally to over 3,000,000 short tons per annum during World War II.

For the last years of the nineteenth century and almost three decades of the twentieth (1894–1926), United States mines contributed more than 50 per cent of the world total, and even during recent years domestic properties have produced a third of the new copper mined. The Michigan deposits were the first major United States field to be developed and, until the railroads were extended to the Montana and Arizona fields around 1882, consistently produced three-quarters or more of United States output. As late as 1907 one-quarter of domestic copper came from the Michigan lodes, and in spite of a gradual decline to virtual insignificance following World War I, the industry can boast of having produced 14.6 per cent of all copper mined in the United States since 1845, a total of some 9.6 billion pounds, valued at $1.5 billion. At the peak of the district's development, around 1907, the companies furnished employment for more than 21,000 workers and provided the economic core for a community of 95,000 people. That same year the stocks of the six significant producers were valued at $185 million in the market. During the whole century of production, shareholders in the two-dozen-odd Michigan copper mining companies which did better than break even received $350 million in dividends.

Not only has the history of the industry significance for its own sake; it may also prove useful in understanding developments which are likely to take place in the evolution of other United States extractive industries. The Michigan copper district was one of the first major domestic non-ferrous metal mining fields to be opened up, and its history provides a full century of development for study, including an almost complete cycle of growth and decline. The problems of each extractive industry will certainly differ in accordance with peculiar conditions of time, locale, and other special circumstance, but it seems probable that many will show a similar pattern of growth and decline, each phase of which may present a number of parallel problems. A period of establishment may be expected in which risks are very great, profits are small — or nonexistent — for all but a few concerns, and the flow of capital into the industry is heavy and is very largely lost to the immediate investor. The next period will be one of substantial growth, both in scale of enterprise and number of successful units, and again the flow of capital is likely to be toward the industry, but this time primarily in the form of reinvestment of earnings, rather than new market flotations. Growth is followed by maturity, a period when new investment opportunities are unpromising and output remains fairly stable. An increasing interest in consolidation schemes may be expected, and earnings are likely to be exceptionally high and to be paid out as made. Finally, decline of the industry brings with it inability to earn enough to meet depletion and even depreciation charges,[1] and an effort to rescue as much sunk capital as possible, often through planned shifts by the companies into other stages of the metals industry.

The history of Michigan copper mining is rich in more general laboratory materials. It has its monopoly elements, constantly reappearing in one form or another. It forcefully underlines the importance of technological change in economic

---

[1] Since these charges are expenses, but not expenditures, failure to cover them does not necessarily indicate financial stringency; it does indicate an unfavorable change in total asset values.

evolution; presents three sets of war control problems; and provides an interesting example of the operation of the free enterprise profit incentive system in opening up difficult natural resources. Finally, it includes a case study of the critical problem of labor reallocation in a declining industrial area, and poses the problem of the effects of benevolent paternalism upon industrial relations and the general pattern of life in a one-industry community.

The author is a firm believer that all too little economics has been used in approaching problems in economic history. The rewards from such application of theoretical tools are likely to take the form of much clearer insights into economic development and a much more meaningful over-all historical picture. This is a limited objective, and the real revolution in the analysis of economic history, and even in economics as a whole, will probably be wrought by that much abused — often justifiably so — advance guard of social scientists who are attempting to develop methods of analyzing the dynamics of institutional change. It is the first of these methodological objectives which has been set as a goal in this study. The economic techniques used are by no means complex, but the author has attempted to write an economic history with the idea constantly in mind that he is, first of all, an economist.

So many people have contributed time and ideas to this study that it is all but impossible to make adequate thanks in a preface. The study began when the author ran across a splendid book entitled *Boom Copper* by Angus Murdoch and later had occasion to talk with him and absorb some of his feeling for the Copper Country. At the University of Chicago, where most of the work was done, I am deeply indebted to Professors Chester Wright, Gregg Lewis, Melvin de Chazeau, and Frank Knight — all of whom spent long hours going over early drafts of the manuscript and taking me to task on its deficiencies.

My greatest debt, perhaps, is to my many friends in the Copper Country who unstintingly made available to me their knowledge of the locality, the historical documents they had collected, and, above all, their understanding of technological aspects of the industry. Among those who gave freely of their time are Professor James Fisher of the Mining College, John W. Rice of the *Mining Gazette*, Benjamin D. Noetzel, long associated with the Isle Royale and other Lake copper companies, and Gene Saari, local representative of the Mine Workers Union. Without the wholehearted coöperation of President Endicott R. Lovell and numerous officers of the Calumet and Hecla Consolidated Copper Company (including J. H. Elliott, C. H. Benedict, A. E. Petermann, and Ocha Potter), the research for the study would not have been possible. The company saw to it that the author spent several days going through the Copper Country works, did special statistical studies at his request, made available to him its magnificent files at the Boston office, provided photographs from its collection, and had an early draft of the manuscript read and criticized by a number of company officers.

I am particularly grateful to Professors Arthur H. Cole and Edward C. Kirkland who read the manuscript, made suggestions for its improvement, and were its sponsors for publication by the Committee on Research in Economic History. Without the constant encouragement and guidance of Professor Cole, completion of the last draft might have been delayed for years.

Finally, my sincere thanks are due to Helene P. Gans, who read the manuscript for matters of style and typed one of the early drafts, and to my wife, Nancy Gans Gates, who constantly encouraged me in this endeavor and somehow remained patient when I gave way to temperament at the more difficult stages.

W. B. G., Jr.

Williamstown, Massachusetts
March 1, 1950

CONTENTS

LIST OF TABLES   xiii

LIST OF ILLUSTRATIONS   xiv

I OPENING THE MICHIGAN LODES, 1845–1866   1
  Discovery and Exploration · The Challenge and the Accomplishment · The Copper Cake beneath the Icing · Roads and Canals or Bust · An Early Technological Revolution · Financial and Managerial Organization and Controls

II MICHIGAN DOMINATES THE UNITED STATES MARKET, 1867–1884   39
  The Postwar Depression, 1867–1871 · The Rise of Calumet and Hecla · The Protective Tariff and the Pooling Arrangements · Revival of the Industry, 1873–1884

III THE STRUGGLE FOR DOMESTIC AND WORLD LEADERSHIP, 1885–1904   64
  Twenty Years of Continued Vitality · Consolidation and Integration · Attempts at Market Control and the Price Boom at the Turn of the Century · The Competitive Position of the Michigan Industry at the Turn of the Century

IV LABOR AND THE COMMUNITY TO 1904   93
  A Frontier Mining Community · A Settled Mining Community and Benevolent Paternalism

V THE INDUSTRY AND MATURITY, 1905–1918   116
  The Pattern of Maturity · The Battle to Hold Costs Down · The Labor Shortage Problem and the Strike of 1913–1914 · War Controls — the Allocation Problem — and the Question of Profiteering

CONTENTS

VI MICHIGAN COPPER MINING IN DECLINE, 1919–1938   143
    The Pattern of Decline · Decline of Michigan Copper Mining in a Period of General Business Prosperity, 1919–1929 · Decline of Michigan Copper Mining in a Period of General Business Depression, 1930–1938 · The Impact of the Decline upon the Community

VII WORLD WAR II AND THE FUTURE   170
    Michigan Copper Mining on the Eve of United States Entry into the War · War Controls and the United States Copper Mining Industry · Operations of the Michigan Industry during the War Years · The Michigan Copper Companies Face the Future · The Michigan Copper District Faces the Future

EPILOGUE   188

APPENDIX   193

NOTES   235

BIBLIOGRAPHY   273

GLOSSARY OF MINING TERMS   284

INDEX   287

TABLES

1. UNITED STATES FOREIGN TRADE IN UNMANUFACTURED COPPER, 1870–1882 — 47
2. MONTHLY MICHIGAN WAGES FOR COPPER MINERS COMPARED WITH WAGES FOR IRON MINERS IN THE EAST, 1845–1866 — 101
3. MONTHLY MICHIGAN WAGES FOR COPPER MINERS COMPARED WITH WAGES FOR IRON MINERS IN THE EAST, 1867–1904 — 108
4. MICHIGAN COSTS COMPARED WITH THOSE OF THE REST OF THE DOMESTIC INDUSTRY, 1909–1918 — 121
5. MICHIGAN COSTS COMPARED WITH THOSE OF THE REST OF THE DOMESTIC INDUSTRY, 1928–1930 — 154
6. WORLD, UNITED STATES, AND MICHIGAN OUTPUT OF NEW COPPER, 1845–1946 — 197
7. UNITED STATES FOREIGN TRADE IN AND CONSUMPTION OF NEW COPPER, 1916–1946 — 202
8. MICHIGAN OUTPUT OF COPPER AND VALUE OF OUTPUT, 1845–1946 — 203
9. MICHIGAN COPPER MINING COMPANIES CLASSIFIED BY SIZE OF ANNUAL OUTPUT, 1845–1945 — 207
10. MICHIGAN COPPER MINING COMPANY EMPLOYMENT, 1850–1946 — 208
11. POUNDS OF COPPER PRODUCED ANNUALLY PER MICHIGAN COPPER MINING COMPANY EMPLOYEE, 1850–1946 — 212
12. DIVIDEND PAYMENTS — ALL MICHIGAN COPPER MINING COMPANIES, 1845–1946 — 215
13. ANNUAL HIGH-LOW STOCK QUOTATIONS OF SEVEN MICHIGAN COPPER MINING COMPANIES, 1848–1946 — 223
14. COPPER COUNTRY POPULATION DATA, 1850–1940 — 228
15. OUTPUT OF THE CALUMET AND HECLA COPPER MINING COMPANY, AND PERCENTAGE OF MICHIGAN OUTPUT, 1867–1946 — 230
16. FREIGHT RATES FOR WATER TRANSPORTATION OF COAL AND COPPER BETWEEN LAKE SUPERIOR AND LOWER LAKE PORTS, 1887–1940 — 231
17. EQUALIZED ASSESSED VALUATION — ALL PERSONAL AND REAL PROPERTY OF HOUGHTON COUNTY, 1900–1946 — 232

ILLUSTRATIONS

Map of the Michigan Copper Country   2
Copper Mining in Michigan during the 1850's   *Following page*   16
Copper Mining in Michigan about 1915   *Following page*   48

CHARTS

General Wages at Calumet, Michigan, Compared with Those at Detroit, 1908–1919   137
Wage Trend at Calumet Compared with U.S. Wholesale Price Trend, 1908–1919   137
Michigan Production and Percentage Michigan of U.S. Total Production, 1845–1946   195
Michigan Copper Mining Company Dividend Payments Compared with Average Annual Copper Prices   195
Population of the Michigan Copper District Compared with Mining Company Employment, 1860–1946   196
Production of Copper per Man-Year of Labor Employed in the Michigan Copper Mining Industry, 1850–1946   196
United States Copper Production, Consumption, Net Imports and Exports, 1845–1880   201
United States Copper Production, Consumption, Net Imports and Exports, 1880–1933   201

MICHIGAN COPPER AND BOSTON DOLLARS

CHAPTER I

Opening the Michigan Lodes, 1845-1866

Were it not for the chance of some great prizes, all this necessary work of exploration would not have been undertaken. Under such conditions a high return on the lucky venture does not constitute a true surplus. Nor is it easy to say whether, on the whole, the gains in successful mining ventures suffice to offset the losses in the unsuccessful. Prizes often have an undue effect on the imagination. The unfailing attraction of a lottery (in which it is obvious that the speculators as a body must lose) proves that where there is a chance of great gain from a lucky stake, men will often pay for the chance more than its actuarial value.[1]

— *Frank William Taussig*

The Michigan Copper Country is located on Keweenaw Peninsula which reaches out like an index finger from the southern shore line of Lake Superior. As shown by the map on page 2 all of the known copper deposits lie along a mineral range which runs a hundred miles through what today are the Upper Peninsula counties of Ontonagon, Houghton, and Keweenaw.

DISCOVERY AND EXPLORATION

Early exploration. The deposits were known to the Indians at the time the French began to explore the Lake Superior region and had been worked by a forgotten race of miners long before Columbus discovered America.[2] The Indian tales were passed along with embellishments by the early French explorers and missionaries, but it was not until 1771 that an Englishman, Alexander Henry, organized the first mining expedition of modern times to reach the Copper Country. The enterprise failed after a long winter spent in the southern section of the Peninsula, and interest in the district lapsed until 1800 when the United States Congress directed the President to appoint an agent to investigate the copper deposits of Lake Superior. No action was taken under the bill, and the next authentic report of the existence of copper on the shores of the lake came from Henry R. Schoolcraft in 1820, who found the indications so promising that he suggested the government should work the deposits. Twenty years more elapsed before scientific exploration was undertaken by Douglass Houghton, first geologist of the newly admitted state of Michigan.

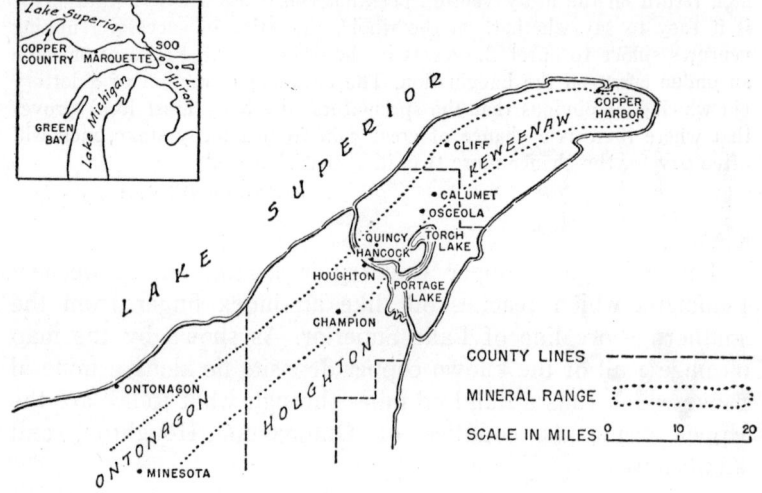

Fig. 1. Michigan Copper Country

The surveys and land laws. In 1840 Houghton began a careful examination of the district and by late 1841 had issued two reports to the State Legislature in which he gave a cautious but encouraging appraisal of copper mining potentialities of the Peninsula. Congress showed sufficient interest in 1841 to appropriate funds for the purchase of the lands from the Indians, and in the summer of 1842 a treaty was negotiated with the Chippewas by which they ceded some 25,000 square miles of territory to the Federal government.[3] Shortly thereafter an agreement was concluded with Houghton to take charge of a linear survey for the United States in addition to the topographical and geographical survey upon which he was already engaged for the state of Michigan.[4] Work on the surveys went forward rapidly, and by 1843, when the first mining permit was issued, locations and boundaries could be designated in something resembling an orderly fashion.

By that year interest in the district had become intense, particularly in the East, and the federal government was under pressure to throw the area open and designate rules under which the deposits might be worked. Following the precedent set in leasing early western lead lands,[5] permits were issued by the War Department — first for nine square miles, and, later, in March, 1845, reduced to one square mile. After a location had been made the permit holder was to apply to Washington for a lease and forward surety bonds amounting to $20,000.[6] The lessee was "allowed one year for exploration, and three more years to mine, with the privilege of two renewals of three years each, making the whole term ten years."[7] He was required to send in returns to the Mineral Agency giving the amount of copper raised and to pay the government 6 per cent royalties for the first three-year mining period and 10 per cent thereafter.

The first major United States mining boom. A few hardy souls came overland into the district from the Wisconsin lead lands as early as the summer of 1843, but it was not until the spring of 1844 that the real boom began. Several schooners owned by the fur companies were operating on Superior at that time, and during the following two years, a half dozen more, including the propeller *Independence* and the sidewheeler *Julia Palmer*, were hauled over the portage at Sault Ste. Marie to carry explorers, miners, speculators, and their supplies up to Keweenaw, and small quantities of copper and hundreds of disillusioned failures back.

Twenty to twenty-five days were required to send mineral from the mines to Buffalo and thence to Boston — the cost running from $18 to $20 per long ton.[8] (At about this same period the rate on a long ton of ore from Chile to Boston was

$15; from Cuba to Boston, $6.) [9] Cargoes had to be hauled by human or animal labor almost a mile across the portage at the Soo and then reshipped on the other side. Even worse, navigation was impossible for at least five months of the year as a result of winter storms and ice formations along the shore of Lake Superior, and was apt to be risky even during the summer season. Although there were a number of harbors at the Peninsula, most were blocked by sand bars to all but the smallest vessels, and passengers and supplies often had to be transferred to lighters before shore could be reached. Finally, the phrase bandied about among returning prospectors of "a howling wilderness" was perhaps a harsh generalization but was, nonetheless, a fitting description for some of the conditions encountered once the Copper Country had been reached. The Peninsula was heavily wooded, swampy in many places, and cut off by land from the outside world by over 200 miles of virtually uninhabited wilderness. Only experienced woodsmen or those fortunate enough to have at their command a sleigh and dog team could reach civilization once the snows began in November.

During the first two years of prospecting and mineral land speculation, there was little that could be dignified by the term "mining." Hundreds of men tramped the wilderness, each equipped with a pick and a few pounds of gunpowder, and with one eye on speculation in land permits where the real money lay. What little copper they found was lying on the surface or easily blown loose from outcropping rocks. But even in these early days there were a few beginnings at real mining, and by 1847 the main outlines of prevailing technology are discernible.

In general discarded methods drawn from the earlier history of other mining fields of the world, particularly Cornwall, were employed. Drilling was by hand, one man holding the drill and one or two others driving it into the rock with sledges. Blasting was done with ordinary gunpowder, and both processes required much skill to get effective results. As the shaft went down into the vein, rock and copper masses were hauled to the surface in an iron bucket, known as a "kibble," which was attached to a heavy chain and powered by men at a windlass or by one or more horses at a whim. The whim was a seventeenth-century Cornish invention, used for both hoisting and pumping, which had been very largely replaced in England by steam power.[10] Copper rock was transported underground to the shafts by wheelbarrows rolled along boards, in contrast with the carts pushed along wooden or iron rails which had been adopted in older fields of the world. Finally, Michigan miners, trammers, and laborers climbed in and out of the shafts by ladders, whereas their Cornish counterparts were already beginning to use man-engines as early as 1841.[11]

The main items of surface equipment usually consisted of a small farm, a blacksmith shop, a carpenter shop or small sawmill, a log bunkhouse or two, a storehouse, a rockhouse, and sometimes a stamp mill. The early prospectors searched for lodes made up of copper masses, almost pure chunks of metal, often weighing ten tons or more, which were laboriously cut up underground and usually shipped directly to the smelter. Barrelwork, copper in very small masses which was detached from its rock matrix by hammering at the rockhouse, was also valued, in part because it did not require milling. But even in 1847 a certain amount of stamp work, or low copper content rock, was considered worth treating. During the summer and fall of 1845, a stamp mill operated by an overshot water wheel was working at Eagle River.[12] These early stamps were of Cornish design with wooden stems and iron heads weighing around 200 pounds, which dropped on the rock some twenty-odd times per minute. Copper mineral[13] was extracted from the resultant sands by hand treatment — the washing and jiggling on boards being about the same technique as that used in the early gold fields.[14] Mass copper was often roasted in kilns or small ovens in order to eliminate waste rock. The rock was piled upon a layer of crossed cordwood, allowed to burn for several days, and then cooled by water which helped to complete the splintering of the matrix.

But during this initial boom period serious mining attempts

were the exception rather than the rule. Not only was the district difficult to reach, even worse to open up, and conspicuously lacking in *easily discoverable*, rich lodes, but the leasing system soon proved extremely detrimental to successful establishment of the industry. By May, 1846, approximately 1,000 permits had been issued, and claims had been staked on every spot that showed signs of copper and even, for speculative purposes, on locations where the existence of the metal was known to be impossible. As one old-timer put it in speaking of permit speculators, "Some of their permits are located where they can't touch land up, nor down, nor sideways — and others ain't nowhere."[15] Having a permit turned into a lease was an expensive step, particularly with the surety bond requirement, and there is evidence that a good deal of politics entered into approval at Washington.[16] Finally, a ten-year maximum leasing period did not represent secure enough tenure to justify the heavy capital investment required to open up a mine. The net result was a wild speculative spree in the selling and buying of permits, very little serious mining, and a marked absence of royalties for the government.

In May, 1846, the President suspended further issue of permits, and by late 1847 the speculative bubble had burst, and the district was all but deserted. Congress came to the rescue in that year with an act which shifted custody of the mineral lands from the War to the Treasury Department and authorized outright sale of the full extent of a lease for $2.50 an acre and of a 40-acre lot within a lease for $5.00 an acre.[17] In September, 1850, the minimum price was reduced to $1.25,[18] and that same year a United States geological survey was completed which provided the first adequate geological maps of the district and enough basic scientific knowledge to permit rational exploration and development work.[19] The feverish prelude to the history of the Michigan copper mining district was over. An enormous amount of work remained to be done before the industry could be placed on a paying basis, but at least the initial task of developing favorable land laws and of providing basic geological knowledge had been accomplished by 1850.

OPENING THE MICHIGAN LODES

THE CHALLENGE AND THE ACCOMPLISHMENT

Domestic and world copper background. Before turning to a consideration of developments after the initial speculative boom, it will be useful to sketch the more general domestic and world copper picture of the period, particularly since some of these outside developments tended to make the task of opening the Michigan lodes an even more difficult one. In the early forties, just before mining began in Michigan, United States output of copper was running around 200,000 pounds per annum. Scattered, sporadic producers in the East — namely in Connecticut, Vermont, and Maryland — were the only domestic sources of the metal. Theirs was an insignificant production even in terms of the copper needs of that day, and the United States annually imported some 3,300 short tons of unmanufactured pigs and bars, plates and sheets, and various manufactures of brass and copper. Since raw copper could enter free of duty and manufactured articles were subject to high rates, over three-quarters, by value, of these imports took the form of pigs, bars, and old copper from the United Kingdom, Chile, and Peru, and plates and sheets from Britain for the domestic shipbuilding industry.[20]

The major sources of world copper of the period were Cornwall and Devon which had reached their peak by the 1840's and were entering a period of gradual decline.[21] Substantial increases elsewhere, notably from Chile, which was soon to surpass England as a copper producer, and from Spain, Australia, and the United States more than doubled world annual production in the two decades following 1845, and had begun, by the mid-fifties, to exert a downward pressure upon world copper prices.

During the forties and early fifties consumption of copper increased rapidly for sheathing wooden ships and for use in the expanding engineering trades, but shortly thereafter the red metal began to run into competitive difficulties in a number of old established lines. Application of steam power to the manufacture of iron and steel, as well as improvements in foundry technology, had cheapened iron to a point where it was offering serious competition in the pot and pan trade, brewery equipment, sugar refining machinery, and similar lines.[22] Engineering demands continued to increase, but by the early sixties, iron ships had begun to supplant wooden vessels which resulted, a few years later, in a reversal of the rising demand trend for copper sheathing.[23]

These developments not only tended to dampen the demand for copper but temporarily increased the amount of scrap flowing back into the supply stream. After 1855 there was a gradual weakening in the world price of the metal — the situation reaching crisis proportions in the London market by late 1865. The domestic economy was partially protected by the passage of a tariff in 1861 of two cents a pound on pigs, bars, and ingots, and of 5 per cent ad valorem on copper ores. Civil War needs for the metal also proved a boon, but gradually weakening world prices hung like a dark cloud over the newly established industry throughout much of its developmental period.

Internal problems involved in opening up the Michigan lodes. Internal problems were quite serious enough without the complication of a world copper glut. The Peninsula comprised approximately 3,000 square miles of territory within which were scattered some 400 lava flows and conglomerate and sandstone beds which the early prospectors might have discovered. And of these 400 possible locations, not more than a dozen or so were destined to yield copper in commercial quantities.[24] Careful exploration of the range had barely begun, and it was still not known that the mass deposits, which, in the forties, had been considered the only lodes worth mining, were geological freaks representing little more than icing of the main copper cake. The really significant deposits were of finely disseminated metal in amygdaloid and conglomerate rock,[25] running to great depth, and seldom outcropping in a fashion which would make proving of potentialities rapid or inexpensive. Past mining and metallurgical experience of the world had little to offer in the way of adequate methods for handling these new problems, and tremendous uncertainty, springing from technical and geological ignorance, was the greatest handicap to be overcome.

Only a little less important were transportation difficulties which were closely associated with those of obtaining an adequate labor supply. For many years the problem of getting copper out and supplies in at something less than prohibitive cost was too much for many of the infant companies and a severe handicap for all except the two or three with bonanza finds. Copper content of all shipments had to be high; in 1847 the trustees of the Copper Falls Company were advising their agent that his first consignment of some 7,000 pounds of mineral had not paid costs. As a result of high transportation charges, nothing yielding less than 40 per cent metal should be shipped.[26]

The industry approached these problems with a number of factors in its favor. Bad as the transportation problem was, the Great Lakes waterway represented an incalculably great asset, as did the fact that the copper discoveries were of pure metal, uncontaminated by sulphur or other undesirable elements which greatly complicated the refining of copper ore found in other parts of the world. In addition the corporate form of enterprise was available from the beginning, as well as stock exchanges in the East which tapped the meager store of speculative capital available in the young nation. Finally, there came to the district a steady stream of high-class labor from older mining and industrial centers of the world. The immigrants brought to Michigan not only their youth and skill, but a highly favorable incentive wage system and the best mining knowledge the world had to offer.[27]

The accomplishment by 1866. From a production standpoint the accomplishment in this first period of 22 years was an impressive one. By the early 1860's the new district was producing about 14 million pounds of copper per annum,[28] an amount equivalent to 60 per cent of domestic requirements, which had tripled since the early forties.[29] Actually, since 1855 the United States had become an exporter as well as an importer of refined copper. The Lake product was of particular value for military and artistic purposes and sold at a premium in foreign markets. From 1855 to 1861, 30 to 80 per cent of annual Michigan output was shipped abroad. The less expensive fire refined metal from Chilean and other foreign and domestic mines continued to be good enough for the requirements of most domestic manufacturers.

The most rapid increases in output were made between 1854, when production stood at about four million pounds, and 1861, when it topped 15 million. By the peak inflationary year of the Civil War, some $5.8 million worth of copper was flowing Eastward from the distant shores of Lake Superior where five thousand men worked for the mining companies in a community which now numbered 19 thousand.[30]

In marked contrast with the production record, the financial operations of the industry can hardly be called a success. From 1845 through 1865, 94 Lake copper companies made capital calls on their stockholders for a total of over $13.1 million. During the same period these companies paid in dividends $5.6 million.[31] It seems probable that there had been at least 20 other enterprises whose bitter history is not included in this statistical summary as well as hundreds of prospectors and miners who came to the district, lost their savings, and were obliged to leave. A few companies were established which paid substantial sums in later years and whose capital investment in 1865 represented a real asset for stockholders, but they numbered at most three or four, and their total assessments had amounted to about half a million dollars.

But such an accounting leaves the whole nature of the problem in obscurity. Eight out of the ninety-four companies paid dividends at one time or another, and six of the eight were successful in the limited sense of paying out more money than they took from stockholders in the form of assessments.[32] Five of the six paid over 300 per cent on invested capital; one of the five paid almost 500 per cent; and the bonanza of the day almost 2,000 per cent. It is extremely important to understand in terms of dollars and cents just what it meant to get in on the ground floor of an exceptionally rich mine.

Let us suppose that an investor was fortunate enough to own 500 of the 6,000 shares of the Cliff mine in 1845. In the course of the next few years, he would have been assessed $9,170. By 1866, the mine would have paid him $175,000 in dividends, or even better, he might have been astute enough to have sold out at the stock market peak in 1859 for $167,000, having already received a little more than $88,000 in dividends. Thus, it is conceivable that an investor might have maximized his return at $255,000 on a 13-year investment of a little over $9,000 — or more than a 200 per cent return per annum. In any case, this was the stuff men's dreams were made of. It proved incentive enough for a more or less continuous flow of capital into the Copper Country. The gambling element is the key to understanding, and it is even a mistake to measure pecuniary success of individual stockholders chiefly in terms of dividends. The game was so uncertain, and there was such a substantial lapse of time between the day a mine was opened and the day it was finally proven a success or failure that there were plenty of opportunities to make (or lose) a fortune by speculating in the securities of even those companies which ultimately ended completely bankrupt.

Nor can the extent of the accomplishment be measured adequately in terms of an immediate dollar-and-cent accounting. This was a period of spade work on a grand scale — of capital loss for all but a few of the early shareholders, which represented, in large part, a capital investment for the more fortunate shareholders who followed them. By 1866, the three major types of copper rock formation of the Peninsula had been discovered, and a beginning had been made in exploiting two out of the three richest copper bearing lodes. An adequate water route to the East had been developed, and during the last few years of the period, real progress was made in solving the problem of internal land transportation. Years of trial-and-error fumbling were required to gain detailed geological knowledge and to adapt the technology of other mining fields to new mining and metallurgical problems. The financial record to the contrary, the accomplishment had been an enormous one, and it will be discussed in more detail in the remainder of this chapter.

THE COPPER CAKE BENEATH THE ICING

The major discoveries. The first discoveries to be developed into paying mines were located in what later constituted Keweenaw County, or the northern third of the mineral range, and Ontonagon County, or the southern third. The section opened up last was Houghton County, lying between Ontonagon and Keweenaw, and containing the Pewabic amygdaloid lode near Portage Lake and the famous Calumet conglomerate, which was to prove one of the richest copper deposits in the world.

The mining attempt in this forbidding country might well have been given up for another quarter of a century if two early prospectors had not stumbled upon lodes containing fabulously rich copper in an uncomplicated form, from both a mining and metallurgical standpoint. The Cliff lode, discovered in 1845, and the Minesota, discovered in 1848, were deposits of mainly mass copper. Similar formations were found elsewhere in the district, but nothing comparable in richness to these first two bonanzas.[33] The Keweenaw section led in production until well into the fifties when the Minesota boosted Ontonagon into first place, and by 1856 the Ontonagon mines were accounting for a little less than 50 per cent of Michigan output, those of Keweenaw probably around 45 per cent, and the small properties near Portage Lake not over 5 per cent.[34]

That same year, the main body of the great Pewabic amygdaloid lode was discovered by one of several old companies which had been working relatively minor offshoots of it since the early fifties. Not only did a geographic shift in the production balance to the Portage Lake section result, but the shift was geologic as well. The new mines were working beds of amygdaloid rock containing some 2 to 4 per cent finely disseminated copper. Their rise was very rapid, and it was apparent as early as 1860 that the future of the district depended upon exploitation of such low content rock. Houghton County established production superiority by 1865, when its output was ten tons more than that of Ontonagon and Keweenaw combined.[35] A falling-off of production at the Cliff and Minesota brought with it not only a relative, but an absolute, decline for the two older sections of the district.

As the period covered by this chapter was closing, a mine was being opened on the third main type of lode found at Superior — a mine which was soon to startle the copper world and make the mighty Minesota seem like a trivial discovery. In 1859, a surveyor named Edwin J. Hulbert had stumbled across a curious pit containing copper rock (apparently stored there by some forgotten race of miners) and a year later had bought a substantial piece of property near that site. On September 17, 1864, the main body of the Calumet lode was discovered on his property. The rock was conglomerate — a tough pudding stone, which, at the new mine, was still low in copper content, as compared with the mass lodes, but much richer than the softer Portage Lake amygdaloids.

Throughout these first twenty-two years, silver was found along with the copper in many of the Lake mines. The Minesota and Cliff were famous for what Swineford calls "silver waifs."[36] Even the Portage Lake mines produced enough silver so that it paid to employ silver pickers at the stamp mills. But the gray metal was not significant enough to make or break a Michigan company, even when the company owned a marginal property. It did, particularly in the early days, add to the speculative aura which hung over the district. Until much experience indicated the contrary, the companies always hoped that the next blast of gunpowder would turn their copper into a silver vein.

Growth in the size of enterprises. Discoveries of new lodes and the establishment of new producing companies (the number rose from eight in 1850 to twenty-three in 1860)[37] was the most important factor in increasing output during these years. But there was also a trend toward larger scale of production of the individual enterprises making up the industry, particularly until the Civil War years. Whereas only one of the eight companies recorded as having a significant output in 1850 produced over 500,000 pounds of copper, nine of the sixteen producers in 1861 had outputs of over 500,000, and six of the nine produced between one and four million pounds. This represented a substantial change since the late fifties when the Minesota and Cliff had stood alone as giants in the industry with annual outputs of two to four million pounds, while the rest of the companies accounted for only a few hundred thousand each per annum. Growth of the Portage Lake mines was tending to place a half dozen enterprises on just about an output par.

These new mines began to reach significant size around 1859–1860, and their continued growth through 1861 provides an interesting problem in output-price relationships. In spite of slowly declining copper prices after 1856 (which were accompanied by three years of gradually declining output) and the lowest copper prices in ten years in 1861, between 1859 and 1861 the Michigan field scored its heaviest gain in output of this 22-year period. The explanation of this phenomenon emphasizes the importance of the development of new properties, which on several occasions brought about rapid increases in Michigan production in spite of falling copper prices.

About the time that the Minesota and Cliff began to decline, in consequence of lower copper prices and depletion of copper reserves, a half dozen new mines were opening up, mainly in the Portage Lake section. (The most important of these new enterprises were the Quincy, Franklin, and Pewabic.) Their combined output increased rapidly between 1857 and 1859, in spite of falling copper prices, but was still so small that their production increase was overbalanced by declines at the Cliff and Minesota. The low copper content of the rock which the new mines were working and the depth of their lodes called for a large scale of operations if the ventures were to succeed. Between 1859 and 1861 their combined output increased by over two and one-half times, a substantial enough gain to raise the Michigan total in spite of falling output at older, "mass-copper" properties.

Copper for War. The initial impact of the Civil War upon the Michigan copper mining industry was very similar to that of the first World War over a half century later. The domestic copper market was completely disorganized, and trade lines with Europe were threatened by Confederate privateers. Alfred Swineford, writing in 1866, characterized those first few months of the war as "one of the darkest hours we remember for the copper mining interests."

Everyone supposed the end had come — that the mines must close down — that nothing was left to do but shoulder the musket and march to the South. Copper stocks fell to a zero point; nobody would want our copper . . . the price of copper fell to seventeen cents.[38]

But recovery came with amazing rapidity; government orders for brass buttons, copper canteens, bronze cannon, and naval equipment [39] replaced the foreign demand, and the annual average price of Lake copper went from 19.1 cents a pound in 1861 to 46.3 cents in 1864.[40] Expressed in gold prices, the increase was not at all that great — corresponding figures being from 19.1 cents in 1861 to an annual average of 23.0 cents in 1865. But the sudden inflationary rise was tremendously stimulating, and it was not until late 1864, or early 1865, that rising labor and other costs caught up with, and then passed, the level at which the companies could sell their product.

Dividends were immediately forthcoming. From $120,000 in 1860 they rose to $1.2 million in 1864, and even more significant, the number of companies paying jumped from one in 1860 to eight in 1864.[41] Three of the Portage Lake mines had just about reached dividend paying status when the Civil War began. One of them, the Quincy, would doubtless have paid money until the world crisis of 1865, even if domestic prices had continued to decline in step with world copper prices. But it would be safe to say that well over half of the suddenly expanded dividend payments owed their existence to the Civil War.

By the time the War ended in 1865, the prospect of paying

the piper was not a pleasant one. In 1865 and 1866, the domestic price for copper began to fall — to 36.3 cents a pound in 1865 and 31.8 cents in 1866. Even worse, with world copper prices down to 17.6 cents, domestic copper was overvalued at 21.5 cents gold and was due to fall in price a good deal further. Costs were being reduced, but were lagging substantially behind the price decline. The net result was a 50 per cent drop in dividends in 1865, and only two dividend paying companies in 1866, for a total of $170,000.

The years 1862–1866 saw the greatest price increase for copper in the whole history of Michigan production. Furthermore, the mines reached a high level of success by the standards of these early days — paying stockholders in the four years 1862 through 1865 over half of the total amount paid in dividends during this 22-year period. Yet production fell by 1.5 million pounds in 1862, a half million in 1863, and another half million in 1864. Two explanations have been offered for this anomaly. The first is that the district suffered from a labor shortage caused by the draining away of men to the army, and the second that: "Some of the 'old' mines were already beginning to show decreasing returns, both physically and in terms of profits under the then existing conditions of cost of production and marketing." [42] Whereas a number of new mines were just getting into production and had not reached a point where their output was significant in the total for the district.

The second explanation is much better than the first, but both, or even a combination of the two, leave much to be desired. It is true that productivity at the Minesota and the Cliff was declining, and between them they accounted for a drop in production of about two million pounds between 1861 and 1864. But their output had been falling off for some time, and this precipitous decline — in spite of an inflationary boom and, in the case of the Cliff, at least, very high dividends — does not make sense unless some other factor was operating. The "new" mines had already become large producers, and, as a whole, their output trend reversed and was either stationary or declining between 1861 and 1864.

Copper Mining in Michigan during the 1850's

(*Harper's New Monthly Magazine*, March, 1853.)

Copper Mining in Michigan during the 1850's

(*Harper's New Monthly Magazine*, April, 1853.)

The answer lies in a labor shortage, not in the sense of a drain of men to the army, for that drain was small and probably significant only indirectly in creating fear and instability, but in the drawing away of labor from all mines working at depth, particularly in Keweenaw and Ontonagon counties where the Cliff and Minesota operated, and in a steady deterioration in the quality and stability of labor as a whole.[43] In 1861 there were 16 producing companies in the industry; by 1865 the total had reached 36 — 29 of which were producing less than 500,000 pounds each. As soon as the price rise began in 1862, developmental work was commenced throughout the district, and men were bid away from the older companies. The great majority of the new enterprises were strictly "war babies" and never had a chance to prove themselves. But they did pay high wages, and perhaps just as significant, their employees worked on the surface, or at worst, less than 100 feet underground.

The proportion of total output contributed by companies producing over one million pounds annually was steadily falling after 1861. By 1865 it had reached the lowest point in ten years with the large mines producing only 54 per cent of the total. The new enterprises were soaking up labor without being able, as yet, to increase substantially the total flow of copper.[44] The old mines were getting the short end in a labor market which was on an inflationary spree, with the workers having their first real opportunity to choose the kind of conditions under which they would labor. In 1865 the over-all production trend was reversed as the new mines reached a point where their output was becoming significant, and the district as a whole turned in a two million pound gain for the year. Some of the deep mines still showed declines, and others seemed to have reached a point of stability. But even as early as 1864, labor and other costs were beginning to catch up with the price of copper, and by 1865 copper prices began a decline which was partially responsible for falling output of the district as a whole in 1866.

Between 1845 and 1946, the Michigan industry produced

copper for three major wars, during each of which domestic production of the red metal declined. In the case of the Civil War, Michigan output represented such a large proportion of the domestic total (around 70 per cent) that the reasons for the decline should be sought in the Lake Superior district alone. Apparently, inflationary copper prices raised prospective profit margins so substantially that labor was bid away from those mines capable of a short-run increase in output. This is an example of misallocation of resources, assuming that the national objective was a short-run increase in copper production.

ROADS AND CANALS OR BUST

Although the industry's output had grown substantially since the early fifties and proved adequate to meet the wartime needs of the North, the most significant accomplishments were those laying groundwork for the future. First among these was the development of a cheap transportation system from the Copper Country to the metal markets and sources of labor and material supply of the East. The waterway system, as completed during these years, not only gave the Michigan mines a competitive advantage over the California copper mining industry (which boomed in consequence of high Civil War prices) and even over isolated districts in the East, such as Ducktown, Tennessee, but assured Michigan preëminence over potential competitors in the West, until the railroads opened up that country in the early eighties. Even after that date it continued to represent an asset which compensated, in some part, for western advantages, such as precious metal content in copper lodes.

Development of the Lake transportation system. It was immediately apparent that the worst link in the transportation system was at Sault Ste. Marie. Not only was it necessary to unload all cargoes, consign them to one of the two forwarding houses, and reload them on the other side of the portage, but the vessels operating on Superior were enabled to charge monopolistic prices in consequence of their small number and of the expense involved in hauling ships over from the Lower Lakes. A few more were brought across between 1846 and 1854, including another sidewheeler and another propeller, but the operating fleet remained small. An improvement was made in the early fifties by the laying of a railroad across the portage,[45] but this was nothing more than a palliative; the Copper Country had to have a canal.

About this time Congress granted Michigan 750,000 acres of land to be disposed of in defraying the cost of such a project, and work was begun by contractors in June, 1853. Two years later the canal was completed at a total cost of $875,000, and on June 18, 1855, the first boat went through the locks.[46] The impact of the opening of the canal was just as substantial as had been anticipated. For a year or more before 1855 purely developmental work had been under way on a large number of locations whose owners now felt able to ship their product eastward.[47] Lower Lake vessels were attracted to the trade, and rates fell by 1860 to $11 per ton to Boston and $9 to New York. Charges of monopoly were still rife since all of the tonnage was owned by a few Cleveland and Detroit shipping firms, but rate reduction was substantial enough to represent real progress.

The second major improvement was made shortly after the Portage Lake district was opened up. Until 1862 the channel from Superior to Portage Lake was so shallow that vessels drawing more than 4.5 feet were obliged to anchor off the entry and transfer their cargoes to lighters, which were towed to and from the mine landings some 14 miles away.[48] In 1859 and 1860 the mines of the district joined together and spent $30,000 dredging the mouth of the entry.[49] Later, in 1862, they formed a company to deepen the 14,000-foot channel and to collect tolls on all outgoing and incoming cargoes.[50]

Thus, by the end of the Civil War it was possible to ship copper and copper mineral direct from the mining company docks at Portage Lake to the Lower Lake wharves. The port of Ontonagon was still handicapped by sand bars, necessitating flat boats to load and unload the larger vessels outside the harbor and run the 12 miles up the river to the mine landings. But the Federal government had begun work on the harbor entrance, and real improvements were expected within a year.[51] Even the Detroit and Cleveland shipping monopoly seemed to be weakening, partially as a result of the competition of a Chicago line. In April, 1866, the *Portage Lake Mining Gazette* reported that the steamship companies were offering contracts for the full season.[52] Formerly the fall rate had been more than twice the summer rate,[53] in part because shipping risks were greater at that time of year. The *Lac La Belle* was lost in 1866 with a heavy load of copper aboard, and three vessels were lost in 1865, two by fire and one by collision,[54] but most of the mining companies carried insurance against such contingencies and had a great deal of explaining to do to stockholders when they lost shipments which had not been covered.[55] As far as water transportation went, the main battle was over. Future improvements were to be refinements and enlargements of the already existing system.

Developments in transportation by land. Adequate land transportation facilities were developed much more slowly; in fact, the first far-reaching improvements were completed during the Civil War years. Until that time the mines continued to build and rebuild their own roads, connect them when feasible, and forward complaints to their representatives in the State Legislature. The most impressive of these private road-building enterprises was that of the rich Minesota mine which completed in the early fifties a plank road about 12 miles to Ontonagon harbor.[56] In 1855 the route by land through the length of the mineral range from Copper Harbor over 100 miles to Ontonagon was still impassable except to a man on foot or, when weather conditions were exceptionally favorable, on horseback. Seven miles were classed as good roads, over 50 as footpaths and bridle paths, and much of the rest as only adequate for a team and wagon during the winter months.[57]

Lack of progress was not, however, due to a dearth of legislation in Lansing. Bill after bill was passed and signed to appropriate land and appoint commissioners to construct state and county roads. Swamp land was placed at the disposal of the counties to defray costs; [58] joint resolutions were forwarded to Washington appealing for grants for military roads; [59] and the counties were authorized to appropriate all nonresident highway taxes for construction projects.[60] But what was needed were substantial amounts of hard cash, and those were not forthcoming until the winter of 1863–1864, when the State finally decided to return to the counties all funds accruing from the specific tax on copper output.[61] Feeling had run high on the question of State reluctance to spend the proceeds of the tax on local improvements, and the Legislature was finally stirred to action when the representative of the district obtained a violent condemnation of State policy from the House Committee on Mines and Minerals: "The history of the Upper Peninsula, from its first settlement to the present time, exhibits a spectacle of unmerited wrong and injustice, which can hardly find a parallel in modern times." [62]

As late as the fall of 1864, however, the *Portage Lake Mining Gazette* was still concerned about the new mines only three to ten miles from Portage Lake, which, during most of the year, were badly handicapped by wholly inadequate roads.[63] Similar new enterprises near Ontonagon were in even worse difficulties, being 12 to 30 miles from port and paying from $5 to $20 per ton for teaming to Ontonagon.[64] The overland winter mail from Green Bay, some 260 miles away, took from five to eight days by dog team, and more often than not the bulkier items were scattered along the trail at points where the going had become particularly difficult.[65]

What progress was made came during the years 1864–1866. Construction was begun on a through route from Houghton to Ontonagon, and a much improved road from Hancock to Keweenaw County was completed, as was the main highway from Houghton to L'Anse and thence southward to Green Bay and the railroad.[66] In 1865 the American Express Company established a daily winter run from Green Bay, and the mails began to come through in less than three days.[67] In

March, 1866, the telegraph lines reached Houghton, and for the first time rapid communication was established with the East. Although an outside railroad line did not reach the Copper Country until the eighties, the iron rails were drawing close enough to have some influence on developments. A railroad had been constructed in the neighboring Marquette Iron Country between 1852 and 1858.[68] During 1863 connections were made with a line from Escanaba on Lake Michigan, and a Lake shipping service was established from that point to Green Bay, which was connected with Chicago by a direct railroad line.[69]

AN EARLY TECHNOLOGICAL REVOLUTION

Technological innovation should be listed as a third major dynamic of this period — surpassed only by discovery and transportation improvements in the significance of its impact upon the development of the industry. With one major exception, the technical processes of every department of the industry underwent fundamental changes during these years. In evaluating the relative importance of the various innovations, it would be useful to have the breakdown of the industry's production dollar. Unfortunately company reports of the day cast little light on many aspects of that problem, but they do permit of enough analysis so that main outlines may be sketched in as guide posts.

The reports provide adequate data for a division of costs into two major categories: expenses at the mine (including construction, mining, and milling) and expenses thereafter for smelting, freight, insurance, and marketing. The usual situation was for the first category to run from 80 to 85 per cent of total expenditures. The classification "expenses at the mine" was seldom broken down for the benefit of stockholders, but occasionally an insight was given into its makeup. The Central Company's report for 1861 showed the following: [70]

	Dollars	Percentage of Total Expenditure at the Mine
Mining expenses	25,926.09	52.9
Surface (general)	14,604.08	29.8
Stamping	4,641.52	9.5
Teaming	2,354.04	4.8
Construction	1,516.57	3.0
Total	49,042.30	100.00

Not only was the Central a small property at this time, but the company was working a fissure vein, which detracts from the general validity of the example. Nevertheless, the figures are useful in establishing an order of importance. Expenditures at the shafts and underground were unquestionably the major cost category. Milling was likely to be a substantial surface item, particularly for mines working low copper content rock. Finally, teaming in these days of poor transportation facilities was perhaps the second most important item of surface expense. Smelting and water freight were generally the most significant categories of the remaining 15 to 20 per cent of the production dollar, but it seems clear that there was a reduction in their relative importance toward the end of the period. During the fifties the Cliff and Minesota often paid out as much as 8 to 12 per cent of total expenditures for freight. By the sixties 7 per cent was high, and the Quincy spent a little over 2 per cent in 1864. Smelting accounted for 7 to 10 per cent of total expenditures at the Minesota throughout the period, but at some of the newer mines which relied heavily on milling it represented as little as 3 to 5 per cent.

The major factor cost at the mining end of the business was undoubtedly labor. Since company reports seldom gave wage payments, it is difficult to assess its exact importance. Two of the early Minesota reports did give such figures, wage payments accounting for about 36 per cent of total expenditures in 1852 and 1853. This percentage seems low, and estimates for various mines during the sixties indicate that 45 to 55 per cent are more reasonable figures for later years.

Developments in underground technology. Between 1847 and 1866 less technical progress was made in drilling, blasting, tramming, and other underground departments than in any other aspect of the Michigan industry. Drilling and blasting techniques were virtually the same in 1866 as they had been in 1847. A new substance called "nitroglycerin," developed by the Swedish engineer Nobel, was just beginning to attract interest at the Lake as the period ended.[71] Tramming techniques had improved somewhat with the general adoption of iron rails during the fifties, but the motive power was still human labor except at the Isle Royale which was using a few horses underground by 1864.[72] Light continued to be provided by candles stuck in bits of clay, and timbering was being resorted to increasingly as the workings reached greater depth.

But many of the mines had become large enough, and enough knowledge had accumulated concerning the geology of the mineral deposits, so that longer range underground development plans could be made. In February, 1863, the *Portage Lake Mining Gazette* announced that the Central and several other mines had adopted the policy of keeping openings fully a year in advance of stopes.[73] This was an important development since only by an advance knowledge of the variations in richness of potential stoping ground and, in consequence, the ability to change rapidly the speed and selectivity of stoping, was it possible to guide mining in response to price changes.

Depth of shafts and hoisting developments. By far the greatest progress was made in the various aspects of hoisting. The Michigan lodes slanted down rapidly, and the problem of raising large quantities of material from depth had to be met, or the companies would perish. In 1849, nine mines were operating some twenty-five shafts which had reached depths of from 57 to 260 feet — only two of them having gone below the 150-foot level.[74] By the early sixties prevailing depths for a number of the larger mines were: the Central, 300 to 500 feet;[75] the Minesota, over 900 feet in five out of eleven shafts;[76] the Pewabic, 647;[77] and the Cliff, over 1500 feet.[78]

Depths such as these had sounded the death knell on hoisting by horse power. Foster and Whitney reported the horse whim almost universally used as late as 1849,[79] but in September of 1850 the Cliff installed its first steam powered winding engine, and the North American had one in operation by 1853.[80] Four years later the shift had been completed throughout the district, and the companies were operating 47 steam engines for hoisting at the mines and stamping in the mills. The average horsepower of the engines was not over 30, and their aggregate cost was estimated at about $300,000.[81] But installing steam engines was not enough of a change to solve the problem. Not only were the shafts becoming deeper, but they were not designed for raising large quantities of rock rapidly. As early as 1850 the Cliff workings were so choked with rubble that production was falling off. More shafts were sunk and more lifting engines installed, but the problem had become so serious again by 1858 that the entire system was revised.[82] Shafts were straightened and enlarged, and skips [83] holding 2.5 tons of rock and running on tracks down the shaft were substituted for the one-ton capacity kibbles.[84] Other mines soon met with the same difficulties, and the Minesota made similar improvements in 1861, to be followed a few years later by the rest of the large producers.[85] At about this same time one-inch wire ropes were substituted for the clumsy chains, and all of the basic essentials for modern hoisting had been developed. It was not safe to haul men up and down the shafts in skips, and as late as the early sixties, miners at the Cliff were still climbing 1,000-foot ladders to reach the surface. This was such a hardship that the deepest mines were losing labor, and the Cliff led the way by installing a man-engine which cut time of ascent from an hour to 15 minutes.[86] Man-engines had been adopted by the Pewabic and the Quincy before the period ended.

Developments in stamping and washing. The shift to amygdaloid beds of 2 to 3 per cent copper content around 1858 placed a real burden on the milling end of the business. In the very early days the rock had been stamped dry, but it soon became apparent that milling in Michigan would require enormous quantities of water.[87] A stream of water met the rock at the stamp head, carried the product on through the washing and jiggling process, and finally disposed of waste sands in a lake or dump stream. The country was well adapted for such a process; streams and small lakes abounded. But even so, hardly a season passed without a half-dozen complaints of mills closed because of lack of water and speculation as to the feasibility of doing milling for the whole district at Portage Lake. Long hauls on low content rock were not practicable, however, and the mines of Ontonagon and Keweenaw found a partial solution to their problem by building dams on nearby streams. The new Portage Lake companies were dependent almost entirely upon stamp-work, and it was there that real progress was made in solving the mine to mill transportation problem.

By 1862, four mills were in operation on the shore of the Lake, handling a total of some ten thousand tons of rock monthly.[88] Tracks were laid from the mines to the mills, often a distance of two miles or more, and teams of horses were used to pull rock cars to a point where the steep slope down to the Lake provided natural motive power. (The loaded cars going down pulled the empty cars up.)[89] In 1865 the Franklin revolutionized existing procedure by installing a locomotive which, with a crew of two men, was able to do the work formerly done by four men and four horses.[90]

But most attention of the day was focused upon the techniques for stamping and washing. Apparently there were three strands to the stamping story. During the early fifties progress was made in improving the small Cornish pestle stamps. Iron was substituted for wood on the shafts; the number of units to a battery was increased; and the stamps were driven by more powerful engines.[91] The Quincy continued to use an improved version of this Cornish method throughout the period, having seventy-four heads operating in their mill by 1862.[92] As early as 1856, however, much larger steam stamps had begun to be introduced, among them the Ball — an improved version of which was to gain almost universal use during the seventies. By the middle sixties the Ball machinery was in operation at several of the mills, the advantage being much heavier pounding with a great reduction in the number of units.[93] About this time the fundamental issues were obscured by an unfortunate tack taken by the Minesota, adopted shortly thereafter by the Huron, and later proven an utter failure by the Calumet. The idea was that stamping could be eliminated by using crushers and rollers. Extensive equipment was installed at the Minesota and Huron mines, and the *Mining Gazette* hailed the invention as a major technical improvement.[94] Everything seemed to be going well until February, 1866, when the Minesota crusher broke down completely and irreparably.[95]

Diversity of technique was just as common in the washing end of milling. The old hand method using ties, buddles, and keeves [96] was still considered most efficient by a new company surveying the field in 1858.[97] Even in 1865 it was recognized as the only method which took full account of the different sizes of mineral particles being washed and saved a maximum of copper in the finely ground sands.[98] But increased speed and resultant savings in the labor cost were beginning to override all objections to more mechanized techniques. In the early sixties most of the mills replaced the old ties with automatic jiggling machines, called "Collums washers." [99] The companies were extremely conscious of the losses they were taking as a result of inadequate milling, but each attempt to get a larger percentage of the copper out of the waste going into the Lake seemed to cost more than the value of the additional metal obtained. In hope of stimulating inventions, some of them let out their waste sands on tribute, but progress in mill recovery was to come very slowly, and the problem was not satisfactorily solved until a half century later.

Fuel and foundry service. The Copper Country was well timbered, and for a number of years wood served as the only fuel. But surprisingly early, coal began to be imported, and quite a debate developed as to their relative merits. The Cliff mine was burning substantial quantities of coal as early as 1856 — apparently because the forests near the mine were being depleted.[100] By the Civil War, a number of other companies were carrying out experiments and finding that, from a technical standpoint, a ton of soft coal was equal to two cords of first-class wood.[101] With coal being delivered at Portage Lake for from $3 to $4 a ton, local labor costs for chopping and high teaming charges favored a good deal of substitution.[102]

In 1860 a foundry was built on Portage Lake, and for the first time major machinery repairs could be made within the district. For sixteen years any breakdown which a company blacksmith could not repair with the crudest of tools had involved sending for parts, or more likely, shipping the machinery itself to Detroit.

Smelting. For a number of years after the first mines were opened, smelting continued to be done at East Coast furnaces, but that arrangement did not prove satisfactory. The Boston and Baltimore works were not well equipped to handle the masses and mineral mined at the Lake, and apparently made little effort to adapt their technology to the new demand. Furthermore, if smelting could be done closer to the mines, a substantial reduction in freight expenses could be gained — only pure ingot would be sent on to eastern markets. Finally, the East Coast smelters were deep in the import game and often had conflicting interests with Michigan producers concerning such matters as a protective tariff on copper ores.

Between 1844 and 1848 several attempts were made to establish works in the Copper Country, but all of them proved abortive.[103] In 1848, Dr. C. G. Hussey and other directors of the Cliff mine decided to go into the smelting end of the business, and two years later established a works at Cleveland, Ohio, which handled the product of the mines in which they were interested until it was closed down in 1867.[104] About this same time (1850) the Detroit and Waterbury Copper Smelting Works was built at Detroit with capital provided by four large brass manufacturers who were anxious to secure a brand of copper on which they could depend.[105] Five years later the Central mine was having its mineral smelted there at an average cost of $18.32 per ton.[106] The first successful local attempt came in 1860 when the Portage Lake Smelting Works was established at Hancock and almost immediately began to handle the major part of the product of the Houghton County mines.[107] Works were also built at Lac La Belle and Ontonagon during the Civil War, but proved short-lived enterprises. Apparently one of the reasons for their failure was the fact that several of the largest mining companies of the Keweenaw and Ontonagon sections were interested in Lower Lake smelters and were not prepared to shift their furnace work to local industries even though it meant substantial shipping savings.[108]

By 1866, over half of Michigan copper was being smelted locally and the rest by establishments in Cleveland, Detroit, and Pittsburgh. The locational factors involved in establishing smelting works were quite complex. In the long run, smelting near the mine sites was to prove most economical, but throughout the greater part of this period relatively high labor and coal costs in the Copper Country and lack of internal transportation facilities by land favored shipment of masses and mineral direct to Lower Lake works.

One of the greatest advantages held by the Michigan industry was the relative simplicity of the smelting of its copper in contrast with the complicated processes required for the treatment of copper ores in other fields of the world.[109] Dr. Hussey of the Cliff made his first attempt in an ordinary cannon furnace with disastrous results, but soon hit upon a reverberatory furnace [110] with a movable roof.[111] Once established, there was little change in technique, and the Portage Lake works of 1861 may be considered as representative of those in Detroit, Cleveland, and Pittsburgh.

The copper mineral was placed in small reverberatory furnaces and brought to the melting point at which time the slag, or molten rock, could be skimmed off. Impurities were then burned out by oxidation — that is, by splashing the copper up in the air. Finally, oxygen was eliminated by poling, allowing carbon in hard wood to unite with the oxygen in the molten mass. By this process the concentrate as shipped from the mill was reduced from a mineral of 65 to 75 per cent copper content to a metal of 99 per cent purity. Small, long-handled iron ladles were used to dip the molten metal out of the furnaces in 15 to

20 pound lots which were carried across the floor and poured into molds.[112]

Evaluation of the accomplishment. Certainly with the major exceptions of drilling, blasting, and tramming, the technology of 1866 was worlds apart from that of 1847. The man-engine, the steam hoist and pump, underground rails, and the Welsh reverberatory furnace were all known in older fields before copper mining began on the Upper Peninsula. They were adopted in Michigan when conditions warranted their use. The wire cable and the skip were new inventions, installed by the Michigan mines at about the same period they were introduced elsewhere. What progress was made in stamping and washing was probably more indigenous to the district — the result of much trial-and-error fumbling toward better methods of solving the special problems of the native, low-content rock.

As for the motives for the introduction of changes, it is possible to break down the cover-all phrase of "cost reducing." Conditions arose which called for either technical change or closure — most of the hoisting and shaft renovating developments were clearly of this character. The man-engine was introduced by the deeper mines to maintain their share of the labor market. Certain other innovations such as the steam hammer, the automatic jigger, and perhaps the mine to mill transportation system were chiefly labor saving in character. There was much discussion of technical problems in the newspapers of the day. Each mine seemed anxious to prove to the public the benefits to be derived from the changes it was introducing, and inventors from the East came to the Copper Country, machinery in hand, to challenge competitors. Throughout the period the highly successful Cliff mine tended to lead the way in introducing important changes. But there was no monopoly on technology, and, by the end of the Civil War, all of the large producers were more or less on a technological par. The innovations had certainly not been capital saving; the ante to take a seat in the game was constantly rising. Perhaps they might best be characterized as the application of increased quantities of capital in the form of steam power to hoisting, pumping, stamping, and washing — and in the form of iron rails to aid men and animals in transporting materials below ground and on the surface.

FINANCIAL AND MANAGERIAL ORGANIZATION AND CONTROLS

The corporate and regulatory framework. From the beginning the Michigan copper mining companies were organized as corporations. During the first few years they were formed under the laws of various states and "issued such numbers of shares or stock certificates, as suited the convenience of each individual set of incorporators."[113] The majority, however, chose Michigan, and special acts were passed by the Legislature granting charters to applicants.[114] In 1850 a general mining law was passed, and revised in 1853, which laid down requirements and procedures for incorporation,[115] and all but half a dozen companies reorganized under its provisions.

The maximum term for a charter was set at 30 years, and capital stock was not to exceed $500,000 divided into 20,000 25-dollar shares. The affairs of each company were to be managed by a board composed of three to nine directors, one of whom was required to be a resident of Michigan. Stockholders were liable for company debts up to the full face value of shares held, but, as long as a concern was not bankrupt, the amount actually paid in was left to the discretion of the directors, who could levy assessments from time to time up to the face value of the stock. The directors were empowered to put the shares owned by a stockholder up for sale if he failed to meet a properly advertised assessment within 60 days. Finally, annual meetings and reports were required, and a copy of each report was to be filed in Lansing.

The State revised its regulatory system from time to time in response to changing conditions and the growing demand for more extensive corporate powers. By an act of 1857, the copper companies had been limited to total land holdings of 3,000 acres, but two years later the legislature amended the law to read 10,000, placing the industry on a par with Upper Peninsula iron mining companies.[116] In 1855 mining corporations were empowered to subscribe to stock in plank road and railroad companies,[117] and two years later authority was granted them to consolidate with other mining companies on the consent of a majority of the stockholders of both corporations.[118] Finally, in 1865 they were authorized to increase capital stock to $1,000,000, divided into 20,000 50-dollar shares.[119]

The first state tax on mining companies was a 4 per cent levy on value of smelter output,[120] but until 1853 state taxation usually took the form of a levy on invested capital. For example, the mining law of 1851 provided for an annual tax of one per cent on paid-in capital, invested earnings, and money borrowed.[121] The companies considered such taxation highly discriminatory against a new industry in which risks were great and substantial periods of prospecting and development were necessary. But it was not until 1853 that the general mining law substituted an output tax of one dollar per ton in lieu of all other state levies.[122]

Thus, by the end of the Civil War the companies had acquired very considerable corporate powers with a minimum of state taxation and control. The mining law contained no provision for audit or inspection of accounts, and there was every indication that the Legislature was prepared to grant any powers which the companies considered essential for successful operation. Development of a favorable (actually lax in some respects) regulatory and tax system had come slowly; just as in the geological and technical ends of the business, experimentation had been the keynote.

Stock financing and the assessment system. By the early fifties, a copper mining section was in full operation at the Boston Stock Exchange and had already become the main source of capital for the Lake mines.[123] As might be expected, the stocks fluctuated markedly, particularly during the Civil War years when more than a tripling of values was not uncommon. (For annual high-low quotations on the stocks of individual companies, see Table 13, p. 223.) During the boom of the middle fifties, trading in the shares of eight of the companies aggregated over 85,000 shares in a single year, and high-low fluctuations often represented a quadrupling of share values.[124]

None of the companies of this period issued fully paid stock; the assessment system was a recognition of uncertainty as to what capital requirements would be, as well as a "come-on" device in dealing with a flighty capital market. The prevailing method of opening a mine was to keep initial assessments as low as possible and to rely on raising enough copper during the first two years to pay exploration and developmental expenses. The Minesota is a good example of how successful the system could be when applied to an exceptionally rich mineral body.

During the first three years, 1848 through 1850, total expenditures amounted to $100,000, and copper sold brought in almost $45,000. The next year, expenditures and receipts were just about in balance. By 1855 receipts were almost twice expenditures, and the company declared its first dividend.[125] The Cliff mine survived on $110,000 in assessments during the five years before it began paying dividends. The system almost failed, however, and a loan from the president of the company was necessary to keep the mine alive during one grim year when the stockholders were reluctant to provide further capital.[126] Part of the explanation of small initial capital requirements in these two cases was the extremely high copper content of the rock mined. Initial requirements for successful Portage Lake amygdaloid mines were somewhat higher. It took the Franklin five years and $170,000 of the stockholders' money to reach dividend paying status. The Quincy spent $200,000 over an even longer period. But still it cannot be said that heavy initial assessments on stockholders were a requisite of success.

It would be a mistake indeed to assume that the 120-odd producing companies operated as completely independent enterprises, each with its own small group of financiers and directors. Interest groups and interlocking directorates with substantial ramifications flourished throughout these years.

There were several reasons for such a development. Mining

was a highly speculative game, and a financier did well to spread his investment over a series of claims and companies. In addition, the number of men of means interested in copper mining was limited, and once a few of them had worked together in one enterprise, they tended to continue their association when something else which looked good came along. It is true that similar ends might have been attained by forming giant corporations with large and scattered holdings, but that presented financing difficulties, to say nothing of the fact that Michigan State mining law limited both the capital stock and land holdings of any one company. Much the better method was to wait until a likely claim had been staked out, or a promising new company formed, and then buy in.

As early as 1854, a Boston financier by the name of Horatio Bigelow was serving as treasurer of 14 different mining companies, among them the Copper Falls, Phoenix, Toltec, and Huron — all small, unsuccessful, but promising properties.[127] At a later period, during the early sixties, he was a director of at least four mines and was associated with the financial group which was struggling to open up the great Calumet conglomerate lode.[128] But the most successful interest groups of the day were those which centered about the Cliff and Quincy. They might well be designated as the Hussey-Howe and Mason-Perkins groups.

Thomas M. Howe and Curtis G. Hussey had reached success as directors of, and heavy stockholders in, the Cliff mine. They, with other directors of the company, made substantial investments of their profits in other properties of the district as well as in Lower Lake smelting establishments. By the early sixties the two men were serving on the boards — usually with one or the other of them as president — of seven mining companies besides the Cliff.[129] Most of their ventures proved just as unsuccessful as the usual run of mines in the district, but one, the National, was a Civil War dividend payer, and together with the Cliff accounted for 35 per cent of total dividends declared in 1864.[130]

T. Henry Perkins and Thomas F. Mason were associated

with an Eastern brokerage house as well as being the most important directors of the rising Quincy mine. By 1865 the seven companies on whose boards they served were accounting for over 38 per cent of Michigan output and paid in 1864 over 50 per cent of the district's dividends.[131] Thus these two financial groups were heavily represented on the boards of companies that paid around 85 per cent of the money made in Michigan copper during the peak inflation year of the Civil War.

Sometimes there were managerial savings to be gained from such interest groups. Most of these were probably in the East, at the financial end of the business, but the Northwestern Mining Company was supervised by the agent of the Cliff mine for a number of years, and the Minesota agent managed the affairs of a number of smaller companies established by financial interests in the mother corporation.[132] The Franklin and Pewabic — both large mines for that day — were operated practically as one property until 1866, when there was a shift in financial control.[133] Nevertheless, it is probably safe to say that companies, even in the same interest group, operated for the most part as independent units.

Administration and selling. New York and secondarily Boston continued to be the markets for Lake copper. Sales were made there, and refined copper in ingots and bars was distributed to Eastern manufacturers or consigned for shipment abroad. The mining companies retained ownership of the product through delivery at Boston or New York — smelting being done on a commission basis. Occasionally a special contract might be made, such as those negotiated with the Government during the Civil War, for specific forms of copper products. The Pewabic made a contract in 1862 with the Navy Department calling for 100 tons of copper bolts, which the *Portage Lake Mining Gazette* declared to be the first contract for a specific form of copper which the mines had ever made with the Government.[134] And again some sales were made direct to Western manufacturers. The Quincy made its first shipment to Chicago in 1866, and the Cliff was selling some of its product to manufacturers in Pittsburgh in 1863.[135] But, in general, the flow of mineral and unwrought copper was eastward with a small stream returning westward again as finished products.

Actual sales were made by brokers or agents on a commission basis — the brokers' board sometimes including important directors of the mining company concerned. In the early days it frequently took an embarrassingly long time from the mining of copper to receipt in Boston of cash from its sale. Throughout the winter months, masses, minerals, and bars were piled up at the ice-locked docks in Michigan. When spring came, the product was shipped eastward, often to be smelted along the way at Cleveland or Detroit. On arrival in New York some time might elapse before a satisfactory sale could be made, and during the fifties the usual credit extended was four months. It seems probable that the larger mining companies were soon able to do better than this. In 1853 the Cliff made its first cash-on-delivery arrangement covering about two-thirds of its annual shipment, and in 1857 the National reported a similar contract.[136]

Up at the Lake, a company's representative was known as the agent — responsible only to the Board of Directors. His authority was very great, in part because communication with the East was slow and often all but impossible for substantial periods during the winter months. However, he was always required to send a monthly report of operations to the Eastern office, and usually was expected to write weekly on current developments.

For administrative purposes, each mine was divided into underground and surface activities, the agent usually having superintendents under him to direct the two branches. Occasionally the underground superintendent, or head mining captain, would have an independent status with direct responsibilities to the Board. But such a situation was unusual and only obtained when the agent was considered more of a businessman than a mining man. At some of the larger properties the organization pattern had become more complicated by the Civil War period. In the case of the Cliff each activity was

OPENING THE MICHIGAN LODES 37

highly systematized under a separate department head,[137] but at most of the mines lines of control were still quite simple and allowed of much flexibility.

Undoubtedly the Lake had its share of bad business management,[138] intensified by the gambling aura which hangs over new mining camps. The Minesota is supposed to have suffered from that curse: during its heyday in the late fifties, everything was done on a grandiose scale which set an unfortunate example for many less well endowed companies.[139] A rich mine can stand a lot of mismanagement, but even the Minesota was obliged to change its policies when mineral reserves began to run low in the sixties. In contrast, the Cliff management was sometimes criticized as being too conservative. In any case, Dr. Hussey and his associates were much more circumspect in their operations.

Dependence upon stock financing tended to encourage a variety of manipulative practices, particularly in the very early days and during the Civil War, when there was a general lowering of financial ethics in an atmosphere aptly characterized by the Springfield, Ohio, *News*:

Fortunes are made and lost annually at the stock board. The object of mining operations frequently is to develop a large yield with a view less to the profits at the mine than at the stock board.[140]

Speculators cornered the Franklin stock in 1866 and almost tripled its value in spite of a generally declining market, and two directors of the Quincy were accused of using their dual position as board members and brokers to sell the 1865 product of the mine to themselves below market prices and then to resell at a $40,000 to $50,000 profit. (The charge was hotly denied from Boston.) [141]

Nonetheless, such practices were not as prevalent as might have been expected in the opening up of an early mining field, and the harm done to legitimate enterprise was not nearly as serious as that which characterized the opening of Western fields several decades later. It seems probable that the greatest difficulty with the stock financing system was that it tended to foster a peculiar form of capital rationing. The investing public was completely lacking in criteria for judging relative potentialities of the early enterprises and, as a result, new companies were established by the dozen whenever market conditions were favorable, with thin financing for all — whether legitimate enterprises with excellent potentialities, at one extreme, or well advertised fly-by-nights, at the other.[142]

CHAPTER II

Michigan Dominates the United States Market, 1867–1884

Legislation can neither be wise nor just which seeks the welfare of a single interest at the expense and to the injury of many and varied interests at least equally deserving the consideration of Congress.[1]
— *President Johnson, February 22, 1869.*

The eighteen years of Michigan copper mining following 1866 were, in many respects, the most paradoxical period of the district's history. Output quintupled between 1866 and 1884, and for somewhat more than the last decade of the period the industry was in a position to dominate the United States copper market. Yet the Lake companies (with one major exception) were in desperate financial difficulties until the early seventies, and the industry as a whole was able to recover late in the period only in consequence of the exploitation of rich new mineral bodies, revolutionary technological developments, and more favorable copper prices.

THE POSTWAR DEPRESSION, 1867–1871

When the Civil War ended, United States copper producers found themselves in most difficult straits. In 1866 Lake copper had sold for 22.5 cents a pound gold or about 5 cents a pound more than Standard copper in the London market.[2] In 1867 the differential dropped to 2.9 cents and the following year to 1.7. At that time (1868), Lake was selling at an average gold price of 16.9 cents a pound, the lowest level since 1851. Not only were domestic prices being forced into line with world prices by the import trade and growing United States output, but the Federal government was disposing of some 5,000 tons of copper from old war material — enough metal to meet a third of a year's domestic demand.[3]

The industry in crisis. In spite of the fact that virtually no money was being made in copper mining, annual output of the Michigan field doubled between 1866 and 1869. The explanation lay in the opening up of the Calumet conglomerate lode. The rest of the industry was clearly declining.[4] Output, other than that from the Calumet and Hecla properties, fell from 16 million pounds in 1867 to a little over 8 million in 1872. Of the 29 recorded companies in 1867, more than a third had closed down by 1872; only four had a larger output by that date than in 1867; and of those four, only one was a significant producer. About a dozen new or reorganized companies had attempted to establish mines, and over half of them had been closed as failures.

According to the *Mining Gazette* most of the properties which remained open took steps to "retrench" — which meant a sharp reduction in underground force, stoppage of all developmental work in advance of stoping, and concentration of remaining miners on the richer runs of ground. For two or three months there was usually no fall of product, but by the sixth month output was likely to be dropping steeply.[5] The next step often was to retire from direct management of the mine by leasing it out to tributers on a royalty basis. By 1870 most of the small properties had been leased, and even some of the larger mines, among them the Franklin and Pewabic.[6] Terms of the contracts varied, the royalty at the Franklin being fixed at an eighth to a sixth of all copper shipped.[7] One result was that the tributers invariably continued the process of stoping only rich ground and spent little or no time opening up the mine — a dual policy which was known as "gutting" or "robbing" the mine of its eyes.

> But these are dubious times, my boy,
> So look out for the eyes of the mines, my boy,
> And after a while, perhaps you'll smile,
> At the rare assortment of "blinds," my boy.[8]

Tributing hung on for a number of years at even the larger properties — the tributers at the Franklin and Pewabic surrendering their lease in 1874 [9] — and the practice was still common at many small mines in 1878.[10] Alexander Agassiz, the brilliant young scientist who came out from Boston in 1867 to save the infant Calumet and Hecla companies, found the managerial class of the district in a completely disorganized state of mind and so divorced from Eastern controls that profitable operation had almost ceased to be a mining aim. He summed up his observations in a letter to Eastern associates: "I don't wonder mines don't pay, for the people up here care very little whether they do or not as long as they keep open." [11]

Nor were things going well at the Eastern end of the business. Early in March, 1867, Mellen Ward and Company, bankers and leading operators in the Copper Falls Mining Company, failed, and it was rumored that the Huron was in difficulties and had borrowed $80,000 from the Copper Falls.[12] Two months later, H. Tracy Arnold and John Leighton, prominent operators in mining stocks, were arrested in Boston — Leighton to face charges of an overissue of stocks in the Franklin and embezzling funds from the Franklin, Dana, and Huron.[13] Charges of private speculations with company funds, cornering operations, and "outrageous deception" were common.[14] Stockholders in the Isle Royale appointed a Committee to investigate their company's affairs, and the future of the young Calumet and Hecla seemed to be imperiled since their most important financier, Quincy A. Shaw, was deeply interested in the ill-fated Huron. The period of managerial and financial disorganization came to an end when copper prices recovered in 1872, but it left most of the mines in a run-down condition and resulted in the passage of a mild regulatory measure by the State Legislature requiring a three-fifths share vote before division or sale of company property and more publicity as to date and place of shareholder meetings.[15]

The search for remedies. Two panaceas were widely discussed during these years — an increase in the protective tariff and consolidation of properties. The first of these will be treated at length later in this chapter; the second may be disposed of rather briefly. When first proposed, consolidation was thought of primarily as a means of reducing surface expenses.[16] A producers' association was set up in the spring of 1869 with the avowed purpose of pooling information concerning "subjects connected with the production of copper" and of fostering consolidations and improvements of unsuccessful properties.[17] There is no record of the association's accomplishment, but about this time the focus of the problem was broadened to include the advantages of consolidating land holdings along workable lodes for mining reasons. Much more was known about geology, and companies which operated on the same lode had clear evidence of that fact and realized that their future was limited by neighbors. In addition, there were sometimes sections of a mine's property which might better be worked from another company's shafts.

In spite of wide recognition of these factors, very few consolidations took place, and practically none except when one or both properties had been shut down as failures, or ownership of both was in the same hands. The Calumet and Hecla represented the latter type when it was formed in May, 1871, by the consolidation of the Calumet, Hecla, and two minor properties.[18] The Atlantic represented the former, incorporating in December, 1872, to operate the combined South Pewabic and Adams properties.[19] The closest case to a consolidation of independent operating mines was that of the Pewabic and Concord with shares being exchanged on a one-to-five basis.[20] This agreement was hailed as a portent of great things to come, but in spite of the passage of an act by the State Legislature which encouraged consolidation by increasing the capital limit to $2.5 million and maximum land holdings to 50,000 acres,[21] nothing more was accomplished. The greatest obstacle was said to be equalization of value, but disagreement as to which party was to retain active management may have been equally important.

Consolidation did prove to be a practicable answer in the smelting end of the business. In 1867 the Waterbury and

Detroit Copper Company merged with the Portage Lake Smelting Company, the consolidation adopting the name, "Detroit and Lake Superior Copper Company."[22] With the decline of the Cliff and other Hussey-Howe mines, the Cleveland and Pittsburgh smelters were gradually frozen out of the business, and by 1882 all Lake copper, with the exception of an insignificant amount still handled by a Hussey plant in Pittsburgh, went to the Detroit and Lake Superior Copper Company furnaces at Hancock and Detroit.[23] The opening of a Mineral Range Railroad in the Copper Country removed any doubt as to the most advantageous smelting point for the Keweenaw and Houghton mines. It was clearly better to use the furnaces at Hancock and ship pure ingot eastward than to ship mineral of 75 per cent copper content to the Detroit works. Throughout most of this period the standard smelting rate was $18 a ton for mineral and $15 for slag, but by the late seventies a substantial differential had been set up favoring Detroit.[24]

	Mineral	Slag
Hancock	$17.00	$12.50
Detroit	15.00	10.00

Despite the lower Detroit rate, three-quarters of the company's business was being done in Hancock by 1882, and the only consistent Detroit customers seemed to be the fast declining mines of Ontonagon, which lacked rail connections to the local smelter.

THE RISE OF CALUMET AND HECLA

The most important development in Michigan and United States copper mining history during the years 1867 to 1884 was the opening up of an exceptionally rich and vast mineral body by the Calumet and Hecla Mining Company. The rise to national supremacy of this concern affected every section of the industry's life: successful price control by a combination of Michigan copper producers, a swift advance in labor productivity in the district, and substantially heavier dividend payments are all characteristics of the period which find primary explanation in the exploitation of that fabulous lode.

Dominance in the Michigan district. In 1867 the Calumet and Hecla companies were shipping only 8.4 per cent of Michigan copper; five years later the percentage was 65.3. After that date the proportion fluctuated somewhat, but with recovery and rapid growth of the rest of the industry during the middle and late seventies, there was a gradual decline to 55.9 per cent of the Lake total by 1883.[25]

The new property was a tremendous financial success as early as 1870, and between 1869 and 1884 declared over $25 million in dividends on a paid-in capital of $1.2 million, or about 80 per cent of all dividends paid by the industry during the 18-year period covered by this chapter.[26] Another 17 per cent of total dividends was paid by the Quincy, Central, and Osceola which left only 3 per cent for the rest of the companies. Great disparity in financial success continued to characterize the development of the field.

The new control group. The rise of Calumet and Hecla brought to prominence a relatively new financial group which tended to be a family affair and could boast of some of Boston's most distinguished names. Management of the properties was entrusted to Alexander Agassiz, while financial affairs were directed from Boston by his brothers-in-law, Quincy A. Shaw, Henry Lee Higginson, and H. S. Russell. Shaw, Agassiz, and Higginson were important names in their own right; the Agassizs had Cabot connections; and Higginson was associated with the well-known Lee-Higginson investment banking firm.[27] In 1875, the 80,000 shares of Calumet and Hecla stock were owned by about 800 shareholders, 13 of whom controlled 34,000 of the total. A very substantial block was held under the various family names.[28]

Shaw	14,800 shares
Agassiz	7,802 "
Higginson	4,574 "
Cabot	525 "

A 20 per cent interest in the company was more than enough to make a multimillionaire. By 1884 such an investor would have received $5 million in dividends — and his shares would have been valued at close to another $5 million in the market.[29]

Significance in terms of national copper developments. The combination of the postwar depression and passage of a 5-cent protective tariff in 1869 gave the rise of Calumet and Hecla a special significance. Copper mining developments in other sections of the United States were substantially curtailed, which increased the Michigan proportion of the total, and the smaller Lake properties were prepared to follow any leadership which was strong and promised a way out of their difficulties.

From 1869 to 1876 the Michigan field consistently produced over 85 per cent of domestic output, Calumet and Hecla alone contributing over half of the United States total. Even after 1876, the decline in relative importance of the Michigan district (in consequence of the rise of Western fields) was gradual, and as late as 1882 the Lake producers were accounting for 63 per cent of the national total. Such percentages represented an excellent statistical base for monopolistic agreements, particularly in conjunction with the protective tariff. There still remained the problem of dealing with an export surplus — after 1869 the United States became a copper exporting nation in all except years of unusually brisk trade conditions.

THE PROTECTIVE TARIFF AND THE POOLING ARRANGEMENTS

Passage of a protective tariff. In February, 1867, a drive for more protection was launched by a joint resolution to Congress from the Michigan Legislature,[30] and by the spring of 1868 the matter was under congressional consideration. Senator Howard of Michigan spoke of the general depression which had come to the Copper Country, leaving 1,500 boarded-up tenements in its wake,[31] and Congressman Driggs contended that the Lake producers were unfairly handicapped by the tariff on iron and steel — products which they used in machinery and drills — and protested against the competition of copper produced by "peon" South American labor.³² In the course of the debate, the bill was supported by congressional representatives of the California copper producers and those of the Tennessee district and opposed on behalf of the Maine shipbuilding interests, the Connecticut brass manufacturers, and the Baltimore smelters.³³ Protection was the rule of the day, and when the final voting came, the bill passed over President Johnson's veto by 38 to 12 in the Senate and 115 to 56 in the House.³⁴ The new law provided for the following duties: ³⁵

Ores	3 cents per pound of fine copper content
Regulus	4 cents per pound of fine copper content
Old copper	4 cents per pound
Bars, ingots, and plates	5 cents per pound
All manufactures of brass and copper	45 per cent ad valorem

The immediate effect of the tariff was to cut off imports of foreign ores and deal a death blow to the Seaboard smelting industry. The works at Baltimore, Boston, New Haven, and New York were obliged to close,³⁶ particularly since the West Coast mining boom had collapsed soon after the end of the War, and by 1869 United States production other than that of Michigan had contracted to less than 1.5 million pounds per annum. The measure was imposed at a time when domestic production had reached a point where it could be equated with domestic demand at a price which was no higher than the world price on the metal. Such being the case, it might well have had no effect upon the domestic price. What gave it teeth was the formation of a pool, the members of which functioned under a strict enough discipline so that, whenever necessary, output could be restricted or "domestic excesses" dumped abroad.

Operations of the pool. The first indication of future events was in early 1870 when a policy of clearing the domestic market of "surpluses" was agreed upon.

A meeting of all the mining and smelting companies of the country was held at New York last Tuesday, to take into consideration the depressed state of this branch of trade. After an interchange of views, it was resolved to export during the present year not less than 5,000,000 pounds of American copper, all pledging themselves to carry into effect the resolution.[37]

From this time on, the Michigan industry was acutely aware of the efficacy of dumping copper abroad whenever domestic output was so substantial as to render the duty ineffective. As Table 1 indicates, a substantial differential between world and

TABLE 1
UNITED STATES FOREIGN TRADE IN UNMANUFACTURED COPPER, 1870–1882 [a]

Year Ending June 30	Total Exports	Total Imports for Consumption (In pounds)	Export Balance	Average Annual Domestic Price Premium [b]
1870	8,465,000	1,227,000	7,238,000	3.8
1871	9,332,000	1,011,000	8,321,000	5.2
1872	1,268,000	5,848,000	− 4,580,000	9.4
1873	1,289,000	13,221,000	− 11,932,000	7.3
1874	953,000	1,921,000	− 968,000	3.7
1875	8,123,000	1,675,000	6,448,000	1.8
1876	14,804,000	2,226,000	12,578,000	2.4
1877	14,162,000	1,597,000	12,565,000	3.0
1878	12,398,000	541,000	11,857,000	2.9
1879	17,951,000	165,000	17,786,000	4.5
1880	4,906,000	6,257,000	− 1,351,000	6.4
1881 [c]	7,498,000	1,388,000	6,110,000	4.6
1882	4,480,000	1,375,000	3,105,000	4.2

[a] Pettengill, "United States Foreign Trade in Copper," dissertation, pp. 57a, 79a, 90a.
[b] The premium is calculated by subtracting quotations for English Standard on the London market from quotations for Lake copper in New York. See Knight, pp. 149–150.
[c] Export-import figures for 1881 and 1882 are for the calendar year.

domestic prices was maintained throughout these years, the policy proving particularly effective when coupled with improving business conditions such as those of the years 1870–1871 and 1879. Whenever the differential went above 5 cents (plus the premium on Lake copper as a superior metal, which amounted to about 1.5 cents a pound), the international flow of copper was reversed and the United States became a substantial importer.

In 1874 a technique was tried which smacked of a domestic copper corner. The New York brokerage house of Holmes and Lissberger offered the large Lake companies contracts for purchase of their entire annual output at well above market prices, with the understanding that the broker would make the necessary sales abroad and see to it that none of the copper was reimported.[38] The condition was that all companies accept the offer before it was to be binding with any one.[39] The proposition was accepted and deliveries begun, but within a few months it became apparent that the terms of the agreement were too far out of line with crisis conditions prevailing in the nation at large, and Holmes and Lissberger went into bankruptcy. Most of the cornered copper had been pledged to various banking houses as collateral, and its sale was not forced upon the market. Apparently the Lake producers coöperated with the bankers in a gradual liquidation.

Calumet and Hecla played an increasingly important role in the pool from this time until the organization was disbanded in 1884. Combination sales were made regularly during the succeeding years, apparently not under long-term agreements, but rather with each sale negotiated as a separate contract when market conditions seemed appropriate.[40] The pooling agreements only required the smaller companies to ship a designated quantity of copper abroad (usually an aggregate amount totaling 50 to 100 per cent of that shipped by Calumet and Hecla). The burden of output restriction, if indeed there was such, was carried by Calumet and Hecla alone. It was the general belief in copper circles that the Lake giant could have produced (and profitably) a great deal more metal during these years.[41] Some support for such a contention can be derived from the company's remarkable production increase between 1883 and 1886 when something approaching a price war was being waged with the Western fields. With copper down to 11 and 12 cents a pound, Calumet and Hecla increased output by 50 per cent in the

Copper Mining in Michigan about 1915
(Calumet and Hecla Consolidated Copper Company.)

Copper Mining in Michigan about 1915

(Calumet and Hecla Consolidated Copper Company.)

course of three years and still managed to pay a total of $4 million in dividends. That there was some restriction, at times, is quite possible, but it seems unlikely that a *major* expansion was feasible in the seventies since the record achievement of the early eighties was largely dependent upon the new power drill which was not introduced until around 1880.

The pool agreements seldom covered domestic marketing policy, in part, at least, because Calumet and Hecla preferred to keep a free hand in the home area. Increasingly, the big Lake producer made sales in the domestic market direct to consumers in very large blocks for future delivery, with the understanding that until the contract period expired, any future sales by the company at a lower price would entitle customers to a rebate on previous purchases. Some of these contracts called for as much as 12 million pounds, to be delivered in the course of three to six months,[42] and one result was that much less copper than formerly entered the open market. "The bulk of the trade is done directly between producers and large consumers, and the metal in many cases does not even get to the great centers of distribution."[43] Similarly, foreign sales were negotiated with European brokers in large quantities of three to eight million pounds. After an initial experience in the early seventies of having copper exports returned to the United States market, enter free of duty as a domestic product, and sell at a substantial profit for European shippers, these foreign contracts contained a clause either forbidding reëxport or requiring that the duty be paid.[44] However, when the domestic price got out of hand, as in 1879–1880, the clause was often of little avail; European dealers were prone to ignore it.

By and large, Calumet and Hecla was strong enough to keep the other Lake companies in line. In commenting upon the market situation in 1882, the *Engineering and Mining Journal* declared:

The time is approaching when current contracts expire, and both parties will probably soon commence manoeuvering. As the power of concluding these great transactions rests alone with the representatives of the Calumet and Hecla, the other Lake Superior mines only being allowed to participate by special grace, the questions affecting the deliberations cannot even be guessed.[45]

Attempting to eliminate its Michigan competitors was not considered wise — first, because they could always sell in the foreign market if prices were slashed at home, and, second, because their political support was necessary if the tariff was to be retained. As the engineering firm of Bainbridge, Seymour, and Rathbone aptly reported: ". . . should the Calumet and Hecla attempt to shut down the other mines as it is locally termed, by increasing their output, they could no longer command sufficient influence by themselves to maintain the copper duty, since all the places they shut down would naturally oppose them."[46] The industry was very conscious of the tenuous character of the political base upon which its marketing arrangements rested. As early as 1874, Alexander Agassiz was greatly concerned about the drive in the Michigan Legislature to pass a law requiring the mining companies to print annual reports and to circulate them widely, since it would "inevitably lead to the taking off of the tariff. . . . This is suicidal for Lake Superior, and I hope it will be resisted by all friends of the country. As long as the stockholders have faith in the management of the Companies, let them keep quiet and ask no embarrassing questions. . . ."[47]

By 1884 the pool arrangements had become quite complex. During the early part of 1883, all of the old devices were tried to maintain the domestic price above the world level, without success.[48] Copper prices were falling in step with worsening general business conditions, and, in spite of the fact that almost all of the Montana product of that year was shipped abroad to take advantage of lower Swansea smelting charges on sulphide ore and a better market for by-product silver,[49] the pool succeeded only in increasing the *domestic* market premium on Lake over other brands and thus fostering substitution and loss of old Lake customers.[50] The written agreement in the fall of 1884 made Calumet and Hecla sole selling agent for all of the companies in *both* the foreign and domestic markets.[51] Export quotas were set in line with an agreement with French buyers to purchase a stated annual maximum-minimum amount of metal over a period of three years — the price to be a sliding one — four pounds sterling above the average monthly price of Chile bars on the London market.[52] Domestic customers were to have the same sliding scale price if they signed long-term contracts with the pool.[53] The price ratio was highly favorable to buyers, and in return, domestic consumers bound themselves to purchase no other brand of copper and not to resell any Lake bought.[54]

The officers of Calumet and Hecla were aware of at least some of the dangers inherent in the scheme. But it was felt that a radical step had to be taken to retain the business of old established domestic consumers and to induce new Arizona competitors to shoulder part, at least, of the dumping burden. As early as 1882, it was perfectly apparent that Western developments were something more than a temporary mining craze and that it was highly desirable to include certain Western companies in the Lake agreements. It was rumored in the trade that conversations had been held concerning the 1882 output: ". . . that the Lake Superior people will guaranty not to make more than 55 million pounds, and that the most prominent Arizona mine will not increase its present capacity during the year." [55] Apparently the agreement was not signed, and by 1884 it was not believed practicable to include the Westerners. Calumet and Hecla considered them to be "too widely scattered" to be subject to discipline and dismissed the matter with the comment that it was almost impossible "to find out the cheats" even with a strictly Michigan combination.[56] On September 3, 1884, Calumet and Hecla notified their New York agent: "Let your buyers know that we propose to hold the trade on Lake copper . . . not to allow ourselves to be supplanted by Arizona." [57] The ill-fated experiment was on.

At about the time these contracts were being negotiated, the Osceola left the pool, and their anomalous results were soon to drive the Quincy into revolt. Not only did the price agreement undervalue Lake as compared with Chile bars, but it was alleged that foreign interests were able to depress the price of Chile bars out of line with other brands of copper and thus bring about a situation by late 1884 and early 1885 where pool copper was selling for as much as a cent below Lake copper outside the pool and at a lower price than Arizona copper.[58] In November, the Quincy secretly accepted an offer above pool prices for export, and, when the other pool members got word of it shortly thereafter, an injunction was sought in the Michigan courts. Feeling ran high, the New York representative of Calumet and Hecla commenting after one interview with the representative of the Quincy, "I never talked with a man before who made no excuse whatever for breaking written agreements." [59]

The Quincy successfully defended its action in Court on the grounds that the pool contracts were against the public interest, the judge agreeing with the defendant and adding that, even if the Court was mistaken in its opinion, the proper recourse for the plaintiffs was a suit for damages.[60] No such suit was brought to Court, however, in part because Calumet and Hecla was thoroughly soured on action in common with the rest of the Michigan industry and was casting about for some other price tactic, to be initiated once the Chile bar contracts should expire in 1886. The remaining members of the pool stuck by their foreign and domestic contracts and watched the Quincy sell copper in England at a cent and a half above pool prices; the Arizona producers showed no signs of adopting a more coöperative attitude; and, worst of all, an increasing quantity of Montana ore was being refined at new electrolytic plants in Baltimore and thrown on the domestic market.[61]

Results of the pool-tariff-dumping arrangement. The Lake selling pool was by no means perfectly disciplined, nor was it in continuous operation. There were years when the domestic price averaged substantially less than five cents a pound plus the quality premium, above the London price; short periods when no unity of action at all was apparent; [62] and probably at all times a number of very small producers acting independently. However, as such arrangements go, the combination was surprisingly effective and resulted in a substantial subsidy for the industry at the expense of consumers in the United States.

Interestingly enough, the copper tariff of 1869 appears in the literature in highly divergent roles.

In a study done for the Arizona Tariff Commission in 1932, Hoval A. Smith was lavish in his praise: "This tariff act embodied a cross section of economic fairness, industrial decency and cooperative compensation not excelled by any prior or subsequent tariff schedule enacted during our legislative history." [63] Taussig has pointed out that the tariff made possible a producer's combination and dumping arrangements, and declared it was without justification since production was already substantial when the measure was passed and success was in sight for Calumet and Hecla. "The duty of 1869 was superfluous as a device for encouraging ventures still in the experimental stage." [64] To make a valid case that the public received commensurate benefits for the subsidy paid the Michigan industry, it would be necessary to show that the domestic price differential so stimulated *western* production that copper was substantially cheaper at a later period than it otherwise would have been. At first glance it might seem that such was the case. During the 15 years following 1882, domestic production increased enormously and, in spite of a swift rise in consumption demand, copper prices ruled at a substantially lower level.

It is perfectly clear that the mines operating outside the pool received a higher average price for their copper than did the Michigan producers. The Lake companies carried the full burden of clearing the domestic market of surpluses by sacrifice sales abroad and, perhaps, restriction of output, while other companies were free to produce to capacity for the home market. But it seems extremely doubtful that the tariff had a marked effect in giving Western producers their start. The discovery of rich ore lodes and the extension of the railroads seem to be factors of dominant importance, quite independent of a subsidy which averaged at most about three cents a pound. Taussig's conclusion is probably sound.

The case has only a sort of methodological significance. The fact that an industry has developed after protection was applied does not prove that it developed *because* protection was applied. . . . The extraordinary richness of the natural resources; the prospect of fortunes in return for daring, persistent, able management; the achievement of American mining engineers, — these quite suffice to explain the great development which has taken place.[65]

REVIVAL OF THE INDUSTRY, 1873–1884

The pooling arrangements are an extremely interesting example of a combination to take advantage of a protective tariff, but it seems probable that other developments of this period were of even more significance for the district's history. During the middle and late seventies, the industry staged a general recovery, with output more than doubling in a decade, and this time the gains were more evenly distributed with production of Calumet and Hecla increasing less rapidly than did that of the rest of the industry.

Copper price movements. Depressed conditions in the copper trade came to an end, temporarily at least, in 1871, and for two years copper prices ruled at exceptionally high levels. During the late sixties, domestic demand had been running at about 26 million pounds per annum; [66] by 1871, the *Iron Age* put consumption at 31.7 million pounds,[67] the greatest gains coming in rifle and pistol cartridges, locomotive fittings, trimmings, and fire boxes, bronze doorknobs, and soldering irons for the canned goods trade. Domestic prices increased by over a third between 1870 and 1872, and, although they declined rapidly thereafter, the rise proved extremely stimulating. Substantial earnings were made at even the smaller properties, and, in consequence, funds were available for badly needed improvements and exploratory work.

Just as in the years 1859–1861, rapid increase in output came on a steeply declining market — the industry turning in a 36 per cent production increase between 1872 and 1874. Copper demand had become closely associated with railroad construction, and the crisis of 1873 was severe enough to shake even Calumet and Hecla.

The outlook is so black that we must husband every resource we can lay hold of. It is absolutely impossible to sell any copper, and some

of our best customers are asking for extensions which we shall have
to grant, of course not delivering the copper due them. . . . We
cannot make advances to anyone.[68]

But the industry recovered from the shock exceedingly rapidly,
and, although dividends remained well below the 1872 level
until 1880, output continued to increase.

Development of new properties. In addition to Calumet and
Hecla three other new companies became significant producers
during the years 1867-1884, and among them these four mines
were accounting for over 71 per cent of Michigan production
as early as 1882. That same year another newcomer was engaged in sinking a shaft, which, in the mid-eighties, was developed into the second most important Lake mine. The new
enterprises were all launched immediately following periods of
very high copper prices — three of them getting under way in
1873-1874 and one just as the period was ending.

Most attention of the day was focused upon the great Calumet discovery, and three of the four important developmental
efforts were aimed at finding an extension of the conglomerate
lode outside Calumet and Hecla property. The Osceola Consolidated Company was organized in 1873 to work the southern
extension of the Calumet conglomerate, but found the continuation of the lode so unsatisfactory that by 1877 the company
had turned to the underlying amygdaloid.[69] The Allouez company had attempted to find an extension of the conglomerate as
early as 1869, but the search proved abortive and mining was
discontinued until 1873. After that date the property developed
a one to two million pound annual output but showed no startling potentialities.[70] To the northwest of Calumet and Hecla,
a grandiose attempt to drive a shaft down to an extension of
the Calumet lode was being undertaken by the Tamarack
Mining Company. The magnitude of the task defied all precedent: it was necessary to drive a vertical shaft to a depth of
over 2,200 feet before a pound of rich conglomerate could be
raised. Over three years of continuous drilling was required to
complete the operation.[71]

The only significant new mining development outside of the Calumet section was undertaken by the Atlantic Mining Company on a lode of very low copper content to the south of Portage Lake. The new concern made its first attempt in 1866 but was obliged to close down by 1870, and it was not until 1873 that the company reorganized and carried out successful developmental work. By 1882, the Osceola, Allouez, and Atlantic accounted for about a third of Michigan production other than that of Calumet and Hecla.

There was a speeding up of the trend for the bulk of the industry to be concentrated in Houghton County, and by 1874 that section produced about 79 per cent of Michigan output, Keweenaw 18, and Ontonagon 3.[72] Six years later, Ontonagon was down to 2 per cent and Keweenaw to 9, leaving 89 per cent of total output for the newer Portage Lake and Conglomerate sections. These figures highlight the fact that most of the famous mass mines either closed or ceased to be significant producers during these years. By 1882 the Cliff was shipping a mere 66,000 pounds, the Minesota a little over 10,000, and the National 17,000. The Central remained as the only important producer outside Houghton County, and in 1882 the output of that property was only a little over 1.25 million pounds.[73]

The role of changing technology. It seems probable that technological change was the most important dynamic force of this period, both in making possible successful exploitation of deposits which had had no economic value in earlier years, and in increasing productivity of labor on lodes already being worked.

The mines reached much greater depths during these years. Whereas 900-foot shafts had been considered very deep at the large properties during the early sixties, by 1880–1882 even the newer companies such as the Allouez and Osceola were down to over 1,000 feet, and older properties such as the Pewabic and Quincy had reached depths of over 2,000 — the Calumet and Hecla, 2,900.[74] The general experience at the Lake was that copper content of the rock gradually fell as the veins reached depth. Most of the amygdaloid mines were now getting from 1.2 to 1.5 per cent copper from each ton of rock stamped,[75] in contrast with around 2 per cent in the earlier period. The Quincy was an exception to the general rule, not only because its rock had proven consistently richer than the other amygdaloids, but because the company was working an exceptionally rich section of its lode. Milling returns of as high as 2.6 or 2.8 were not uncommon. The Atlantic was an exception at the other extreme, mining rock at a profit which gave only .7 per cent copper return per ton stamped. Profitable operation was possible due to the unusual degree of uniformity of the lode and the fact that the rock was the easiest to drill and blast in the district. The Calumet and Hecla lode, which Agassiz reported as yielding 15 per cent in 1867,[76] had rapidly fallen to a little under 5 per cent by 1873, and maintained just about that average, with some slight decline, through 1882.[77] Michigan copper of the early 1860's had come from substantially poorer rock than did that of the 1870's, and the high copper content of the conglomerate lode much more than compensated for increase in cost resulting from greater depth of shafts.

By the early eighties, air drills and high explosives had become prime essentials for successful mining and had revolutionized underground work. The introduction of these changes did not come all at once, and in the early years of experimentation, their practicability often looked dubious. Apparently the first power drills were introduced into the Pewabic and Franklin properties just following the Civil War.[78] Other mines began to experiment with the new machinery a few years later, and by 1869–1871 the so-called Burleigh drill was being tried by Calumet and Hecla, Copper Falls, Quincy, and other companies.[79] Experimentation continued in 1872 and 1873, and then came to a standstill. The drills were extremely heavy and cumbersome, usually powered by steam, and most of the mining companies came to the conclusion that the Burleigh was just as unsatisfactory as hand drilling.[80] The Franklin tried a Winchester drill in 1875,[81] and the Isle Royale an Ingersoll in 1876,[82] but the general consensus was to wait for something better. In 1874 the Quincy was doing most of its drilling by hand,[83] and as late as 1878 the same situation obtained at Calumet and Hecla.[84] But in 1879–1880 the new Rand air compressor and drill was introduced and adopted almost immediately by all of the companies, in part as a means of coping with a temporary labor shortage. The Quincy found that production could be maintained with less than two-thirds of the underground men formerly employed; the Osceola announced that by introducing ten drills the company could dispense with 80 to 100 miners; [85] and Calumet and Hecla began to change over in 1879 and by 1882 was producing over 20 per cent more copper with a 20 per cent reduction of underground force.[86]

Blasting improvements were second only to machine drilling in revolutionizing underground work. The *Portage Lake Mining Gazette* first speaks of the use of nitroglycerin in August, 1869, when it was introduced by the agent of the Isle Royale, John Mabbs, in a last-minute attempt to save that mine.[87] Experiments apparently were satisfactory, but the miners objected to the use of the new explosive on the ground that it was too dangerous, and when it was tried at the Huron in April, 1870, the men struck for a week and blew up some of the stock.[88] Anything bearing the name "nitroglycerin" or "dynamite" became an anathema to Lake miners,[89] and a compromise was reached on what was known as "giant powder" containing about 50 per cent nitroglycerin and going under the trade names of "Hercules" and "Excelsior" explosives.[90] In 1874 the Quincy was trying these products, and by 1878 their use had become general throughout the district.[91]

During these years a number of experiments were made with the diamond drill as an exploratory technique. The Quincy was particularly successful in discovering rich sections of its lode by this method,[92] and its use was reported at the Calumet and Hecla as early as 1871, and in prospecting on the Osceola property in 1874.[93] Man-engines continued to be installed at the deepest mines, although ladders and sometimes stairs were still common. Skips were improved by an automatic dumping arrangement introduced by Richard Uren early in the period,[94] and, until the air drill tended to make such installations obsolete, large air pumps for ventilation were occasionally found necessary.[95] Finally, the hoisting engines at the shafts were becoming enormous pieces of machinery. Calumet and Hecla installed one in 1877 which hoisted from four shafts simultaneously, ran all air compressors, and provided power for the rock house tramways.[96] As the period ended, the company was trying out a 2,000 horsepower engine which had cost $100,000 and was alleged to be the largest stationary engine in the world.[97]

Progress continued to be made in stamping, and there was a marked tendency toward standardization of equipment in all of the Lake Superior mills. By 1874 the direct action Ball steam stamp was generally recognized as the most effective machinery, and when the Quincy went over to it in 1881, thereby reducing stamping costs by over 25 per cent,[98] all of the major mills were operating with about the same stamping equipment. The Ball stamp had a 24-inch lift, struck about 90 blows a minute,[99] and could crush from 100 to 120 tons of hard conglomerate or a maximum of 170 tons of amygdaloid every 24 hours.[100]

Washing technology was still the subject of much debate. The Colloms automatic washer became standard equipment,[101] but represented only a first step in the washing process. The greatest difficulty seemed to be with the fine copper carried off as float or in the waste grains of sand, and since the metal was most highly disseminated in the conglomerate rock, Calumet and Hecla was the greatest sufferer.[102] The length of the washing process and the number of separate steps was increased at all of the mills, and in 1880 Munroe reported that Calumet and Hecla was experimenting with restamping of a portion of its sands.[103] Around the mid-seventies, a conical slime table was introduced, called the Evans slime table, and immediately found great favor.[104] It seems probable that the Evans represented some improvement since all six of the important mills had adopted it by 1880.[105] Nevertheless, any progress made in the over-all washing process was not dramatic. Not only does the literature contain many critical judgments of results, but Calumet and Hecla mill employment increased by 50 per cent between 1872 and 1882 with a doubling of output, while in the same period underground employment actually decreased by 14 per cent.[106]

Between 1860 and 1880, there was a tripling of annual output of refined copper per worker employed in the industry, and even between 1870 and 1880, there was a net increase of more than 4,000 pounds, a gain which was greater than total production per worker in 1860.[107] Development of the uniformly rich conglomerate lode and technological improvements had given the industry a new lease on life. Mechanization was clearly the rule of the day. It had become apparent that the Lake rock with its very low copper content could only be wrought successfully by mass production methods, and the formula for successful mining seemed to have been found if only a property contained a large and relatively uniform mineral body. Finally, there seemed to be a correlation between the speeding up of the adoption of technological improvements and periods when copper prices were exceptionally high and the demand for labor such that wage rates were rising steeply. The years 1871–1873 and 1880–1882 had a dual effect in making ready cash available for experimentation and putting the spotlight upon high labor costs and the possibility of substituting machines for men.

Completing the transportation system. The local transportation problem was greatly simplified by the decline of the Ontonagon and Keweenaw mines. A rectangular area comprising less than 70 square miles was now producing the great bulk of the industry's copper. The first bridge between Hancock and Houghton was completed in the spring of 1872,[108] and by 1879 it was possible to travel by good turnpikes and macadamized roads from Copper Harbor at the northern end of the peninsula to Ontonagon, 90 miles to the south.[109] The most important internal transportation developments, however, were in the field of local railroads.

One of the first major undertakings which Alexander Agassiz

brought to completion was the construction of the Hecla and Torch Lake Railroad, a 4-foot 1-inch gauge track running from the mine four miles to the mills at Lake Linden.[110] An even more ambitious project was begun by other parties in June, 1871, when the Mineral Range Railroad Company was formed to connect Hancock and Calumet. Over $325,000 was expended in the course of the next two and one-half years, and the 12-mile track was completed in October of 1873. By 1882 the line was equipped with 4 locomotives, 40 mineral rock cars, and about 40 other passenger-, flat-, and boxcars.[111] Not only did it service the Calumet and Hecla Company, but the Peninsula and Osceola had direct connections, and other properties further north, such as the Phoenix and Allouez, had good wagon road connections. Fifty cents a ton was charged for freight to the Hancock smelter in 1882,[112] and as early as 1876 most of the Keweenaw County mines had found it advantageous to send their copper by road and rail to be smelted there.[113]

During the first half of the period 1867–1884, there continued to be a substantial amount of interest in improving the harbors and canals which served as the Copper Country termini of the Great Lakes waterway. Important harbor improvements were completed at Ontonagon in 1867;[114] the harbor at Lac La Belle was made practicable by a short canal to Superior at about this same time;[115] and by 1875 a company formed under the auspices of Calumet and Hecla had completed the dredging of a two-mile channel through the marsh between Torch Lake and Portage Lake at a cost of $100,000. The largest steamers were now able to tie up alongside the company's docks.[116] The most extensive enterprise of the day, however, was the construction of the Portage Lake and Lake Superior Ship Canal which, when completed in 1873, permitted vessels direct passage through the Keweenaw Peninsula and thus a short-cut to the iron and wheat country of Upper Superior. Incidentally, the canal shortened the haul from the copper mines on the western coast of the Peninsula and made Houghton and Hancock ports of call for almost all of the

Upper Lake traffic. About $2.5 million was expended by the contractors over a period of five years, and the Federal Government granted 450,000 acres of public land in payment.[117]

In 1867 the Detroit and Cleveland steamboat lines combined and reorganized their services. All discrimination between different classes of shippers and different seasons was eliminated, and by November of 1869 the *Mining Gazette* reported that for the first time there were no complaints of exorbitant rates.[118] By the late seventies, the rate on copper to Detroit or Buffalo was $3.50 to $4.00 a ton, depending upon the location of the mine, and the rate to New York was $6.00 to $8.00 a ton.[119] (In 1860 the New York rate had been $9.00 and during the Civil War inflation $8.00 to $12.00 a ton had been charged to Detroit.[120])

Throughout these years the railroad network was drawing closer to the Copper Country, and in 1883 direct connections were established from Houghton to the East coast. In 1872 the Chicago and Northwestern had been connected with the line running from Escanaba to Marquette, and the Marquette, Houghton, and Ontonagon was extended to L'Anse, only 35 miles from Houghton.[121] This was a very important development since it meant that copper could be sent to Chicago and thence eastward with only one transshipment. It was now practicable to ship during the winter months when Superior was closed, and in 1874 about a third of the Lake product was teamed to L'Anse and sent to market at a cost of about a cent a pound more than the Great Lakes rate. The gain in selling price due to off-season marketing was alleged to have been three cents a pound.[122] During the winter months two passenger stages ran daily between L'Anse and Portage Lake,[123] and by 1881–82 there were over 100 freight wagons engaged in the winter haulage trade, handling 8,000 tons of freight a season.[124] During the summer the steamer *Ivanhoe* served as the connecting link, plowing back and forth twice a day to L'Anse.

The first year the railroad charge from L'Anse to Chicago was $25.00 a ton, but by 1874 a standardized winter and summer rate was set at $11.90. Haulage to L'Anse cost $2.00, so that the total charge on copper from Houghton to Chicago was $13.90 a ton.[125] Around 1882 the winter rate for teaming to L'Anse, rail to Chicago and thence to New York ran from $24.00 to $25.00 a ton.[126] That same year the Upper and Lower peninsulas of Michigan were connected by the extension of the Marquette line to the Straits of Mackinac where ferries bridged the gap to the Lower Peninsula lines, and the State Government made a liberal land grant for the extension of the railroad from L'Anse to Houghton.[127]

Just before the final rail connection was made to Houghton, the Michigan mines could ship to New York in the summer at about one-third of a cent a pound, or less than 2 per cent of value of product. Even in winter the cost was seldom over 1.25 cents a pound or perhaps 7 per cent of value. (By 1885 it was down to .7 cent.) As late as 1877, large amounts of Arizona copper were still shipped overland by bull team 750 miles to the nearest railroad and then 2,500 miles to the Baltimore refineries. The wagon freight amounted to about 4 cents a pound and rail fare to a cent a pound, both of these charges on mineral which still had to be refined.[128] Perhaps as high a proportion as 35 per cent of value went into transportation costs. In 1877 the Clifton district on the border of New Mexico and Arizona was paying $60 a ton to ship mineral to the smelter.[129] A little earlier, in 1876, the *Engineering and Mining Journal* estimated that the Butte companies were paying 25 per cent of value to send their product to the East Coast.[130] But by 1884 railroad connections had been made with the big mining camps of the West, and freight rates were tumbling down toward the 1893 rate of .7 of a cent a pound from Butte to New York.[131] The copper world was changing rapidly, and Michigan dominance of the domestic market had already begun to crumble beneath an avalanche of Western metal.

CHAPTER III

The Struggle for Domestic and World Leadership
1885–1904

> When markets become highly oligopolistic in
> structure, the line between fierce rivalry
> and harmonious agreement is but a hair's breadth.[1]
> —W. B. G., Jr.

> The copper supply has become too great for any one or combination to control. Our French friends have been very anxious to have us unite with them and try and control the product of the world — they to take care of Europe and we of America, but I would have nothing to do with the scheme. . . . We must each do the best we can for ourselves and the sooner the supply is reduced the better it will be for those that live.
>
> The managers of our mines are not ready to look with favor on any plan which will take from them the power to control their own product and diminish their importance and in fact almost do away with the necessity for their existence. I think they will have to have a severe lesson in competition for at least one season before any such combination can be brought about.
>
> Our Congressman from Connecticut seems very hostile to the wicked trusts but by degrees I fancy there will come a recognition that combinations of various interests are somehow inevitable.[2]
>
> —*Channing Clapp, Calumet and Hecla, from letters severally of March 23, 1886, January 2, 1886, and September 18, 1888.*

During the years 1885–1904, output of the Michigan district increased more rapidly in absolute terms than in any other period of the industry's history. (See Fig. 4, p. 195.) But with the rise of the great copper fields of the western United States, the Lake producers were unable to maintain preëminence in domestic copper mining. The battle for leadership was a fierce one, and the stakes became highly significant in consequence of the major role which United States production had assumed in the world copper picture. By the 1890's control of the domestic industry, if such could be attained, had come to mean dominance in the world.

TWENTY YEARS OF CONTINUED VITALITY

Evidence of vitality in the industry. Between 1885 and 1904 annual output of the district nearly tripled, rising from a little under 73 million pounds to over 208 million,[3] or an average increase per annum of 6.75 million pounds. Dividends fluctuated substantially in response to copper price movements, and there was a marked concentration toward the end of the period, such that a peak payment of over $12.3 million was made in 1899, and the last five years (1900–1904) saw aggregate payments of over $31 million, compared with about $11.2 million for the first five (1885–1889).[4] Not only do output figures and dividend payments indicate a marked degree of vitality, but important new discoveries were made late in the period which, in 1904, were still in an early stage of development, and around the turn of the century the plants of old properties were expanded and renovated on an unprecedented scale.

The role of new discoveries. New mineral discoveries played a much less significant role in increasing production during this period than in the years 1867–1884. The two important new finds were not made until the late nineties, and even by 1904 accounted for only about a fifth of total Michigan output. In 1896 the Mohawk mine was established upon an extension of the Kearsarge amygdaloid lode in Keweenaw County and by 1904 was producing about 8 million pounds per annum.[5] Vastly more important was the discovery of a large lode a few miles south of Portage Lake which came to be known as the Baltic or South Range. Copper-bearing rock had been reported in that location as early as 1882, but, due to the fact that the incline of the lode was much steeper than that of deposits previously worked in the district, diamond drilling had failed to uncover the main mineral body. In 1897 the deposit was rediscovered, and in the next few years three companies were incorporated to work it.[6] Production from these mines first became significant in 1902 when they accounted for a little over 10 per cent of Michigan output.[7]

Growth in the output of old properties. The major part of

the output increases came from expansion of production at mines which had been the important producers in 1884. Calumet and Hecla increased annual production by about 2.5 times between 1883 and 1904; the Quincy more than tripled annual output; the Osceola jumped from 4.3 to 20.5 million pounds; and smaller properties, such as the Atlantic and Franklin, scored substantial increases.[8] Finally, the Tamarack, which began mining the Calumet conglomerate in 1883, had an output by 1904 of about 15 million pounds. Among them these six relatively old mines shipped about 70 per cent of the total for the district in 1904.

Toward the end of the period, some of the increases in the industry's output were accounted for by new companies which opened up old mines after consolidation of a number of unsuccessful adjoining properties. The Wolverine was the most important concern of this class, followed by the Michigan, Isle Royale, Mass, Adventure, and Phoenix. Together they accounted for a little under 10 per cent of all copper shipped in 1904.

In that year, 7 out of the 19 producing companies had outputs of over 10 million pounds, in marked contrast with the situation from 1883 to 1887 when only Calumet and Hecla was in that class. Calumet and Hecla had continued to expand and still overshadowed the rest of the industry, with an output of 80 million pounds, but its long period of overwhelming preeminence seemed to be drawing to a close. In 1904 the Osceola shipped 20 million pounds and the Quincy 18, and Calumet and Hecla accounted for only 38.6 per cent of total Michigan output, compared with 65.5 in 1885.[9]

The role of technological change. Although technological change played nothing like as dramatic a role in the industry's development as during the years 1867–1884, it does form one of the main strands of an explanation of the substantial and continuous gains in output and, more generally, of the industry's extremely long period of growth. In consequence primarily of falling copper content, in what was at best low copper content rock, and of rapidly increasing depth, the nature of the mining and milling problem was constantly changing at the large Michigan properties. At any given moment the current technical solution was applicable for a fairly short span of time, which meant that the rate of obsolescence on much of the equipment was very high, and made technical change and improvement a matter of first importance. Looking at the period 1885–1904 for the industry as a whole, it seems clear that technological improvements, supplemented by certain secondary factors to be considered later in this chapter, a little better than maintained labor productivity in the face of increasing mining difficulties and perhaps even some decline in the quality of labor. Annual output per worker employed in the industry increased by about a third between 1884 and 1894, and began to decline shortly thereafter in such fashion that over-all productivity in 1904 was not much higher (about 7 per cent) than that of 1884.[10]

There was very little change in blasting and drilling techniques, and in spite of the fact that hand tramming was one of the weakest links in the underground process, only two companies experimented extensively with power haulage. Calumet and Hecla laid plans in 1893 for a system of driving tram cars by compressed air and purchased ten small air-driven locomotives in 1894, and a number more in 1897.[11] But most tramming continued to be done by hand, and in 1904 the company was reported to be considering electric motor haulage.[12] In 1901 the Quincy began experimenting with power haulage and by 1903 had fifteen electric locomotives in operation on main drifts, each of which pulled a train of three to four rock cars.[13]

As in the first quarter century of the industry's history, most technological progress in actual mining was made at the shafts. The Tamarack initiated a major improvement for deep mining in the middle eighties by sinking all shafts vertically instead of along the lode, which greatly increased speed of hoisting at a substantial reduction in cost.[14] The vertical shaft idea was taken over by Calumet and Hecla in 1890 when the company commenced sinking the famous Red Jacket shaft which was finally bottomed 4,920 feet underground.[15] About this same time, the big mines began enlarging existing shafts so that two skips, working in balance, could be run by the same hoist;[16] skip capacity was increased from two to five tons; and man cars, powered by the regular hoists and equipped with safety devices, replaced the old man-engines.[17] All of these changes meant that more powerful hoisting engines were required, and by 1904 the larger Michigan mines were equipped with engines which hoisted seven- and eight-ton capacity skips at speeds of over 40 miles an hour from what had come to be the deepest shafts in the world.[18]

Substantial progress was made in milling technology, the net effect being an increase in productivity per mill worker employed in spite of a substantial decline in the copper content of the rock worked,[19] and more than a 50 per cent reduction of cost per ton of rock milled.[20] Steady improvement was made in the steam stamp, gradually increasing capacity from around 350 tons of amygdaloid rock per 24 hours or 150 tons of conglomerate in 1882 to 550 tons of amygdaloid or 325 tons of conglomerate by 1904.[21] The most important changes were the adoption after 1884 of an improved version of the Ball stamp known as the "Leavitt" which increased capacity by about 50 per cent with a 30 per cent reduction of steam consumption,[22] putting the stamps on solid iron instead of wood foundations during the early nineties,[23] and just as the period was ending, compounding the cylinders which added another 50 per cent to output with a 35 per cent reduction in fuel requirements.[24]

The washing end of milling underwent very little change until the turn of the century when copper recovery was substantially increased and water requirements reduced by the general adoption of Wilfley concentrators and Chilean regrinding mills to replace the old finisher jigs and slime tables.[25] Finally, during the nineties rapid progress was made in the introduction of electrical power for lighting and secondarily for motive purposes. As early as 1891, the Calumet and Hecla and the Tamarack had introduced Brush dynamos to run mine pumps,[26] and by 1903 the shop machinery at the Quincy was driven by electric motors.[27]

Secondary factors tending to extend the life of the Michigan lodes. The discovery of important new mineral bodies at widely spaced intervals of time,[28] and a constantly changing mining problem, successfully met by continuous technological improvements, do much to explain the long period of growth in the Michigan industry.[29] Certain secondary factors tended to operate in the same direction. Lodes of low copper content, running to great depth, and substantial variations in thickness and richness of different sections of each lode made it extremely risky to attempt rapid increases in rate of exploitation. Each shaft driven thousands of feet into a lode told more about the character and future potentialities of the property, and sinking a large number simultaneously usually seemed too hazardous a short-cut to increased volume of output.

Rapid exploitation of successful Michigan properties may have been held back by a form of capital rationing. The mines were financed by conservative Boston interests, and except in very unusual circumstances, a successful operating property was expected to meet capital costs for expansion out of surpluses accumulated in years of high copper prices when earnings rose above stockholders' "normal" dividend expectations. The result was that expenditures to make good current obsolescence and depreciation and for major development tended to be made during and immediately following periods of high copper prices.[30] Conservative Boston financing and management [31] also explains why rapid exploitation of properties for stock manipulative purposes played an insignificant part in the Michigan history, in marked contrast with certain periods of the Montana and Arizona story. Finally, the fact that Calumet and Hecla consolidated ownership of practically all of the land over the rich conglomerate lode relatively early in the industry's history meant, first, that the greatest lode of the district was exploited as a whole,[32] and, second, that in certain periods the big Lake producer had to consider the effect of its output upon price.

CONSOLIDATION AND INTEGRATION

Around 1890, three interrelated developments began to take shape in the Michigan industry — control of producing properties was gradually concentrated into fewer hands; there was an increasing number of consolidations of old properties; and the largest mines and interest groups went into the smelting and even manufacturing ends of the business. In part these developments reflect the maturing of a mining field and the constant search for means of expanding reserves and reducing costs; in part they reflect more general developments taking place in the United States — the growing power of financial groups in a period when capital requirements were rising and, as a result of a more diffuse capital market, maintenance of control required a lower percentage of ownership.[33] They represent the third major strand in an understanding of the industry's continued growth.

Consolidations and land purchases. Each of the large producers of 1883 owed part of its success in continuing to increase output to purchases or consolidations which increased mineral and other land holdings. In 1891 the Quincy purchased the Pewabic property for a little over $700,000;[34] two years later the company acquired 640 acres of adjoining mineral land for $500,000;[35] and in 1897 the Mesnard and Pontiac mines were absorbed at a cost of $38,560.[36] Calumet and Hecla purchased 120 acres of mineral land adjoining the Tamarack in July of 1895,[37] and in 1899 began buying all the land around Calumet, mineral and otherwise, which could be enticed into the market.[38] Finally, the Osceola took steps to assure its future through a major consolidation in 1897 by which the Iroquois, Kearsarge, Tamarack Junior, and Osceola — all Bigelow properties — were merged into one company, the Osceola Consolidated Copper Company.[39]

The consolidation fever was high in 1899–1900 when six new companies were incorporated to work the holdings of some two dozen old, unsuccessful properties. The new producers were the Adventure, Isle Royale, Mass, Michigan, Phoenix, and Arcadian Consolidated Copper Companies, only one of which, the Isle Royale, ever became a successful producer. However, their formation caused an enormous stir in the Copper Country. Over 18,000 acres of mineral land were involved in the transactions, and by 1904 the new enterprises had made calls upon shareholders aggregating over $7 million.[40]

Concentration of control of operating properties. There was a marked tendency for a larger proportion of Michigan output to be controlled by fewer men. Calumet and Hecla and the Quincy continued along their independent ways with no marked change in control groups and little interest in other properties of the district. Two other groups developed to a point where one controlled more of United States copper output than did Calumet and Hecla, and the other a little less than a third of Michigan production.

Albert S. Bigelow and Joseph W. Clark had first reached success in the Osceola mine, which began producing in 1874, and the Tamarack, which shipped its first copper in 1883.[41] During the late 1880's, they became associated with Leonard Lewisohn, the powerful New York coffee and copper broker, in a number of successful Lake and Western mining enterprises, with an aggregate output in 1895 of over 86 million pounds of refined copper, or about 23 per cent of the United States total.[42] The western holdings of this group included the Boston and Montana and Butte and Boston properties at Butte and the Old Dominion Mine at Globe, Arizona, and were even more significant than the Tamarack, Osceola, Kearsarge, and Tamarack, Jr., mines in Michigan.[43]

The second major interest group evolved out of the so-called Stanton-Gay mines, which in 1885 had consisted of three relatively small producers: the Atlantic, Central, and Allouez. In 1890 John Stanton was the main force in the establishment of the Wolverine Copper Company, and in 1898–99 of the Mohawk, Winona, Phoenix, and Michigan. During the nineties the Stanton group became associated with well-known Boston interests, the most active member of which was William A. Paine of the investment house of Paine-Webber, which were laying plans to open up the undeveloped country between Houghton and Ontonagon. The Paine interests incorporated the Copper Range Railroad Company in 1899 to build and operate a railroad from Houghton 41 miles to Mass City where it was to connect with the Chicago, Milwaukee, and St. Paul. The road was opened in 1900 and served, among others, the Baltic, Champion, and Trimountain mines — all three of which had been opened on the newly discovered Baltic lode by the Paine group, in coöperation with John Stanton.[44] In 1901 a holding company, known as the Copper Range Consolidated Company, was incorporated under the laws of New Jersey, with William A. Paine as President and John Stanton on the Board, to hold virtually the entire stock of the Baltic Mining Company, the Copper Range Railroad Company, and the Trimountain Mining Company, as well as one-half of the stock of the Champion Copper Company and a 60 per cent share interest in the Michigan Smelting Company. In 1904 what might be called the Paine-Stanton interest group controlled nine operating mines with a total production of over 62 million pounds of copper, or a little less than 30 per cent of the industry's output. Control of Michigan production had reached a marked degree of concentration.[45]

	Number of Mining Companies	Output in Pounds	Percentage of Michigan Total
Calumet and Hecla	1	80,341,019	38.6
Paine-Stanton	9	62,392,095	30.0
Bigelow-Lewisohn	4	38,227,219	18.4
Quincy	1	18,343,160	8.8
Total		199,303,493	95.8

Integration into smelting and manufacturing. Until 1887, smelting for all Lake companies was done by the Detroit and Lake Superior Copper Company which was "chiefly owned and controlled in Connecticut by three or four of the largest copper rolling and manufacturing companies in the country."[46] By 1904 the picture had changed completely, and all Lake mineral was being handled at furnaces either owned directly by the largest Michigan mines or by subsidiary companies.

The shift began in 1887 when the Detroit and Lake Superior Copper Company built a special works at Lake Linden to handle the output of Calumet and Hecla. Ownership was on a 50-50 basis until 1892, when Calumet and Hecla bought up complete control.[47] At about this same time Calumet and Hecla purchased a tract of land at Buffalo, New York, and established an additional smelter, allegedly to take advantage of lower coal costs.[48] In 1895 the Buffalo works were equipped for electrolytic refining in order to separate out the small silver content of some of the company's mineral.[49]

Meanwhile, the Bigelow interests had gone even further along the integration route. The Tamarack-Osceola Manufacturing Company was incorporated in 1888 to operate a rolling mill and wire mill at Dollar Bay on Portage Lake, and in 1889 smelting furnaces were added to the works.[50] The smelting section of the enterprise was consolidated with the Hancock works of the Detroit and Lake Superior Copper Company two years later, and a new company formed known as the Lake Superior Smelting Company.[51] In 1904, the shares of the smelting company were owned by the Tamarack, Osceola, Isle Royale, and Ahmeek, all Bigelow properties.[52] The Quincy joined the movement in December, 1898, when smelting was begun at its own furnaces in Hancock,[53] and in 1903 the Michigan Smelting Company was incorporated to operate a new works three miles west of Houghton for the Stanton and Paine mines.[54]

Thus, by 1904 over 95 per cent of the industry's output was controlled by two large companies and two interest groups which smelted their own mineral, and one of which had substantial interests in the maufacturing end of the business.[55] In addition, some of the companies had invested heavily in timber lands and sawmills;[56] all owned short railroads for mine-to-mill and sometimes longer haulage; and one, Calumet and Hecla, owned and operated a small fleet of vessels to take copper and mineral to the Buffalo refinery and eastern markets and haul coal back.[57] Consolidation of properties and concentration of control had been highly significant in increasing mineral reserves of old properties, but also were important in making integration into smelting possible, since ownership of smelting furnaces, if it was to mean a reduction of costs, required a fairly large output.[58]

It seems probable that other savings resulting from joint management of properties in the same interest group became significant during these years. Stevens speaks of a substantial lightening of costs in consequence of joint local and eastern management of the Tamarack and Osceola properties,[59] and common capital expenditures were often made within interest groups. For example, the Osceola and Tamarack mills were served by the same pumping plant in 1904, and the Baltic and Atlantic mills were dependent upon a $150,000 dam jointly constructed by the two companies.[60]

ATTEMPTS AT MARKET CONTROL AND THE PRICE BOOM AT THE TURN OF THE CENTURY

The Michigan copper mining industry ended the period 1885–1904 with what was, in many respects, a real surge of new life. This rejuvenation, stimulated as it was by an intensification of the consolidation and integration movements, was partially the result of the copper price boom at the turn of the century.

The price boom, 1899–1901, and its effect upon the industry. In 1894 prices on Lake copper reached a record low for the first half century of the industry's history, an average selling price of 9.6 cents a pound, and then began a steady recovery to 12 cents by 1898. In 1899 the average price jumped to 17.6 and remained slightly above 16 cents for the next two years, followed by a decline to 11.9 in 1902.[61] These were the highest copper prices since 1880–1882 and were sustained for a long enough period to have a marked effect upon the industry.

Gradually rising prices in 1897 and 1898 were followed by substantial output increases in 1898. In 1899 and 1900 total

Michigan output declined and then began a notable rise, but it was not until 1902 that production surpassed the 1898 level, and the heaviest increases came during the years 1903 and 1904.[62] As in other periods of sudden price rises, one reason for the inverse correlation between price movements and output in 1899 and 1900 was a labor shortage at many of the older mines in consequence of heavy development work at both new and old properties.[63] An additional factor was involved in this case since Calumet and Hecla was badly crippled in May of 1900 by a severe underground fire.[64] However, the delayed impact of high prices upon production does much to explain the substantial gains in output, which amounted to over 17 million pounds per annum during the last three years of the period.

As might be expected, there was no delay in the effect of high copper prices upon dividend payments and share quotations. Dividends rose from $5.4 million in 1897 to $12.3 million in 1899, and during the four years 1898–1901 the companies paid out a total of $36.5 million, an amount equal to the aggregate paid in the first 44 years of the industry's history.[65] Finally, a stock market boom developed in 1897 and by 1899 had doubled and tripled the value of the shares of the major companies.[66]

High copper prices, exceptionally large profits, and a booming share market turned a flow of capital into the district, which served to open up the newly discovered Baltic lode, made possible the consolidation of a score of old unsuccessful properties into half a dozen new enterprises, and renovated the plants of successful old producers on an unprecedented scale. In the two years 1899 and 1900 the Quincy spent over a million dollars for improvements, an annual rate of expenditure two and one-half times that of 1897. The Atlantic more than quadrupled annual expenditures for improvements between 1897 and 1901, and the Osceola increased that cost category from $91,400 in 1898 to over $483,000 in 1901.[67]

The copper price boom of 1899–1901 began as nothing more than a free interplay of market forces with demand rising sharply against a relatively inelastic supply. As early as the end of 1897 the domestic electrical industry was expanding much more rapidly than the general rate of economic recovery in the United States, and by 1899 the requirements for copper in electrical railroads, power transmission, lighting, and various shipping industries were increasing in a phenomenal fashion.[68] Pettengill estimates that domestic copper consumption increased by almost a third between 1898 and 1899, the sudden shift in demand being met in large part by a 100 million pound reduction of the export balance.[69] But even in 1899 there was another strand to the story. In May of that year rumors were confirmed of the formation of the Amalgamated Copper Company of New Jersey under the aegis of important men in Standard Oil circles whose broker announced their intention of ultimately consolidating all of the important United States copper properties.[70] The activities of this group had a profound effect upon share values during the following three years and a substantial effect upon the price of the metal, particularly during the years 1900–1901. To understand how such a development was possible, it is necessary to go back to the breakup of the Lake pool in 1883–1885 and trace through the history of alternating periods of fierce rivalry and attempts at market control, and Michigan's role in the more general story.

Copper at ten cents a pound. Although the Court decision brought an official end to the pool in January of 1885, Calumet and Hecla continued to fill the Chile bar contracts until March 31, 1886, when they finally expired. The company was pressed for copper to meet its commitments during most of 1885, and no real plans were laid for future action until the fall. In April Channing Clapp, the vice-president in charge of marketing policy, was declaring, "I wish in the future to be free from any entangling alliances, but beyond that I have decided on no policy." [71] But by December his views had clarified:

We have soon got to go into a fight in which our only weapon will be a lower price than anyone else, and until we inaugurate that it makes but little difference about the feelings of our customers toward us — the lower price will make them all our friends at once.[72]

In the spring of 1886 the Lake giant launched a campaign to teach the rest of the domestic industry where its interests lay. Output was increased substantially in spite of the lowest copper prices in 40 years, and the dumping policy was reversed — the company reducing exports and filling foreign orders, allegedly, only at prices above those in the domestic market.[73] May brought the final bombshell — future contracts with domestic consumers to deliver copper at 10 cents a pound.[74]

The immediate results were gratifying; three of the largest Arizona mines closed down by July, and Anaconda stopped producing from August until December.[75] The decline in copper production was general in mid-1886, the United States and world totals for that year showing a sizable sag. By the fall, Calumet and Hecla felt able to reverse its course and began exporting — in order to take advantage of domestic curtailment, drive the home price above that in the world market, and liquidate its remaining stocks in the United States at a higher price. The victory was, however, a fleeting one. By the end of the year, the Western companies were opening up again, and, even worse, Lake copper was pouring in from Europe, the customs people allowing it to enter free of duty.[76] With noteworthy Bostonian restraint, Clapp commented, "After the loss we have sustained in order to get this copper out of the Country, to have it come back as soon as we have succeeded in getting up the price on this side is very vexatious." [77]

When navigation opened again in the spring of 1887, the situation became even more precarious. Not only were the Westerners in full production again, but the smaller Michigan producers signed selling contracts with Leonard Lewisohn, and under his expert guidance pushed sales in the domestic market.[78] Channing Clapp complained that the Calumet and Hecla New England broker did not "run fast enough outside the (Connecticut) Valley," [79] and that:

It will now be a constant struggle between us with all the chances in favor of Lewisohn as he keeps his salesmen out all the time, and when the buyers find out the arrangement he has made with the Lake producers we shall be very likely to get left with our stock on our hands and the other mines sold out.[80]

Calumet and Hecla drove the price down to 10 cents again and even made secret contracts for future delivery at 9.75 cents a pound. But in August a fire closed half of the big company's shafts for five weeks, and hardly had the debris been cleared than an even more serious blaze broke out in November, reducing output to half the normal amount.[81] The battle was a stalemate — Calumet and Hecla was pressed even to fill its contracts, let alone keep up the fight. The questions of who should curtail, or shoulder the dumping burden, and who should serve the big domestic consumers were no nearer solution than ever. The time was ripe for a fresh approach.

The possibility of another combination had never been far from the minds of the leaders of the industry, least of all from the mind of Channing Clapp. He was by no means opposed to combinations — just disillusioned with the kind the industry had had in the past — and he even indicated from time to time that a period of bitter rivalry might result in a more satisfactory arrangement. (See quotation at the beginning of this chapter.) The first requisite was an agreement which would be binding and include everyone. In early 1886 he was suggesting that any future combination must provide for a money forfeit; [82] in July he rejected an ingenious proposal to form a combination and then sell enough copper to the small companies to keep them idle,[83] and in October, 1887, he was writing to Lewisohn, turning down the latter's overtures on the grounds that Lewisohn had shown a profound lack of good faith.[84] But the surprise move came from abroad.

The Secretan Syndicate, 1887–1889. From October of 1887 to March of 1889, world copper history was dominated by the operations of a group of French capitalists brought together by M. Secretan, director of the largest European copper manufacturing company, the Société Industrielle et Commercialle des Métaux, and backed by the Comptoir d'Escompte (the second most powerful banking establishment in France), the

Paris Rothschilds, the Crédit Lyonnais, and the Banque de Paris et Pays-Bas.[85] The Syndicate offered the great mining companies of the world three-year contracts for their entire output on highly favorable terms, which varied somewhat in each case. The one with Calumet and Hecla (concluded in late December, 1887) covered a three-year period during which the company agreed not to exceed production limits somewhat above current levels (1888, 25,000 long tons; 1889, 27,000; and 1890, 28,000) and guaranteed a price of 13.5 cents a pound, or about 3 cents more than the average price in 1887. Profits derived from that part of sales receipts above 13.5 cents were to be divided equally between the contracting parties. Calumet and Hecla was to manage sales in the domestic market and the Syndicate those made abroad — the company to export approximately a quarter of its annual product.[86] By mid-1888, 37 companies, including all of the important Michigan producers, were bound by such agreements,[87] and about 80 to 85 per cent of world copper output was cornered.[88]

Within the United States, a selling pool was formed to handle all Lake copper, and the first combined sale was successfully negotiated in May at 16.5 cents a pound, the Syndicate covering the operation by taking up all odd floating lots.[89] As the year drew to a close, the domestic picture was quite encouraging. A second sale had been concluded at the same price — once the lion had been seized by the tail no lower price was feasible since any signs of weakness would lead consumers to expect a further fall and postpone buying.[90] The only real difficulty seemed to be with the Tamarack and Osceola, which were raising hob with consumers by giving their own rolling mill more favorable prices than those offered by the pool.[91]

Difficulties were encountered abroad, however, almost immediately. The contracts set limits on the output of the largest producers, usually at levels well above current production, but did not impose limits on smaller properties.[92] Prices were driven up to such high levels that a mining boom got under way all over the world; huge amounts of scrap copper began to appear in the market, some of it coming from distances as great as Russia and India,[93] and purchases were restricted in both the United States and European markets.[94] In October, 1888, the Syndicate was reported attempting to extend contracts from six to twelve years with strong curtailment provisions,[95] and by early 1889 it was apparent that the load was too great and complete collapse imminent. In April of 1889 Lake copper was quoted at 16 cents a pound; a month later 12 cents was the going price. The operation closed dramatically with M. Secretan committing suicide.

From the Michigan point of view, the results of the Syndicate's operations had been quite satisfactory. Dividends rose from the unusually depressed level of $1.37 million in 1887 to $3.26 million in 1888; profits were available for much needed renovations; and there was a brief share market boom which carried security values up 50 per cent or more. The difficult question was how the copper of the defunct Syndicate was to be disposed of, particularly since a substantial amount (35 million pounds of Lake alone) was stored in the United States.[96] The French bankers were holding about 140,000 tons of copper,[97] and throughout the early months of 1889 representatives of the Lake companies were busy trying to organize the American producers and come to terms with the European interests holding the Syndicate stocks.[98] Representatives of all the major copper producers of the world assembled at Paris in March of 1889 to consider the interrelated questions of how far the price should be allowed to sag, how quickly the stocks should be liquidated and on which side of the Atlantic, and whether an agreement could be reached as to output restriction. Excitement was intense — all the domestic interests conferring frequently throughout the Spring[99] — the greatest stumbling block being Lewisohn.

Everyone was so frightened by the prospect of a price collapse that conclusion of a far-reaching agreement seemed probable (by midsummer Haggin of Anaconda had called in lawyers to make a plan for the Westerners and eliminate Lewisohn)[100] when a bombshell fell from other quarters. The Rothschild interests began liquidating stocks of Lake at 11.5 cents a pound in the United States market.[101] Talk of a combination immediately subsided, but the expected copper glut failed to appear; general business conditions were surging upwards so rapidly that, in spite of liquidation of Syndicate stocks, increased demand for copper carried Lake up to an average of 15.8 cents a pound in 1890 to the general astonishment of the trade.[102]

The producers' associations. Relief was only temporary, and when business conditions worsened, bringing the price of copper down in 1891, Calumet and Hecla initiated a new foreign policy — attempting to establish direct contacts with consumers abroad instead of selling through dealers. Their hope was to compete more effectively with electrolytic bar. Arrangements were made with special agents in England, France, Germany, Austria, and Italy, and all sales were made under the "C. & H." brand name.[103]

By the fall of 1891 a new combination was in prospect, primarily in consequence of vastly improved relations between the directors of Calumet and Hecla and Haggin of Anaconda.[104] In November, Colonel Livermore, successor to Channing Clapp, wrote his English agent:

Haggin is disposed to effect an arrangement by which all American mines and the large European mines shall restrict production until consumption increases, and unless this is accomplished I shall expect to see a campaign opened in January which will knock some of the weaker ones into quietude.[105]

And direct to Haggin:

My London correspondent writes me under date of 1st inst. that Henry R. Merton has said to him that if you and I so desire he thinks he can get the European miners to agree to restrict output, that he is sure of Tharsis, Rio Tinto, and Cape.[106]

During December, Anaconda apparently prepared the ground by "destroying confidence in prices" so that the other Montana and Arizona mines would feel coöperative,[107] and there was a good deal of correspondence with Haggin as to the proper way of handling the ever-recalcitrant Lewisohn.

The gentleman we spoke of says that he would be willing to agree to sell all over 90% of his product of last year to any responsible person for 5 cts a pound for next year. This seems to be the most feasible plan. Are you in a position to ascertain from the foreigners whether they would restrict ten per cent? If you can do this it would seem worthwhile to have a conference.[108]

Meetings were held throughout the first half of 1892, dealing primarily with the thorny problem of output restriction, but it was not until June that a formal agreement was reached.[109] On June 22, 1892, Livermore wrote to his London agent:

There seems to be no doubt that beginning July 1st production of all the principal copper mines in Europe, America, and Australia will be so proportioned as to prevent the production of the world from exceeding its production of 1891 by more than 7,000 tons.[110]

Word of the agreement began to circulate in the trade and soon reached Congressional ears, made sensitive thereto by the recent passage of the Sherman Act. In July, Senator Nelson W. Aldrich made inquiries of Calumet and Hecla and received a reply stating, first, that the company was not a member of a trust to control output — and, second, that to their knowledge there was no such trust in existence; however, it did state:

For your own information but not for public use, I will add that there has been much negotiation between American and foreign mine owners recently with the view on the part of some of them of agreeing to limit production, but there are some of us who have always been persuaded that such an agreement could not be made without violation of the law and we have declined to engage in one, but the discussions have resulted in a conviction that a certain ratio of production among the chief mines would be of benefit to all, and it is the belief that the desire to encourage each other to conform to that ratio will induce each one to conform to it, and in order to furnish evidence of what is being done I believe that it is the intention of each one to report his production to the others at stated intervals. You will see that this involves no promise to limit production and each one is at liberty to conform or not to the proposed ratio. But there are so many people

THE STRUGGLE FOR LEADERSHIP

who would torture this state of affairs into the semblance of a trust that I for one should not like to make it the subject of discussion.[111]

The next year saw the operation of the first really effective world copper combination to curtail production. World output was reduced in 1893 by some 35 million pounds — that of the United States by 16 million and of Michigan by 10 million. (This was, however, not nearly enough to prevent copper prices from falling to the lowest level recorded before 1932.) All of the important United States producers entered into an agreement to form the American Producers Association which was to collect sworn monthly statements from each member as to output and exports and to deal with a newly formed European Producers Association. Between them the two organizations represented over 75 per cent of world copper production.[112] Monthly output allotments were set up for each mine, the understanding being that each had to conform to 12 times its monthly quota by the end of the year. As an example, one of the reports Calumet and Hecla received from the Association is presented below.[113]

Monthly Allotment	Company	Actual Production
	(In Thousands of Pounds)	
6,250	Anaconda	6,169
5,000	Calumet and Hecla	4,855
3,569	Butte and Boston / Boston and Montana	4,125
1,283	Tamarack	1,253
1,136	Parrot Silver	852
1,125	United Verde	917
1,035	Copper Queen	1,114
815	Quincy	1,914
602	Arizona Copper	900
509	Osceola	544
429	Detroit Copper	384
253	Buffalo Copper	none
158	Long Island	none
137	Kearsarge	71
958	Small Lake Companies	1,300
3,302	Other	2,684
26,561		27,082

In the fall of 1892, Livermore wrote his English agent, with what approached awe, that restriction was being carried out in good faith.[114]

However, the agreement was not renewed in the late spring of 1893. Livermore reported developments as follows:

Copper producers in this country have determined to discontinue their arrangement excepting so far as to make returns and hold monthly meetings if the European mine owners will do the same. My own view is that this will prove to restrict production all that is necessary because as long as Haggin and we are assured that other mines are not producing extravagantly we are disposed to keep within bounds, and he and I have agreed not to increase without notice to each other. We think that we can hold a club big enough to keep the rest in order.[115]

Such was apparently the case until the spring of 1894 when Lewisohn and Haggin substantially increased output, to be followed in August by Calumet and Hecla. Throughout the following year there was constant talk of a new curtailment agreement — the proposals apparently being initiated by the London Rothschilds — [116] but no joint action was taken except for the continued exchange of monthly output data and "cordial rivalry" between Calumet and Hecla and Anaconda. Apparently the great stumbling block was Lewisohn, who, according to other members of the trade, had not lived up to his agreements. When the European producers called on the Americans to give them "an honorable assurance that we would limit output," Livermore commented that there were two insurmountable objections. It was impossible to coöperate with Lewisohn unless he could be bound to his understandings and the anti-trust laws made such binding impossible.[117] Calumet and Hecla showed a growing respect for the anti-trust laws (particularly the Michigan Act) during these years — not as anything to be feared if agreements could be kept informal but as prohibiting combination agreements which could really be enforced.[118] (Other members of the industry seemed to be in a much more uninhibited frame of mind.) The next major attempt at combination was to come a few years later from a group of real professionals. In the meantime, domestic and world output were rising in step with general business recovery and increased copper prices. In looking back, Livermore commented in May, 1896:

> My impression is that the statistics which are collected by the Association of Copper Miners and exchanged have been of some benefit in steadying the price of copper. It seems to me that with the information which they give buyers have been less liable to the influences which speculators are accustomed to set at work to unduly raise or depress prices.[119]

And again, to his French correspondent:

> We are not working with the Anaconda and Rio Tinto. We are now, as we have been for a long time, on friendly terms with the Anaconda Company. Sometimes we have conferred with them as to the true policy of prices and production but such has not been the case recently.[120]

Operations of the Amalgamated Copper Company and the United Metals Selling Company, 1899–1901. During the nineties efforts at organizing world copper producers into an effective association had fallen short of complete success primarily because of difficulties encountered in the United States. By 1899 it was clear that any interest group which could speak for United States producers, with their 55 per cent of world output, would have little difficulty in coming to terms with the major companies in other parts of the world. In 1899 Thomas Lawson, a Boston stockbroker, together with William Rockefeller and Henry H. Rogers, both associated with Standard Oil, set out to consolidate the important United States properties.

As early as February, Livermore wrote his French correspondent of the desire on the part of a group of capitalists to combine all the great copper properties and expressed doubt as to their ability to do so.[121] In April he wrote him again to pass along the recent news of the combination and to give assurance that "there is no disposition on the part of the Calumet and Hecla Mining Company to merge itself in such a combination." [122] According to Thomas Lawson, the first section of the proposed consolidation was to consist of the Boston financed mines, with which he had had extensive experience.[123] The companies concerned and their relative standing in 1899 were as follows:

		1899 Output	Dividends
Calumet and Hecla		89,610,963 lbs.	$10,000,000
Bigelow-Lewisohn	Boston & Montana / Butte & Boston	79,000,000	5,400,000
	Tamarack	18,565,602	600,000
	Osceola	11,358,049	558,450
Quincy		14,301,182	950,000
		212,835,796	$17,508,450

The production of these mines represented about 38 per cent of United States and 23 per cent of world output. Apparently Lawson had already begun to buy up their shares when the plan of campaign was suddenly changed.[124] Lawson implies that a chance meeting between Marcus Daly of Anaconda and Henry H. Rogers brought about the shift. In addition, there were doubtless enormous difficulties encountered in acquiring the shares of the Quincy and the Calumet and Hecla, which were both closely held. As events transpired, the first section, which was launched as the Amalgamated Copper Company, was based upon majority ownership of the shares of the Anaconda and other mines in which Daly had substantial interests.[125] Livermore's comment at the time indicated very little concern:

Rockefeller and his associates by extensive advertising have endeavored to persuade the public to buy the shares of the Amalgamated Copper Co. Whether they intend to retain control of the Company we do not know, (but we think it probable that they do, and if they do,) we think they will be more conservative in regulating the output of copper than the former owners . . . have been.[126]

But this was by no means the end of the operation. During the fall of 1899, Lewisohn became selling agent for the combination, which, with his mines, now controlled about 95,000 tons of copper per annum.[127] A year later the Lewisohns were thrown out by Henry Rogers, losing control of their selling agency as well as their great Raritan refineries. A new company under Amalgamated control was set up, known as the United Metals Selling Company, to handle sales for the Amalgamated and "associated interests" totaling about 70 per cent of United States output.[128]

In 1900 the prospects of the great combination looked exceedingly bright. The Bigelow-Lewisohn mines were considered an associated interest of the Standard Oil group and were selling their copper through the United Metals Selling Company; the Rockefeller interests had bought 3,000 acres of land in Houghton County, including about 17 old mineral tracts, and were equipping their new Arcadian Consolidated Copper Company property on a scale never before witnessed in the Michigan district; [129] Thomas Lawson allegedly was holding large blocks of shares in a number of Lake companies; [130] and the sky seemed to be the limit on what the combination was prepared to spend — important stockholders of Calumet and Hecla were reported to have received offers of over $1,000 a share for a controlling interest in the company.[131]

Calumet and Hecla felt called upon to deny the rumors current in the trade:

> The rumors that this Company has come under the control of the Amalgamated Co. are entirely unfounded. Our situation remains the same as it always has been, and I see no reason to suppose that it will change during the lifetime of those who are now in control of this Company.[132]

Nevertheless relations seemed to be cordial — Livermore meeting with the Standard Oil people in New York,[133] and on one occasion writing somewhat mysteriously to Rogers: "If you and Mr. Dodge find your views in accord I hope that I shall be able to acquiesce in the judgment you and he form." [134] In any case, he seemed content with the way things were going:

> The United Metal Selling Co. seems to be controlled by a more conservative policy than that which the Lewisohns used to follow, and it

now seems to us that the influence of the Company is likely to prevent the violent fluctuations in the price of copper in which Lewisohn used to participate.[135]

In 1900 and 1901 the Amalgamated adopted the policy of maintaining "a firm price." Lake was quoted at 17 cents and electrolytic at 16.25, and during 1901 the output of the Montana mines was restricted by about 25 million pounds.[136] Production in the rest of the country increased substantially, however, and the net effect was a reduction of about 4 million pounds in United States output, an amount which was not substantial enough to maintain prices in the face of a slackening of the European demand.[137] All of the Michigan companies, with the exception of the Bigelow group, undersold the trust price until December, when the United Metals Selling Company slashed Lake to 12 cents a pound.

Apparently Calumet and Hecla came within an ace of formally associating with the combination just before the price was slashed. The company had increased output steadily all through the 1901 restriction period, and in the fall Rogers approached Livermore with a proposition to make a combined sale.[138] Calumet and Hecla first held out for a 20 per cent share, which Rogers considered too high. Livermore then proposed on November 22, 1901, an arrangement, subject to renegotiation after three months, by which the Calumet and Hecla share would be 17.5 per cent.[139] Apparently the only answer Amalgamated made was to plunge ahead alone.

The new policy was to force the price down and keep it there. Early in 1902, Lake sold at 10.9 and electrolytic at 10.6. Murdoch reports that Calumet and Hecla, certain Arizona interests, and the Rothschilds retired from the market and adopted the policy of storing all copper mined.[140] Livermore believed that United Metals was attempting to depress the shares of the Rio Tinto to persuade the Rothschilds to engage in an agreement to reduce production and maintain copper prices.[141] Just as in 1887 when Calumet and Hecla attempted a punitive expedition, a demand boom set in and Amalgamated was unable to stay a price rise. The average price of Lake went to 12.2 in 1902 and 13.7 in 1903 in spite of the liquidation of substantial stocks held by the independents. By that year it was apparent that the Amalgamated storm was blowing over. The copper world was being shaken by great new producers opening up at Bisbee, Arizona; Ely, Nevada; and Bingham, Utah; and the anti-trust feeling of the times seemed to preclude substantial extension of the Amalgamated consolidation. In Michigan, the Arcadian Consolidated Copper Company had gone down to miserable failure with a magnificent surface plant and little copper below ground, and it was clear that Lawson had drawn a blank in his attempt to buy out the holdings of Boston's copper aristocrats.

THE COMPETITIVE POSITION OF THE MICHIGAN INDUSTRY AT THE TURN OF THE CENTURY

At the turn of the century, the Michigan copper district was showing marked vitality and was increasing output at about the same rate as United States producers as a whole. The proportion of United States output accounted for by the district had fallen steadily from 51 per cent in 1886 to 25.8 per cent in 1899, but after that date had practically stabilized. In the year 1902, Michigan companies mined 53 per cent of the rock tonnage raised in United States copper mining, employed 53 per cent of the wage earners and 69.4 per cent of the horsepower used in the industry, but produced only 25.6 per cent of domestic output of refined copper.[142] These last statistics cast dark shadows for the future.

The problem of increasing mining difficulties. In spite of increasing output and a high level of dividend payments, the Michigan field was on the threshold of maturity. The year 1900 saw the Tamarack with all five vertical shafts down to 3,200 to 4,600 feet;[143] the Calumet and Hecla Red Jacket shaft reached 4,920 feet in 1902, and the company's deepest inclined shaft 6,900 feet;[144] while the deepest Quincy shaft in 1904 was down to 5,280 feet on the dip.[145] These were the deepest mining shafts in the world, and even the Anaconda, after 20 years of successful history, was working most of its shafts at less than 2,000 feet.[146] Greater depth had brought a continued fall in copper content. The conglomerate lode, which had yielded a 4.5 per cent mill return in 1883, was down to less than 3 per cent by 1900,[147] and the return from the old amygdaloids, which had yielded 1.2 to 1.5 per cent in 1883, was around one per cent by 1900.[148] In 1905 the Anaconda was getting over 3.25 per cent copper return and the Boston and Montana about 5 per cent.[149]

The major new Michigan discovery, the Baltic lode, carried a much lower copper content than had been the case in the early days of the Pewabic lode, upon which the Franklin and Quincy had thrived. Returns of around 1.4 per cent were considered good in 1904,[150] and the lode slanted down to great depth much more rapidly than did earlier discoveries in the industry's history. The clearest sign of maturity, however, was an actual decline of production from the Calumet conglomerate lode which had served as the backbone of the district for so many years. Calumet and Hecla reached its peak output for the period 1883–1904 in 1899, and in spite of the fact that an increasing quantity of amygdaloid rock was treated after that date, in 1904 the company fell short of the 1899 production total by about nine million pounds. The only other major conglomerate producer was the Tamarack, and output from that property reached a peak in 1898 and steadily declined thereafter.

Years of mining at the older properties meant that vast areas underground were honeycombed and left with millions of board feet of timbering which dried out and became as inflammable as tinder. Calumet and Hecla began to have difficulty with fires in old workings as early as 1884, and had major conflagrations in 1887, 1888, and 1900,[151] while around the turn of the century the Quincy began to be troubled by air blasts, caused by the shifting of rock around old workings.[152]

It is something of a mystery why Calumet and Hecla did not invest in some of the new copper properties of the West, particularly since the company was showered with offers throughout these years. Apparently the answer lies in a combination of contentment with current income — increasing age of the top personnel of the big Lake producer, making them unwilling to assume risks and take on new responsibilities — and, finally, sheer bad luck when the search was belatedly undertaken. As early as 1892 Livermore laid down the policy in a letter to his English correspondent: "We have good ground enough for this generation and one or two more, and we therefore are not looking for further fields for our energies." [153] In 1894 Haggin approached Calumet and Hecla with a proposition that Anaconda and Calumet and Hecla should purchase jointly a newly discovered six million dollar western property. Livermore was favorably inclined but was ill at the time, and Alexander Agassiz finally wrote Haggin that "Mr. Shaw was getting old and hard to move to anything new and that I [Agassiz] was always away and could not run anything new." [154] The following year, however, the company did join with Anaconda in keeping two young geologists in the field looking for promising new claims.[155] But it was not until 1897 that Calumet and Hecla really became interested and began sending representatives all over the West and as far afield as Mexico, British Columbia, and Alaska.[156] Apparently, nothing of real merit was turned up.

Quality of copper, metallurgy, and precious metal content. Lake copper continued to draw a premium as a superior metal, but by 1904 it seems probable that the premium over electrolytically refined western copper was due more to old established custom in the trade than to real differences in quality. The Special Census of 1902 reported the average Michigan price for the year as half a cent higher than that of Montana copper and seven-tenths of a cent above that of Arizona copper.[157] Livermore commented on the situation as follows in 1900:

> The manufacture of electrolytic copper in this country has become so far perfected that the quality of a great deal of it (for example that of the Baltimore Works) is so uniform that manufacturers can now rely upon it, and we now find that the most of them are accustomed to buy electrolytic copper for the manufacture of wire, and they regard the use of our copper as essential only for strong brass, and perhaps some

other special uses. Today we cannot sell our wire-bars in competition with electrolytic wire-bars at any advance in price above that of the latter, although when the market is an advancing one we can get a better price for our copper for the other uses above mentioned.[158]

Such an advantage was more than overbalanced by the value of by-product silver and gold contained in western ores. In 1897–98 Anaconda was getting one dollar for by-product silver and gold for every four dollars worth of copper sold,[159] and in 1902 the value of gold and silver mined as a by-product of copper in the United States was over 10 per cent of the value of the copper.[160] Since practically all of the precious metal content was in western ores, this often represented a premium of two cents a pound or more on copper sold by an Arizona or Montana producer. Finally, the Michigan cost advantage in consequence of simplicity of metallurgy of its native metal was substantially reduced by the adaptation of the Bessemer process for the conversion of western ores into matte and the introduction of electrolysis for final refining.[161] Richter has declared, "It can almost be said that bessemerizing did as much for the copper industry as it did for steel — at least for that major part of the copper industry which was working on sulphide ores." [162] Michigan prospects would have been black indeed if the industry had not had a substantial advantage in the cost of labor. Comparatively low Michigan wage rates had become such an important factor in the industry's competitive position that they call for more detailed consideration.

CHAPTER IV

Labor and the Community to 1904

Rarely is the laboring man better off than in this district. . . . The necessities of life are not high; the climate is healthy; good schools are plentiful; hospitals are easily available; and, on the whole, it is obvious that the miner in this region is better off than the high paid men who live amid the desolation of Arizona and Nevada, or among the even more brutalizing environments of such places as Butte City and Broken Hill.[1]

— *T. A. Rickard*

Sweetness and light, however, didn't reign universal in the middle of the Keweenaw thumb. There were individualists with a holy hate for the company's domination. . . . Cornish shift bosses often threw up steady jobs under the aegis of C. & H. for precarious employment at one of the prospect mines some new company was always developing. Finnish trammers worked for the company only in between their meagre potato crops, and the Irish willingly risked their jobs to run for public office against a company man. Old-time Germans saved every penny until they could go into business and so call themselves independent.[2]

— *Angus Murdoch*

The United States Mining Census of 1902 reported that 95 per cent of all Montana copper mining wage earners were receiving $3.50 a day or more — 11.6 per cent falling in the $4.00 or more category. In Michigan 41.8 per cent were receiving $2.00 to $2.24, and 98 per cent were covered in the rate range of $1.50 to $2.74. (The Arizona rates fell between those of Michigan and Montana.)[3] The wage difference was made even more substantial by the fact that an eight-hour day had become standard in many parts of the West in contrast with the ten-hour Michigan day.[4] The opening up of railroads into the big trans-Mississippi mining camps had slashed the freight rate on a ton of copper shipped from Butte to New York until, by 1893, it amounted to .7 of a cent a pound, but had resulted in no reduction in western wage rates. The cost of living in northwestern mining camps was reported to have dropped by about a third during the decade preceding 1893, but wages for miners were consistently maintained at $3.50 per day.[5]

The difference between Michigan and Montana rates is largely explicable in terms of the difficulties encountered in attracting workers to the Northwest, the highly competitive situation around Butte at both an economic and political level, and early and successful Montana unionism. But certain other factors should be brought in which, by the turn of the century, had begun to operate to hold Michigan rates down. Foremost among these were favorable immigration developments of the 1890's and depression conditions in the neighboring Michigan iron country, but even deeper lay such factors as settled community living in a good climate, cheap transportation to the East and Europe, a deeply rooted incentive wage system, and a remarkably well-conducted paternalism that, among other effects, seemed to preclude unionism. To expose some of these root factors requires an excursion as far back as pre-Civil War days.

A FRONTIER MINING COMMUNITY

Until after the Civil War, the Michigan Copper District was characterized by typical frontier mining conditions, and not until the seventies did it begin to take on the aspect of a permanent community which set it off from most other mining camps of the world and proved a real asset in attracting and maintaining a first-class supply of labor. As Angus Murdoch has said, "Thirty years has been the entire life span of most American mining camps. Many vanished before they outgrew their boom-town dance-hall days. But here an ephemeral boomtown had actually grown to manhood." [6]

Even during the frontier period, however, there were factors affecting the supply and efficiency of labor which were unusually favorable to successful establishment of the industry.

Nationality and sources of labor. Some of the first explorers came overland into the copper district from the Wisconsin lead mines, but almost immediately the peninsula's dependence upon the Great Lakes waterway made the East, and indirectly Europe, the dominant sources of labor. Many of the early miners came from the silver, lead, and copper mines of Maine, Vermont, and other eastern states; some from the Canadian fur trade; and very early, Englishmen, Irishmen, and Germans began to arrive from abroad, driven from their homes by the gradual decline of the great Cornish mines, the Irish potato famine, and the revolutionary upheavals of the late forties in mid-Europe.

From the beginning, the Cornishman established himself as the backbone of the underground force and the supervisor of both underground and surface developments. His educational background was not likely to be as good as that of the early German, but he had mined copper, and experience was what counted. As early as 1844, 20 Cornish miners were working for the Lake Superior Copper Company,[7] and in 1849 most of the miners at the Cliff were Cornishmen.[8] But the real stream began in the fifties after the California gold boom had set off an exodus of mining men from England.[9]

In 1859, a traveler passing through the district reported a great mixture of nationalities — Cornish, Irish, German, and a few Frenchmen. He paid tribute to the sober, educated Germans — 300 of whom were working at the Minesota — as the only immigrants who had a positive resolve never to return home. In his opinion, the Irishman was dominated by wanderlust, and the Englishman was saving up for the great day when he could sail for Cornwall, his pockets full of gold.[10] A few years later, in 1864, an interesting statistical report was published showing the nativity of employees at the Amygdaloid mine.[11]

United States	175
Ireland	76
Germany	70
England	40
Canada	27
Switzerland	5
Total	393

Census figures tend to support a belief that a large percentage in the flow of labor was coming from abroad — although it is impossible to estimate how long the immigrants remained in the East before coming out to Michigan. In Houghton County, five persons out of seven were of foreign birth in 1850 and two out of three, in 1860.

Growth of employment and population. Between 1850 and 1864 the population of the Copper Country increased by over seventeen-fold — from 1,097 to 18,811. (For population figures, see Table 14, p. 228.) But this was not a true reflection of the growth of the potential labor force since there was a highly significant shift in the age and sex makeup of the community as the district became less markedly a frontier area. In the same period the male population increased by fourteen times, and the male population age 21 to 45 by approximately ten times. In 1854, 56 per cent of the people in the district were males, age 21 to 45, whereas only ten years later the percentage had dropped to 33. The pioneer miner was a man in the prime of life, and during the early years there was one such potential worker for each child, woman, and aged member of the community.

During the forties and early fifties, the demand for labor had been seasonal in character — reaching a peak in the open-water months when shipping was possible and exploration of the country was not impeded by harsh winter weather. The last few boats in the fall carried the less hardy souls back to civilization, and if mining company curtailment was more severe than expected, a few more men would drift away over the snows during the winter months. When spring came, labor was usually short, and the first boats which arrived after the ice broke up were as important in replenishing the labor supply as they were in providing food and mining equipment. By the sixties, seasonal fluctuations were becoming less significant since the mines had come to consider the winter months as the period when most progress should be made underground, and the district as a whole had opened up and lost some of its winter terrors. In general, the companies were able to obtain an adequate supply of labor at rates which were not a great deal above those for mining in the

East. Serious shortages appeared only when a large number of new mines were being established at the same time — as in the mid-fifties — and during the Civil War period, when the shortage was severe enough to merit detailed comment.

The Amygdaloid company's report for 1862 speaks of the great labor shortage due to volunteering and emigration to Canada to escape the draft.[12] In 1864 the National blamed inability to increase output on the labor shortage, brought about by the great number of new mining enterprises and the panic caused by the approach of the draft.[13] By the end of 1864, the *Mining Gazette* was declaring that the Ontonagon mines had half of their normal supply of labor and a few months later that the Cliff was having so much difficulty obtaining workers that its mining force had fallen to a quarter of its 1862 average.[14] That there was a shortage can scarcely be questioned; it even seems apparent that it explains the falling output of the district as a whole during the years 1862–1864. But its peculiar nature is made manifest by a number of contradictory facts.

Census figures show the total number of males as 9,181 in 1860 as against 11,278 in 1864. Even more significant the mines are shown as employing 3,681 men in 1860 as compared with 5,447 in 1864. The draft and volunteering took some 833 men from the three counties during the course of the war,[15] some of them experienced miners. On the other hand, the Portage Lake companies, working through foreign agents and the Mine Emigrant Society, were remarkably successful in importing workers from abroad. A small number of Englishmen arrived in May, 1863; 250 Canadians a month later; and 400 Scandinavians in 1864.[16] But the demands for labor at new enterprises were running well ahead of supply.[17] Ontonagon and Keweenaw counties suffered more severely than the Portage Lake sector because they lagged behind in the effort to encourage immigration. Even though many of the men who were imported joined the army, the effect was to fill the Houghton County draft quota and thereby to attract miners endeavoring to escape the draft in Ontonagon and Keweenaw.[18] By the end of 1864, the *Mining Gazette* reported prevailing wages in Houghton as ten dollars per month less than rates in the other two sections of the district.[19] But by the summer of 1865, the shortage had largely disappeared. The spring immigration had been heavy; some mines were already firing men and curtailing output; and for all of the companies the price-cost relationship had changed so substantially that there was no longer an incentive to carry out large-scale development work.

The draft had spread fear throughout the district and created instability and a high degree of mobility of labor. But inflation and the manpower shortage were probably even more important factors in making labor mobile and in loosening mining company controls over the communities. The company reports of the period are full of complaints of indolence, insubordination, and strikes.[20] Swineford has declared, "Intemperance, vice and crime ruled the hour. . . . Mine officers were drilled in the manual, ostensibly for the purpose of fitting themselves for service in the army, but really to be prepared to resist internal commotion." [21] When the war ended, a more orderly and peaceable era succeeded. "Dull times followed; the price of copper fell; many mines suspended operations; and labor was at a discount. Hence, wise men became prudent and circumspect in conduct — they were obliged to or starve." [22]

Wages and working and living conditions. As early as the eighteenth century, the Cornish miner worked under a dual wage arrangement whereby he received tribute, or a share in value produced, when working on mineral bearing rock, and so much a fathom, or "contract payment," when he was sinking a shaft or driving a crosscut through nonpaying ground.[23] It was the second of these institutions which he carried with him to Michigan and established so firmly that elements of it survive in the wage setup of today.

The system was adopted by the early Lake copper companies, apparently from the beginning, and underwent no important changes during the period under consideration. An excellent description is available in the *Mining Magazine* of how it was operating around 1853.[24] Approximately every sixth underground man was a contractor, whose function it was to bargain with the mining captain as to the price per unit of measure for a specific job. Once agreement had been reached, the contractor picked men to assist him and the work was commenced. Terms and the work accomplished were recorded by the company clerk, and credits accumulated under each man's name as contracts were completed. At the end of the month, debits were made for company furnished materials such as fuses, powder, candles, and the loss in weight of drills, and the miners were paid the balance.

This was the basic system for underground work, although a man could, if he preferred, elect "company account" or a straight monthly wage, the rate on which was kept well below the average contract level. The scheme had advantages and disadvantages for all concerned. The companies controlled the level of average payments by keeping duration of contracts short and renegotiating in accordance with monthly rates of pay current in the district. Furthermore, they benefited from an incentive system and from continuous competition among workers. The disadvantage came from the necessity of close, highly skilled supervision as contracts neared completion, since it was part and parcel of the game for the miners to pretend that a job was extremely difficult in order to get better terms on the next bargain. From the miners' point of view, the system offered rewards for exceptional ability or energy. The major drawback was that the rewards themselves tended to depress the average level of future contracts. In any case, it is difficult to conceive of a more individualistic wage institution or one which would be less compatible with the principles of organized labor.

Surface workers were paid a straight monthly wage except when the nature of their job was particularly well adapted to the contract system. For example, teaming was often done by contract, a man with his horses receiving a set amount for a specific job. Occasionally, farming was done under a variation of the system, and the mines experimented from time to time with its application to other surface activities.[25]

Wages were gradually rising from the time the district was

opened until just before 1860, with the heaviest gains coming during the early fifties. About the end of that decade there was a slight decline and then virtually 100 per cent increases from 1861 to 1864, followed by substantial reductions when the war ended. During the first few years a good miner commanded about $30 a month, while unskilled surface labor was receiving $15 to $20, and special craftsmen, such as blacksmiths, as much as $40.[26] By the early 1850's, the monthly rate for miners had increased to about $34, and that for surface men to from $26 to $28.[27] It seems probable that there was some rise after that date. The Minesota was paying the exceptionally high rate of $45 for miners in 1857, and the National, $38 for miners and over $30 for surface workers. But by 1860 the over-all rate apparently had fallen again to just about the level of the early fifties. During the peak of the Civil War inflation in 1864, monthly rates for miners of $65 or more were not unusual, and surface men were often averaging as much as $55.

The incentive nature of the underground system was intensified at some mines due to silver finds which, by tradition, were "legitimate" spoils if a miner was astute enough to conceal them from the company.[28] It seems doubtful if the silver proved a significant supplement to wages in any but exceptional cases, although it has been contended that the prevalence of the metal at the Cliff permitted the company to hold wages below those of other mines of the district.[29]

In general, mobility of labor was such that wages tended to rule the same throughout the district, and there was only one occasion, of which there is any record, when the company agents got together to arrive at a common policy. In the early spring of 1865, the cost-price relationship had become highly unfavorable, and individual companies were attempting to reduce wages.[30] In spite of an increased labor supply, these efforts were not immediately successful,[31] and in May the agents assembled to discuss the situation, in hope of arriving at a general agreement.[32] There is no record of the outcome of their meeting, but wage rates were soon reduced to a point where the directors of one company declared that, although wages had not fallen to anything like the prewar level, "men with families have to live very close to keep out of the poorhouse."[33]

Copper Country wages for miners compared favorably with wages of similar skilled workers in the New York, Pennsylvania, and New Jersey iron mines.

TABLE 2

MONTHLY MICHIGAN WAGES FOR COPPER MINERS COMPARED WITH WAGES FOR IRON MINERS IN THE EAST, 1845–1866

(In dollars)

Year	New Jersey[a]	Cornwall, Pennsylvania[a]	Henry District, New York[a]	Michigan
1845	19.50	22.75	26.00	30.00
1853	26.00	20.80	32.50	34.00
1860	26.00	24.70	32.50	33.00
1864	65.00	44.20	65.00	65.00
1866	42.90	45.50	42.90	53.00

[a] Monthly rates for other than Michigan were derived by multiplying daily rates by 26.

Source: Daily rates for other than Michigan from Nelson W. Aldrich, *Report on Wholesale Prices, Wages, and Transportation,* 52 Cong., 2 Sess., Senate Report No. 1934, 1893, IV, 1567–1568.

The data presented above are by no means adequate, particularly since it is not certain that the job classifications are completely comparable throughout, but, taken in conjunction with other information indicating that the Michigan working day was somewhat shorter, it is probably safe to say that the advantage held by the Michigan miner was substantial until the middle fifties, or even the Civil War period, when gains in the East began to narrow the differential. It cannot be concluded, however, that its full extent was reflected in real wages since living costs were probably higher in this frontier area, particularly during the early days.

During the latter half of the period very few of the mines paid their men in currency.[34] The usual medium was the sight draft, payable at the companies' eastern offices, which found its way to Pittsburgh, Boston, or New York via merchants, boardinghouse keepers, and others who accepted it at face value in the Copper Country. This meant that very little money had to be kept at the mines and represented a substantial short-term credit, particularly during the winter months when communication with the East was infrequent. In 1865 the *Mining Gazette* declared that the drafts had served as the principal currency of the country for ten years or more.[35]

Within each company, employees were divided into underground and surface workers. The chief subcategories of the former were miners, miners' assistants, trammers, and timbermen, while the surface workers were divided into stamp hands, engineers, laborers, smiths, carpenters, teamsters, farmers, and a half-dozen other trades. The proportion of total employment in each of these categories varied substantially from mine to mine, depending in part upon the particular phase of development reached, and it is even difficult to generalize about the underground and surface division. The number on the surface was usually less than the number underground, and it was not exceptional for actual miners and their assistants to constitute a third of all employees.

Hours of work tended to vary somewhat among different sections of the district and even from mine to mine, usually being less for mines of great depth where as much as an hour was often required for the men to reach their place of work. Horace Greeley implies that an eight-hour day was customary for miners in 1847,[36] and in 1853 the deep mines of Keweenaw had an eight-hour shift, while the newer Ontonagon companies required ten.[37] In general, ten hours seemed to be the usual practice for surface workers with variations downward to eight hours for miners when underground conditions called for them.[38] The ten-hour day had won wide acceptance in the United States by 1860, but the national average was still around eleven, and iron miners in Pennsylvania and New Jersey were working anywhere from ten hours up to the traditional sunrise to sunset requirement.[39] It is probably safe to say that the Michigan workers, particularly in the early days, were working shorter hours than the great majority of miners and laborers in other parts of the country.

Copper mining in Michigan has never been considered as dangerous as most underground work since cave-ins are infrequent and noxious or explosive gases almost unknown. Even so, there were many accidents underground. During 1866 the *Portage Lake Mining Gazette* reported five deaths and a half-dozen serious injuries in the Portage Lake section, usually resulting from falls and powder explosions.[40] But this could hardly be called evidence of hazardous employment since perhaps 1,500 men were working below the surface during the year.

Working conditions underground were tiring and often unpleasant. All drilling was by hand with heavy sledges; mining materials and rock were laboriously shoved by hand in wheelbarrows or small cars; and at most mines there were hundreds of feet of ladders to be climbed once the day's work was finished. Very little had been done about ventilation, although one company was experimenting with pipes made of tarred paper in 1864, and the air was sometimes foul, particularly at the ends of long drifts.[41] By the 1860's most of the mines had built adequate change houses near the shafts, where the men kept their regular clothes while underground and left their working clothes to dry after their shift was over.

The very early miners had to contend with the rigors of frontier existence in a wilderness that was icy and stormbound for five to six months of each year. They lived in long bunkhouses near the mine shafts, often in communities of as few as twenty-odd men and half a dozen women and children,[42] and sometimes saw the dread shadow of starvation before the long winters broke up.[43] Until the late fifties community life clearly reflected the predominance of single men. Most of the working population lived at boardinghouses, often kept by an agent of the company, where the monthly charge for room and board ran from as little as a fourth to as much as half of their income.[44] But as the district was opened up, community life changed substantially.

Mining communities of the early sixties sometimes contained as many as 1,000 to 1,500 persons.[45] The companies were interested in creating a permanent labor market and would rent, and sometimes sell, land to employees who wanted to build homes.[46] Or, if a worker preferred, a house could be rented from the company at a nominal fee, usually just enough to cover upkeep on the dwelling. Ordinarily, company built schools were available, and always churches.

"Bal surgeons," or what is now called industrial health insurance, was another eighteenth-century Cornish institution which early miners brought to the district.[47] As it operated in Michigan, each man contributed a fixed amount from his monthly pay, usually one dollar for married men and 50 cents for single men, and the company physician looked after the whole family.[48] By the early sixties, the service had been greatly improved as the mines began to build small hospitals equipped with a dozen to 40 beds and with more elaborate instruments than could be stowed in a doctor's cabin.[49]

All of this represented real progress, but life for most people must have continued to be both hard and barren. More often than not, the schools were completely inadequate, even by the standards of the day, and particularly unsatisfactory in the eyes of the German element of the population.[50] There was always the possibility of discharge during the winter months when escape from the district was all but impossible, and company controls of the details of living were close and often inflexible. When the directors of the Minesota reported in 1852 that "good order and sobriety" were maintained by the company agent, they meant what they said.[51] The mine officers represented law and order, and their rulings were enforced by pay deductions or firing at their discretion.[52] Liquor was prohibited in the communities, and except in times of extreme labor shortage, a man found under its influence was discharged.[53] As might be expected, there were reasons for the controls. Many of the early miners were rough and ready, eager to drink and brawl whenever possible. Germans fought Irishmen, and Irishmen fought Cornishmen, and if liquor was available, a mine might lose its best men for two or three days until the supply gave out.[54] The workers must often have seemed like barbarians to cultivated Bostonian stockholders whose agents sent back reports of rigorously enforcing order, to protect not only company property, but the security of the mine officers and their families as well.

The Civil War completely disorganized the "ordered" life of the mining communities, and prices rose so rapidly that it is doubtful if living conditions were bettered by the doubling of wages. Fite concludes that in the North as a whole labor probably suffered by the inflation — prices advancing "approximately 100 per cent and wages from 50 to 60 per cent." [55] In the Copper Country, it seems probable that both wages and prices rose more rapidly than did the national average and that real wages may have been maintained until 1864, after which date they fell to something like a bare existence level. A letter was printed in the *Mining Gazette* in April of 1866 which gives a basis for interesting, if tentative, comparisons.[56]

Staples	Prices before Inflation about 1861	Prices April, 1866
Flour (barrel)	$ 7.00	$11.00
Pork (100 lbs.)	12.00 to 15.00	40.00
Sugar (lb.)	0.08	0.18
Board (1 month)	9.00 to 10.00	20.00
Fare from Detroit	3.00 to 8.00	14.00 to 20.00
Boots (pair)	3.50 to 5.00	6.00 to 9.00

	Monthly Wages	
	1861	1866
Miners on contract	$33.00	$53.00
Surface workers	28.00	47.00

A SETTLED MINING COMMUNITY AND BENEVOLENT PATERNALISM

Population and employment trends. Following the Civil War, the industry moved into its great period of growth — lasting more than a third of a century — and, in consequence, mining company employment and population of the area grew apace. It was a steady, orderly development which, except in a few years of exceptionally high copper prices, seemed to put no great strain on the labor supply.

Mining company employment fluctuated a good deal from the Civil War until the middle eighties in consequence of the depression in the trade and the far-reaching technological improvements introduced in the late seventies and early eighties, and it was not until the mid-eighties that a clear upward trend in employment is discernible. Mining company employment in Houghton County rose from 6,200 in 1887 to 8,170 by 1896 and then to 14,321 in 1904. Total mining company employment of the district was about 16,500 in 1904. (See Table 10, p. 208, and Fig. 9, p. 201.)

Steady population gains were made throughout the seventies and eighties, the total for the district reaching 38,283 by 1890 and then, under the impact of heavy southeastern European immigration, virtually doubling in 15 years — to 75,171 in 1904. The trend toward a more "normal" age and sex distribution continued, although there were temporary reversals when immigration was unusually heavy. The proportion of males continued to fall until the mid-eighties (reaching about 53 per cent) and then stabilized around 55 per cent. The percentage of males aged 21 to 45 was down to 27.3 per cent as early as 1874.

In Houghton County the proportion of foreign born gradually fell from 56.7 per cent in 1870 to 48.9 in 1880, but the actual number increased from 7,869 to 10,991. Irishmen made up nearly a third of the total in 1870, with Englishmen second, and Canadians third. By 1880 a substantial shift had taken place, and Englishmen ranked first, followed in order by Canadians, Irishmen, and Germans.[57] This was the decade when one-third of the mining population of Cornwall emigrated from their homes,[58] and the Michigan Copper District received a substantial share of that skilled labor. Direct immigration to Houghton of Cornishmen and Scandinavians was so heavy in 1873 that it was the subject of special comment in the *Engineering and Mining Journal*.[59] It was during the nineties, however, that the real revolution took place. Population of Houghton County doubled in the 14 years between 1890 and 1904, and for the first time the great bulk of the foreign arrivals was from non-English speaking countries. The Census of 1904 indicates that over

10,000 people came to Houghton during the nineties from Finland, Austria, and Italy.[60] In consequence of this great influx, 40 per cent of the people of the county were still foreign born in 1904. The mining companies encouraged this new immigration development in the hope that language barriers would forestall the growth of unionism and that the new workers would prove to be easily manageable. Such expectations were to be gravely disappointed.

Wages and hours of work. Hours of work remained about the same as those prevailing from 1845 to 1866; if anything, there may have been some increase in the length of the working day. A two-shift system was customary — from 7:00 A.M. to 6:00 P.M. and from 7:00 P.M. to 6:00 A.M., but actual working time at a surface job or in the mine probably averaged about ten hours.[61]

Data on wages for this period are much more precise than those available for the two decades preceding 1866. As indicated by Table 3 (p. 108), rates tended downward until 1872, when rising copper prices injected new life into the district. A substantial amount of development work was undertaken and caused a shortage of labor in 1872 and early 1873, which was reflected in wage increases of about 30 per cent. Heavy immigration in the spring and summer of 1873, combined with falling prices for copper and a speeding up of technological change, drove wages down by 1874 to the lowest level since the early sixties. In 1880 there was a substantial recovery, resulting from high copper prices and increased mining activity. Copper Country wages for miners still compared favorably with the wages of iron miners in the East, although the differential was not as great as that of the years 1845–1860.[62] The effect of good transportation facilities and the elimination of frontier conditions were clearly evidenced by the fact that miners' wages in many Western districts in 1881–82 were $4 a day, or over twice the Michigan rate.[63]

By the 1890's the Michigan copper industry was sharing a labor market with the neighboring iron industry, and since the iron region suffered acutely from the general depression of the

TABLE 3. MONTHLY MICHIGAN WAGES FOR COPPER MINERS COMPARED WITH WAGES FOR IRON MINERS IN THE EAST, 1867–1904

Year	Wholesale Price Index[a]	New Jersey[b]	Cornwall, Penn.	Henry District, New York	Quincy Mine, Michigan[e]	Michigan Weighted[d]
1867	162	$52.00[e]	$46.80	$53.30	$50.83[f]	$31.38
1868	158	52.00	48.10	53.30	50.44	31.92
1869	151	52.00	48.10	53.30	51.10	33.84
1870	135	52.00	48.10	53.30	46.09	34.14
1871	130	45.50	48.10	53.30	47.08	36.22
1872	136	58.50	49.40	53.30	60.62	44.57
1873	133	58.50	53.50	59.80	62.42	46.93
1874	126	45.50	52.00	67.60	43.38	34.43
1875	118	32.50	45.50	45.50	46.74	39.61
1876	110	32.50	41.60	45.50	47.13	42.85
1877	106	26.00	41.60	39.00	43.79	41.31
1878	91	26.00	41.60	39.00	41.50	45.60
1879	90	32.50	41.60	39.00	38.76	43.07
1880	100	52.00	42.90	41.60	49.10	49.10
1881	103	39.00	48.10	45.50	48.54	47.13
1882	108	45.50	53.30	48.10	48.83	45.21
1883	101	39.00	53.30	45.50	46.02	45.56
1884	93	33.80	53.30	42.90	43.35	46.61
1885	85	32.50	49.40	39.00	44.00	51.76
1886	82	45.50	54.60	42.90	45.80	55.85
1887	85	45.50	57.20	45.50	48.40	56.94
1888	86	39.00	57.20	45.50	49.60	57.67
1889	81	39.00	57.20	42.90	49.15	60.68
1890	82	42.90	57.20	45.50	52.60	64.15
1891	82	39.00	54.60	42.90	53.40	65.12
1892	76				53.75	70.72
1893	78				49.60	63.59
1894	70				50.70	72.43
1895	71				50.00	70.42
1896	68				52.00	76.47
1897	68				52.52	77.24
1898	71				52.50	73.94
1899	77				56.72	73.66
1900	82				62.00	75.61
1901	81				62.00	76.54
1902	86				62.00	72.09
1903	87				62.00	71.26
1904	87				62.40	71.72

[a] George F. Warren and Frank A. Pearson, *Prices* (New York: J. Wiley, 1939), pp. 12–13. (The base is 1910–1914.) [b] Aldrich Report, pp. 1567–1568. [c] *The Copper Handbook for 1911*, X (Houghton, 1912), 1442–1443. [d] Quincy mine figures divided by wholesale price index. [e] All figures for New Jersey are the highest monthly rates for the year; other figures are averages. [f] Calumet and Hecla paid higher rates than did the Quincy.

mid-nineties, there was a constant pressure of iron miners seeking employment.[64] It seems probable that the copper mines paid higher wages than those paid in the Iron Country during these years. The State Census of 1894 showed the Houghton copper mine rate for skilled labor as $2.44 a day and $1.45 for ordinary labor, as compared with $1.93 and $1.40 for the Marquette iron range.[65] But around the middle of the decade, a union movement temporarily gained ground in the Iron Country, and by 1902 wage rates were on a par with those of the Copper Country, or even slightly above them for the more skilled workers.[66] Looking back over the years 1883–1904, it is perfectly apparent that there was a marked tendency for Michigan rates to rise. Even the period of general depression in the mid-nineties did little more than level off the advance, and by the years 1902–1904 a Quincy miner on contract was earning about 35 per cent more than his counterpart of the years 1883–1886. The same period saw a 13 per cent fall in the wholesale price index and thus it appears that the rise in real wages was even more substantial than 35 per cent.

The pattern of community living. It was during these years that the Michigan industry, led by Calumet and Hecla, established the reputation of following as enlightened a policy of paternalism as that of any mining district in the world. Calumet and Hecla set up an Employees' Aid Fund in 1877, supported by equal contributions from the men and the company, which provided for sick benefits of $25 a month up to eight months, $500 death benefits, and $300 for permanent disability.[67] This plan represented an extremely advanced conception of company responsibility, and in its first ten months of operation 435 men received aid and four death payments were made.[68] Working conditions generally were probably above average for mining enterprises of this period, particularly since the underground spaces of the Michigan mines were relatively dry and ventilation had become good.

The companies continued to run stores and boardinghouses, or much more often, to lease them out in such a way that some control over prices was maintained,[69] and during the seventies board and room for a single man ran about $20 a month.⁷⁰ Communities in Houghton County continued to grow, and if a family man worked for Calumet and Hecla around 1875, he lived in a village of 5,000 people and could rent a home with a garden plot for a nominal monthly sum. Rent was fixed in accordance with the size of the house occupied — a dollar a month being added for each additional room. House assignment was made in accordance with size of family, responsibility of the tenant, and value of the man in his job, rather than the nature of his employment. In 1874 Calumet was a large, sprawling village with only a few streets graded and drained and long rows of pine-board miners' cottages, "all alike, and painted red, with stove pipes sticking through the roofs." ⁷¹ The company had the reputation of treating its working community exceptionally well — among other things building churches and what was alleged to be one of the finest school buildings in the United States, with 37 rooms, steam heat, and single desk seating for 1,200 pupils.⁷²

The community had become much more diverse in its make-up. Whereas one out of every three males had been copper mine employees in 1864, about one out of six worked for the mining companies in 1880. Not only do these figures reflect a substantial increase in the proportion of children, but it seems quite probable that there was more diversification of employment. In 1874 the State Census listed total employment in Houghton County as 5,831 — 61 per cent of which was at the mines. A substantial proportion of the remaining 39 per cent were engaged in professional, retail, and service trades.⁷³ Perhaps the most significant development in the distribution of employment was the rapid concentration of a large percentage of the district's working force in a single mine. By 1880 Calumet and Hecla was employing about a third of the mining employees of the Copper Country. It seems probable that something more than another third were employed by the Quincy, Allouez, Franklin, and Atlantic, which left about 30 per cent, or at most 1,500 men, for the remaining 22 mines. With the exception of Calumet and Hecla, average employment at the larger properties was about the same as that of the leading mines of the early sixties. By the late seventies mining had been put on a mass production basis without the employment of more men.

The companies encouraged their agents and other officers to enter into local politics, and in consequence were heavily represented on the county boards of supervisors. The agents of the Quincy and Atlantic were on the Houghton County Board throughout the seventies along with the Assistant Superintendent of Calumet and Hecla. The critical committee was that on finance, and in 1876 both the Quincy and the Atlantic agents were members of that three-man board.[74]

By the turn of the century the large Michigan mines had bought up substantial amounts of residential acreage around their properties and were continuing the policy of either building homes and renting them to employees or leasing the land under conditions which permitted the workers to build their own homes. Rental rates had become institutionalized to such an extent that the workers were assured low rates on adequate housing practically in perpetuity.[75] In 1895 Calumet and Hecla made a study of home and land rents in relation to worker income which showed that annual rent of company built houses amounted to 3 per cent of the cost of construction of the dwellings and 4.3 to 5.5 per cent of the wages of the men concerned. Workers who owned their homes on company land paid 8 to 9 per cent of wages in taxes and ground rents, often sublet part of the dwellings, and were on the average better housed than workers dwelling in company built units.[76] The homes were certainly not luxurious, but were good enough so that Horace Stevens could declare in 1900, "There is probably no mining field in the world where the employees of the mines are so well housed as in the Lake Superior copper district." [77] Schools, hospitals, churches, libraries, and health insurance schemes were all subsidized by the companies, and Calumet and Hecla was soon to introduce an old-age retirement plan.

Angus Murdoch has summed up the community living pattern as follows:

Your home was heated with coal brought on company boats, you washed in water from company pumps, had your dinner under company-made electric light. Even your garbage was carried off in company wagons. The books you read were from among the sixteen thousand volumes of the $50,000 company library. The company penetrated your most private life: more than likely your wife would have your children at the company hospital.

No one could deny that, for the most part, company infiltration into your life was good and most economical. The schools in which your children were educated were among the best in the United States. The Froebel system of kindergarten teaching was adopted by the Calumet schools long before it was accepted by the school systems of great cities. . . .

The simpler lives were good ones, but the white-collar workers, living a more complicated social existence, were inclined to resent the Boston caste system, superimposed on Calumet Township. A clerk was a clerk all twenty-four hours a day, and his wife couldn't expect to be included in the afternoon whist parties of ladies whose husbands bore such titles as Assistant Geologist, Associate Metallurgist or Mill Engineer. And these ladies, in turn, draped by Red Jacket couturiers, were apt to feel uncomfortable as they passed down the reception line at Calumet's yearly balls. This impressive line was invariably made up of transplanted Bostonians who brought the airs and graces of an older world to what they considered frontier functions.[78]

It was a well-ordered social pattern indeed — with a few elegant Bostonians at the top, leading the company officers and their families into the Red Jacket opera house to applaud Modjeska, Sarah Bernhardt, Maude Adams, and Lillian Russell, while down at the bottom of the social pyramid a wife of an extrammer exclaimed: "The company was wonderful — a man always came and fixed the toilet." [79]

There were abuses, of course, besides the intangible one of bringing up immigrants with a very mixed conception of a democratic way of life. In 1901 the central office of Calumet and Hecla carried out an investigation of foremen selling jobs to the men,[80] and as early as 1894 the petty bosses were being called down for the ten-year-old practice of having men on special duty at their homes.[81]

The labor movement and repression. It was also during these years that the industry settled firmly on the principle that collective action by workers was not to be tolerated, particularly if it had anything to do with the national union movement.

The district had its first major strike in 1872. A number of grievances accumulated during the hard times from 1867 to 1870. Real wages had been driven down to an unusually low level immediately following the Civil War; the 90-day draft system had caused resentment; and nerves had been frayed by the depressed state of the industry and insecurity of employment. When a labor shortage developed in 1872, dissatisfaction continued, and there was much shifting of workers from mine to mine in spite of general and heavy wage increases.[82] In May the employees of the Portage Lake and Calumet sections went out on strike, apparently for wage increases and an eight-hour day.[83] The men refused to let their places be filled by workers who would accept company terms and had recourse to force in preventing them. The strike lasted three weeks and then collapsed shortly after a company of infantry was sent to Houghton from Detroit. Strike leaders were haled into court,[84] and the *Mining Gazette* warned the workers against radical eastern ideas. "Nothing more thoroughly un-American, in practice and in principle, can well be conceived than trades unionism." [85] The strike must have come as a shock to the mine managers, and it seems probable that they began to watch closely for signs of unionism. When an "outsider" appeared on Calumet and Hecla property in 1874 and "incited" their employees, he was promptly arrested, and the *Gazette* came out with the statement: "It is high time a class of men in this country were taught that the rights of a corporation are just as sacred as those of an individual." [86] The companies were quite prepared to see that such was the case. When there was a strike of new immigrants from Finland and Sweden in January of 1874, President Agassiz wrote Superintendent Wright:

We cannot be dictated to by anyone. The mine must stop if it stays closed forever. . . . As I have written you before we have always treated our men fairly and honestly, they have received higher wages than any other corporation. I have attempted formerly to try and get their good will by offering them a share of the profits. They spit in my face as it were and all we can do is to sit quietly and await results. Wages will be raised whenever we see fit and at no other time (if they don't like it they must go and get employment elsewhere. . . .)[87]

In the late eighties and early nineties there was quite an intensive Knights of Labor scare. Not only were the companies suffering from an increasing number of short sporadic strikes, which aroused the suspicion that organized labor was stirring, but in casting about for the cause of the great Calumet and Hecla fires the question of outside labor saboteurs was raised. In June, 1887, a private detective hired by the Company reported that all efforts to organize the mining company employees had failed — that the only foothold the Knights had won was in two local foundries.[88] As a security measure, however, Calumet and Hecla set up a company union, and Alexander Agassiz wrote to Wright: "We ought not to hire any new men who are K. of L. and any of our men who belong should be discharged. The men have their own union now and they cannot belong to two, they must make their choice."[89] Fear continued for a few years and was intensified in the summer of 1890 when there was an organized demand for shorter hours, culminating in a strike at the stamp mill in July.[90] In early 1891 a final drive was launched to eliminate whatever vestiges remained of the Knights: "Every means possible should be taken to ascertain which of our men have joined and then to discharge these men as fast as any breach of our regulations or their contracts or duties gives the occasion. . . . If this is too slow then use express reason of joining K. of Ls."[91]

Heavy immigration of non-English speaking workers from Finland, Austria, and Italy was increasing the difficulties of the employer-employee relationship and creating a new nationality problem since the Cornish and Irish workers tended to draw together in face of the new arrivals.[92] In 1890 and 1904 the district suffered from widespread strikes; all of the mines were closed for short periods in the summer of 1890,[93] and the Quincy, Atlantic, and Baltic lode mines lost about three weeks' production in 1904.[94] The years 1892, 1894, 1896, and 1897 saw occasional short strikes at different properties, almost always among trammers, and company reaction usually was to grant compromise wage increases, and sometimes to refuse to take back the strike leaders.[95] These short strikes had very little effect upon the industry's output, but probably did indicate a good deal of underlying dissatisfaction. Part of the trouble was due to nationality and language difficulties; part to the fact that tramming was extremely hard work; and another part doubtless was due to unionization in the Iron Country and the western copper fields. Finally, some people became restive under paternalism, however benevolent, and as Murdoch has put it, had "a holy hate for the company's domination."[96]

As the century ended, the chief lesson which the companies seemed to have drawn from the previous 25 years of labor relations experience was that the difficulties might have been forestalled by a harsher and more alert managerial policy. In 1900 Calumet and Hecla opposed a street railway system connecting the various mining properties because "the men could get together easier in time of strike,"[97] and Alexander Agassiz commented after a strike in 1901: "The trouble at the Lake it seems to me has been fomented by our own officers and the lack of force exhibited in the handling of discontented employees."[98] In spite of an exceedingly liberal paternalistic system (or perhaps even, in part, *because of* what it did to men's minds), the seeds of dissatisfaction were sprouting and were to be harvested some 12 years later amid bitterness which demoralized the whole district and left permanent scars.

CHAPTER V

The Industry and Maturity, 1905–1918

A long period of extraordinarily high and sustained dividend payments is often an indication that a mining district will soon decline since it may well represent the shifting of capital out of the industry, which, in days of rapid expansion, had been plowed back to open up new ground on old properties and to develop new mines.[1]

—*W. B. G., Jr.*

THE PATTERN OF MATURITY

During the years 1905–1918 the Michigan copper mining industry leveled off into a fairly long period of maturity. All-time peaks were reached in output, value of output, employment, and dividend payments, in part as a result of exceptionally high copper prices, but these did little more than mask conditions which shortly thereafter were to bring about a substantial decline.

Relative stability of output. From 1905 to 1912 the output of the industry was relatively constant, fluctuating between 216 and 233 million pounds. Major labor troubles caused a substantial dip to a little over 139 million in 1913, to be followed by a record output of almost 267 million pounds in 1916 and a decline to 228 million by 1918.[2] Stability of output meant a constantly falling share of the United States total and reduction of Lake copper to virtual insignificance. The percentage of United States output accounted for by the district dropped from 25.9 in 1905 to 11.9 in 1918, and even the peak production of the industry's history in 1916 amounted to only 13.3 per cent of the national total for that year.[3]

The three largest Lake producers of 1905 (Calumet and Hecla, Osceola, and Quincy) all reached record productions early in the period which they were unable again to equal, even with the stimulus of war prices.⁴ In 1905 these three mines plus the Tamarack accounted for about 65 per cent of Michigan output; by 1916 their combined production had dropped by about a fifth, and their share of total product to 44 per cent. The Osceola and Quincy reached production peaks in 1909 and 1910 and showed some falling off thereafter, but the most serious development for the district was the marked decline at Calumet and Hecla. The Lake giant produced 100 million pounds in 1906, with a peacetime record of 5,734 men on the payroll, and then fell rapidly to 67.9 million by 1912. In 1916 a recovery was made to 76.8 million pounds, but by 1918 the total had fallen back to about 68 million.⁵

No new mineral discoveries of any consequence were made during these years, and absolute decline of the industry was avoided by very substantial production increases at four relatively young properties: the Ahmeek, Allouez, Isle Royale, and Champion. Their combined output amounted to over 80 million pounds of copper in 1916, as compared with 20 million in 1905. The most significant development had been at the Champion which reached a record production of 33.6 million pounds in 1916, becoming the second largest producer in the Michigan industry.⁶

Exceptionally high dividends. The 14-year period of maturity was marked by the heaviest dividends paid in the district's history. A total of over $146 million was declared out to stockholders, which represented payments of slightly under $10.5 million per annum, or about $2 million less than the industry's previous annual record, established in 1899.⁷ Not only were dividends generally high (about $5 million in all but one year of the period), but they were much more evenly distributed among the major producers than had been the case in previous periods.⁸

	Per Cent
Calumet and Hecla	33.1
Champion	16.0
Osceola	8.8
Quincy	8.1
Ahmeek	7.7

	Per Cent
Mohawk	5.9
Wolverine	5.7
Baltic	5.4
10 others	9.3
Total	100.0

About 65 per cent of the payments were made in the six peak years 1906–1907 and 1915–1918, and in 1917 the industry reached an all-time record of slightly less than $24 million. A long production plateau and unusually heavy and general dividend payments present the basic characteristics of this period, and set the over-all framework for more detailed discussion.

The effect of "high" copper prices. One strand of the explanation comes from the demand side: the years 1905–1918 can be characterized more accurately as a seller's market than any other period of the industry's history. The concept of "high" prices for a product is difficult to imbue with precise meaning, and care must be exercised in handling it. The period opened with the Russo-Japanese War, covered a major business boom — that of 1906–07 — and closed with four years of wartime prosperity. It did include several years of depressed trade conditions following the crisis of 1907, but general business conditions were nothing like as serious from 1908 to 1911 as those experienced after similar crises in the seventies, eighties, and nineties.

From 1905 to 1918 world copper output doubled,[9] while United States consumption increased by over two and one-half times.[10] Continued expansion of the electrical industry was still the major factor on the demand side, although shell and cartridge requirements were important around 1905 [11] and the main explanatory factor after 1914 in an increase in domestic consumption from a peacetime high of 833 million pounds in 1912 to over 1,661 million in 1918. During six years of the period the average annual quotation on Lake copper was over 16.5 cents a pound, and the total output for the 14 years was valued at about 18.6 cents a pound, in contrast with 13.1 for the period 1883–1904.[12]

Declining security prices. Stock market evaluation of the industry reached an all-time peak in 1907, Calumet and Hecla selling for $1,000 a share, and then declined steadily until 1911.[13] High copper prices reversed the trend in 1912 and 1915–16. But in 1916, with production at a record peak and dividends some $5 million above the 1906 and 1907 level, the shares of the major companies (with one exception, the Mohawk) were selling at about a third less than the 1907 high, and by 1918 at less than half the peak 1907 prices.

Part of the explanation for this substantial decline was doubtless overvaluation in the speculative fever of 1907; another was recognition of the war as a temporary phenomenon, likely to result in overproduction of copper, but there was a strand dependent upon a falling evaluation of the industry itself, particularly as compared with the newly developed and even more profitable fields of Utah, Nevada, Arizona, and New Mexico. The investing public was becoming aware of underlying developments in the Michigan industry, an awareness which was furthered by a widely publicized reassessment of mining properties by an outside expert in 1911,[14] and the strike of 1913–14, which gave the industry and its problems widespread publicity in magazines, newspapers, and government publications.

With no new discoveries to make the investment of capital a good risk, it seems probable that exceptionally heavy dividends are partially explicable in terms of disinvestment of capital. Construction expenditures equivalent to current depreciation were still being made, but funds which formerly had gone to purchases of more land as a sort of "depletion reserve"[15] and to meet obsolescence of major capital items were being declared out to stockholders. Finlay pointed out in 1911 that, in the case of the Calumet conglomerate, the mine had been magnificently equipped in the bonanza days — underground development work was largely completed — and that as a result, great profits could be expected until exhaustion was reached.[16] In marked contrast with earlier booms, the periods 1906–07 and 1915–16 did not result in a large number of new flotations and heavy investment of stock market funds in new enterprises. There was no widespread movement to consolidate old unsuccessful properties into new mining ventures following the boom of 1905–06, and the year 1916 was marked by a complete absence of new public flotations.[17]

THE BATTLE TO HOLD COSTS DOWN

Although substantial credit for a long period of maturity and inflated profit levels should go to relatively high copper prices, equally important explanations can be found on the cost side. In general, the long-run competitive position of the Michigan industry was worsening, particularly with the rise of the Western porphyry [18] mines around 1910, but integration of operations at producing properties and a speeding up of the rate of technological change were compensating, temporarily at least, for more difficult mining conditions.

Worsening competitive position. It seems unlikely that Michigan's competitive position would have worsened materially in this period if it had not been for the opening up of low-cost mining fields in the West. In 1909 these low copper content, open-cut mines were producing about 14 per cent of United States output — by 1918 they accounted for 38 per cent. Since their costs were relatively low, the rise in average costs for the industry *as a whole* was dampened, and an increasing proportion of the output of older fields was becoming marginal.[19] Around 1920 the United States Geological Survey conducted a study of copper mining costs in connection with a super-power survey, and arrived at the accompanying figures showing the trend from 1909 to 1918.[20] Table 4 shows Michigan costs following the wholesale price trend [21] (with the exception of the strike years of 1913–14) while the growth of the porphyry mines pulled down average costs of the industry as a whole well below the wholesale price trend. Conclusions to be drawn are two-fold. First, average profits per pound of copper produced were falling in Michigan relative to the trend in the industry as a whole; and, second, there is a presumption that, if demand slackened substantially, the proportion of United States production accounted for by the Lake producers would decline.

The movement to integrate operations of producing properties. In Chapter III a good deal of emphasis was placed upon concentration of control of Michigan output into the hands of four interest groups. A concomitant of this concentration had been a certain amount of integration of operations, particularly in such fields as top management, purchasing, and certain major

TABLE 4

MICHIGAN COSTS COMPARED WITH THOSE OF THE REST OF THE DOMESTIC INDUSTRY, 1909–1918

(Cost Figures in Cents Per Pound)

Year	Michigan Average	Entire Industry	Porphyry Mines	Wholesale Price Index
1909	9.9	9.3	9.2	99
1910	9.9	8.6	8.4	103
1911	9.6	8.8	8.1	95
1912	10.7	9.3	8.7	101
1913	13.8	10.2	9.3	102
1914	11.5	9.5	8.3	99
1915	9.6	8.9	7.9	101
1916	12.4	10.4	9.3	125
1917	15.6	12.9	12.7	172
1918	18.9	14.5	14.0	191

capital expenditures, such as pumping plants and smelting works. But there had been only one case where concentration of control of producing properties had been followed by complete integration of operations. (Four of the Bigelow properties were merged into the Osceola Consolidated.) The period 1905–1918 is characterized by a clear realization of the long-run necessity for such integration, in what had become a mature industry, and a deadly battle for its attainment, crowned by only partial success.

The problem appeared in its most acute form in the case of Calumet and Hecla. The great Lake company was equipped with what was alleged to be the most magnificent copper mining surface plant in the world. Between 1905 and 1918 output declined by about a third; all efforts to discover substantial deposits in nearby undeveloped mineral lands were unavailing; and it soon became clear that the company's future, as well as its ability to maintain full use of plant facilities, depended upon gaining control of adjoining operating properties. That most of these properties happened to be managed by the Bigelow interests, which had been associated with the Standard Oil crowd in the heyday of the "trust," made the proposition both more difficult and more enticing.

In May of 1905 the governor of Michigan approved a bill permitting mining companies to hold stock in other mining companies,[22] and Calumet and Hecla began to buy up shares of various old unsuccessful properties, as well as those of its successful neighbors, as a depletion reserve and "to secure economical cooperation."[23] By far the most important acquisition was a quarter interest in the Osceola, which was the second largest mine in the district, adjoined Calumet and Hecla lands, and worked some of the same amygdaloid lodes. Shortly before the annual meeting of the Osceola shareholders in 1907, the directors of Calumet and Hecla notified Bigelow that they had obtained voting power for a majority of Osceola stock and expected to take over the management of the property. In light of these facts, they requested him not to make major commitments for the future. On March 12, 1907, Bigelow filed a bill in the Federal Circuit Court of Michigan demanding an injunction against the calling of a meeting of Osceola shareholders on the grounds of a potential violation of the Sherman Anti-Trust Act. A temporary injunction was granted,[24] and the case was fought up to the Circuit Court of Appeals. The plaintiff's most interesting contention was that so-called "prime lake copper" was produced by only five companies;[25] that it was a distinct product, considered essential by the United States government for cartridges; and that a monopoly, making possible price raising, would result if Calumet and Hecla were permitted to vote its block of stock in the Osceola elections.[26] The final ruling was made in February, 1909, and the injunction raised, when the Circuit Court of Appeals declared that "prime Lake" was not a distinct product since the rise of electrolytic copper, and that the intent of the defendant's action was to prolong the life of Calumet and Hecla and bring about cost reductions at both properties. Apparently Bigelow intended to appeal to higher courts, and shortly following the decision Calumet and Hecla made a settlement whereby they purchased all of his Michigan holdings (some 125,000 shares of stock) for eight million dollars.[27] A good deal had been accomplished, particularly from a control standpoint. About a third of the Osceola stock was now held by Calumet and Hecla, somewhat less than a fifth of that of the Isle Royale, almost half of the Ahmeek, and about a third of the Tamarack. All of these were significant producing properties, and in 1909–10 Calumet and Hecla directors and local management took over their operation. Control and joint management, however, were not enough — the cost logic of the situation called for substantial integration of operations, only attainable by merger.

In December, 1910, the directors of Calumet and Hecla issued a consolidation report to stockholders of their own and subsidary companies, calling for a merger of ten companies on a stock exchange basis, capitalization of the new corporation to be set at ten million dollars.[28] The proposal was hailed in mining circles as thoroughly sound. The relative value of the properties had been determined by outside appraisal; operating savings, among them greater ability to shift mining forces, joint milling, and elimination of 10 per cent of operating shafts, were considered highly significant; and the scheme raised the possibility of intensive prospecting for new mineral bodies on a scale beyond the financial ability of smaller companies.[29] In spite of the fact that management of all of the properties was in the hands of Calumet and Hecla and that the cost reduction contention was never seriously questioned, the plan had fallen through by October of 1911. In March votes were taken at stockholders' meetings of all of the companies except the Laurium (in which Calumet and Hecla owned a controlling interest), and heavy majorities favored consolidation. However, stockholders friendly to Bigelow brought a number of suits in the Michigan courts, contending that the exchange ratios were unfair. Despite the fact that prospects for ultimately favorable court decisions were good, Calumet and Hecla abandoned the plan by voting against merger in the Laurium meeting, on the grounds that prolonged legal action would invalidate the proposal since the exchange terms would become obsolete.[30] Personal animosities, the interest of stock speculators in preserving small, unsuccessful properties, and fear by local people that integration of operations would eliminate a large number of jobs were the fundamental factors behind the opposition.[31] Calumet and Hecla had to be satisfied with savings from joint management and piecemeal purchase of neighboring properties. Copper sales were handled in common;[32] various service functions were consolidated, such as fire protection and central employment;[33] progress was made in joint milling for a few of the smaller mines;[34] and in 1917 the Tamarack, which had lain like a wedge between two sections of Calumet and Hecla property, was integrated by the purchase of all outstanding shares.[35]

As of December 31, 1918, Calumet and Hecla was actively managing companies, the combined output of which totaled 190.5 million pounds of copper per annum, or 60.8 per cent of Michigan production.[36] The situation in 1918 represented the result of a substantial shift of capital from the Calumet and Hecla conglomerate mine to those of its younger amygdaloid neighbors,[37] and, although complete integration had been blocked, events were to transpire in the early twenties which would make such a development so desirable that all opposition would be eliminated.

Calumet and Hecla was not the only company of the district to be concerned with integration of operations and partially blocked in its attainment. In 1911 the Copper Range acquired the property of the old Atlantic mine by stock exchange.[38] Four years later the Copper Range was reincorporated with a capital stock increase to ten million dollars, and the Baltic, in which ownership was 99 per cent, was dissolved. A similar attempt to dissolve the Trimountain, in which ownership was also 99 per cent, was blocked in the Michigan courts on the grounds that economy was not a strong enough argument when minority shareholders could not be induced to approve of a merger.[39] The problem at the Quincy continued to be one of purchasing the land of unsuccessful mines, and between 1907 and 1918 a little over a million and a half dollars was spent in acquiring other properties, including the holdings of the old Franklin and Arcadian.[40] By 1918 the impact of consolidation and integration of operations had concentrated control of Michigan production into even fewer hands than had been the case in 1904.

	Percentage of Michigan Output
Calumet and Hecla and subsidiaries	60.8
Copper Range and loosely affiliated Paine and Stanton mines	23.7
Quincy	8.6
Total	92.1

Speeding up of the rate of technological change. The period 1905–1918 was characterized by a rapid rate of technological change in both underground and surface departments. The underground improvements were second only in importance to those of the years 1879–1882, and the period saw a satisfactory solution to the problem of milling losses, which had plagued Lake producers since early Civil War days.

There had been no real improvements in drilling technique since the early eighties, and in 1910 Lake rock was being broken by cumbersome two-man drills weighing about 300 pounds. In 1909 practical one-man machines came on the market,[41] some of which worked on the hammer principle and weighed as little as 39 pounds. Others, for more general use, worked on the piston principle and weighed less than half as much as the two-man drills.[42] All of the new machines used much higher air pressure, thereby increasing drilling power. The Michigan mines carried on extensive experiments with various makes in 1911 and 1912, and experience soon showed that the one-man drill was at least as effective a rockbreaker as the old two-man machine.[43] Trials at Calumet and Hecla showed the increase in effectiveness to range from 34 per cent in stoping to 91 per cent in drifting.[44] Because of the strike, the impact of the new innovation was delayed until 1915, but by that year Calumet and Hecla was able to reverse a falling productivity trend for underground workers (which dated back to 1905), and raise output per underground employee to the 1906 level.[45] It seems probable that the drill was the main factor in the general cost reduction of 1915, which for most companies carried costs back to 1910 or even earlier years.[46]

In the last chapter mention was made of power tramming experiments at the Quincy and Calumet and Hecla. General adoption of power haulage was delayed at the Lake primarily because stoping points were usually far apart and on a number of levels, which meant that there was seldom enough material available in any one spot to warrant continuous operation of power-driven tram cars.[47] By 1914 almost all tramming on the Calumet and Hecla conglomerate was being done by rope haulage,[48] a technique which was of very limited applicability in the amygdaloid mines because of the winding nature of the drifts. In 1912 electric haulage was being tried on three levels of the Baltic,[49] but it was not until the war years, when an acute shortage of trammers threatened to cripple the mines, that motor haulage came into general use. In 1917 and 1918 the amygdaloid mines introduced storage battery locomotives for tramming as rapidly as they could be obtained from the manufacturers, even though their use meant straightening some drifts and concentrating stoping on fewer levels.[50]

During the years 1905–1917 important changes in mill recovery techniques followed one another so rapidly that almost continuous renovation of plants became necessary. The new Chilean grinders had been in general use at the Lake for only a few years[51] when a much more efficient grinder was introduced, known as the "Hardinge," which operated on the principle of agitating the material to be ground against hard Danish pebbles in a revolving metal drum. Much finer grinding could be obtained by this method, and power requirements were not expensive, since its introduction coincided with the adaptation of the low-pressure turbine, as a means of utilizing exhaust steam from the stamps as motive power.[52] In 1911 and 1912 experiments were made with the Hardinge grinders and plans were laid for their general introduction.[53] The new regrinding plant at Calumet and Hecla had not yet been completed when successful experiments in leaching were concluded by C. H. Benedict of Calumet and Hecla, which promised to double anticipated recovery from the retreatment of sands.[54] Leaching was begun on a commercial basis in July, 1916, and by February of 1917 a 2,000 ton capacity plant was in operation at Calumet and Hecla.[55] As far as the big Lake company was concerned, leaching solved the problem of copper residual left in sands, but there still remained a substantial copper loss in slimes.[56] Just as the period was ending, Calumet and Hecla introduced the froth flotation process, which had been commercially developed by 1912 and had done much to make possible low-cost treatment of the porphyry ores of the West.[57]

There was a two-fold impact from the development of these new milling techniques. First, copper recovery from all rock mined in the district was increased substantially, and, second, it became possible to rework 40 years of accumulated tailings from the Calumet and Hecla mills at a very substantial profit. Copper recovery at Calumet and Hecla rose from around 76 per cent in 1917 to 81 per cent in 1918. (By 1920 it had reached 91 per cent.) In 1915 the company's reclamation plant went into operation, and by 1917 was producing over nine million pounds of copper per annum at a cost of about 6 cents a pound.[58] With copper selling at above 24 cents enormous profits were in prospect, and the extent of the tailing piles in Torch Lake — some 40 million tons of sand averaging 8 to 10 pounds of copper per ton in the newer deposits and 12 to 20 in the older — was equivalent to the discovery of a new and very low cost mine.[59]

Continued importance of "low" labor costs. High copper prices, integration of operations of producing properties, and a speeding up of the rate of technological change would have been of little avail in maintaining Michigan output and making possible substantial dividend payments, if it had not been for a continuation of relatively low wage rates. In 1909 the Michigan industry produced 11,882 pounds of refined copper for every man employed in the industry, while the corresponding average for Montana was 23,983 and Arizona, 26,312.[60] Cheaper transportation and simpler metallurgical problems were not enough to redress such a balance: Lake producers had to have cheaper labor. Finlay, in his cost study of 1908, gave average Butte wages from 1901 to 1907 as 47 cents an hour, whereas 25 cents was the going rate in Michigan. He considered it probable that Butte miners were more effective than those at Lake Superior, and estimated that, all factors considered, Butte labor was 50 per cent more expensive.[61] The Census of 1910 shows Michigan copper mining employees receiving an average of $2.36 a shift, as compared with 3.87 in Montana and $3.40 in Arizona.[62] Any development which tended to reduce this differential was of critical importance to the Michigan companies.

THE LABOR SHORTAGE PROBLEM AND THE STRIKE OF 1913–1914

There were many more years of so-called "labor shortage" between 1905 and 1918 than had been the case in any previous period of the industry's history. Underlying this new development was the fact that the flow of immigrants into the district reached a peak during the boom of 1906–07 and, shortly thereafter, began a steep decline. Between 1904 and 1910 the population of Houghton County increased from about 71,000 to 88,000, but had declined by 1920 to slightly under 72,000.[63] Even more significant was the fact that the number of foreign born declined from about 33,000 in 1910 to 21,000 in 1920, or about 7,000 less than the 1904 total, and that the number of males, age 18 to 44, fell by about a third between 1904 and 1920. The first major shortage [64] appeared in late 1910 and became increasingly serious during 1911, 1912, and the first half of 1913. The second shortage was the result of the war, became general in late 1916, and reached an acute stage in the spring of 1918. When the facts are examined, the mystery is not so much why these shortages developed in the Michigan copper district,[65] but rather why the wartime shortage was not much more severe, since the copper district maintained much of the all important differential vis-à-vis the western copper fields, in spite of the fact that wages in the neighboring Michigan and Minnesota iron fields and the new industrial area around Detroit rose to levels equal to, or above, that of wages in the West.

A labor shortage develops, 1910–1912. Michigan copper mining employment reached an all-time peak of 21,000 men in 1907, and, as a result of the sharp decline of copper prices late in the year, wages were reduced by about 10 per cent.[66] In 1909 the relative wage situation was approximately as presented below, and, if the past was any criterion, represented an employment-wage *status quo*.[67]

Industry	Average Wage Per Day All Employees
Michigan copper	$2.36
Michigan iron	2.28
Minnesota iron	2.37
Detroit (general wage)	2.02
Montana copper	3.87
Arizona copper	3.40

By 1911, however, the Michigan copper district was experiencing its first real net emigration. Apparently, Irish and Cornish miners, who were attracted to the western camps, formed the core of the exodus,[68] while a more general run of labor was leaving for the Michigan and Minnesota iron ranges.[69] Copper mining employment in Houghton County fell from 17,974 in 1909 to 15,361 in 1911, in spite of the fact that the mine managers claimed that the companies needed men.[70] The reasons behind the exodus are not altogether clear, although there is evidence to support a belief that hourly wage rates in the Iron Country were rising somewhat above those in the Copper Country,[71] and that a substantial amount of dissatisfaction was being engendered among Michigan copper miners by Western Federation organizers, who appeared in 1909 to tell the men of the wage wonders of Butte.[72] The Michigan companies raised wages 10 per cent in the spring of 1912, with a resultant increase in employment of a few hundred over 1911, but there continued to be a shortage, particularly of trammers.

The Western Federation of Miners and the events leading to the strike of 1913–1914. As early as 1904, when the Northern Mineral Mine Workers' Union became a part of the Western Federation of Miners, local unions had been set up in the Copper country, but by 1906–07 the movement had died out, and the district was even more of a non-union camp than the neighboring Iron Country. In 1909, however, organizers were sent in by the Western Federation,[73] which had recently split with the Industrial Workers of the World and was moving to a somewhat more conservative position, finally resulting in affiliation with the American Federation of Labor in 1911.[74] Not only was the Michigan field a rich plum and a good base of operations for future organization of the iron fields, but it seems possible that Federation leaders considered low Lake wage rates (as compared with those at Butte) detrimental to continued success of unionism in western copper fields, particularly in light of weakness within western labor's ranks engendered by bitter controversy over the I.W.W.[75] Organization of the Michigan field did not prove easy, and on the eve of the strike, after about four years of campaigning, the Federation had signed up perhaps a third to a half of the underground employees of Calumet and Hecla and its subsidiaries, a very small minority of the company's surface workers, and a somewhat higher percentage of the employees of the other mines of the district.[76]

The slow progress made was surprising in light of a number of factors favoring an organizational drive. The industry had become more and more dependent upon non-English speaking immigrant workers, who had gravitated to the lowest paid jobs.[77] Not only had this made the petty boss and nationality problems more acute, but the Finnish element, which amounted to about a third of the foreign born, contained a large Socialist group which was ripe for organization.[78] Hours of work were longer than those required in the West or in the neighboring

Iron Country, on the average by about an hour,[79] and the minimum underground wage in Butte was higher than the average underground wage in Michigan.[80] Within the Michigan district wage differences were substantial among different nationality groups, and Calumet and Hecla, which employed a majority of the Cornish and Irish workers, paid average wages substantially higher than those of the other companies.[81] In spite of the factors favoring organization, the Federation's efforts came close to bogging down in a district in which the possibilities for individual attainment were stressed by the contract wage system and in which workers received real benefits from paternalism. According to one study, home rentals in the Copper Country were about a fifth those of Butte, fuel 50 per cent less, and the general run of foods about a third less.[82] The mining companies had continued expenditures to improve community living, and, beginning in 1911, the State government passed a series of laws to assure more extensive protection of workmen, among them acts providing for the election of county mine inspectors,[83] workman's compensation for accidents resulting in death or serious injury,[84] and settlement of wages twice a month or partial payment in case a contract system was used.[85] It is conceivable that the organizational movement would have died out in a fashion similar to that of 1904 [86] if it had not been for the introduction of the one-man drill in 1911 and 1912. In addition to having the usual fear of a major laborsaving device, many of the men considered the new machine dangerous, in that its use often required the driller to work alone in a stope.[87] It was also contended that no clear-cut system was provided in case a man needed help in setting the machine up.

Apparently the mine operators had known for a number of years that the labor situation was boiling up to a major strike.[88] They did little actively to oppose the organizational drive, but evidently made up their minds to break the Federation's hold on the district if and when a strike came. In their eyes, the Federation not only represented a threat by radical outsiders to a paternalistic system in which they firmly believed, but its recognition inevitably would increase wage costs and might even eliminate the wage differential between Michigan and the West, to say nothing of the fact that it threatened to hold back the general adoption of the one-man drill.

Their potential power for a showdown was enormous. The mines owned practically all of the land in the district and had few employees who did not live on company rented property or in company rented houses, under contracts which could be terminated within 15 days.[89] All community facilities were dependent upon their bounty, and the Board of Supervisors of Houghton County was clearly dominated by mine managers and their associates.[90] Finally, two acts had been passed by the State legislature in 1911 which served to strengthen strike-breaking efforts. The first amended an act of 1909, in such fashion that a county in which there was a riot was relieved of the financial burden involved in supporting the state militia,[91] and the second repealed an act of 1889 which called for State investigation of major labor disputes and a full public report in case the parties refused arbitration.[92]

An account of the strike — July 22, 1913, to April 14, 1914. Western Federation leaders were against strike action until more strength had been consolidated in the district. Local feeling ran high, however, and in July an action vote was taken which resulted in the forwarding of a letter to the various mine managers, declaring that the Federation represented a large number of their employees who were dissatisfied with existing conditions and that a strike would be called unless the mine managers met with representatives of the Federation. The letter was ignored, and on July 22, 1913, the strike was on.[93]

During the first few days there was a good deal of rioting, occasioned by successful Federation attempts to prevent nonunion men from working, but by July 27 the entire National Guard of the State, numbering 2,600 men, was encamped at the various mine sites, and a short period of peace ensued. Initial union demands were for recognition of the Federation, two men to a drill, an eight-hour day, an improved system for presenting grievances, a pay increase, and the establishment of a minimum wage. The mine managers took the stand that the

Western Federation was an alien organization, known for violence and irresponsibility; that the companies owed it to their stockholders and to their non-union employees to eliminate this "monster" from the district; and that the striking employees would be taken back only if they had committed no illegal acts and were prepared to give up membership in the union.

Beginning in August, attempts were made to reopen the mines, and a new period of violence ensued. Interestingly enough, the "bloody" Federation, although it was guilty of a certain amount of physical intimidation of nonstrikers, destroyed no property [94] and lagged far behind the mine dominated sheriff's office in the use of violence. During the strike about 1,700 men served as deputies, and the sheriff hired 52 men from the Wadell-Mahon strikebreaking organization of New York. Fifty-seven other men were hired from this organization by various mining companies, and Calumet and Hecla employed 120 guards from the Ascher Detective Agency of New York.[95] Eviction notices began to be served on strikers early in September by the Copper Range and Quincy, but this strikebreaking technique was tied up in the courts by injunction.[96]

In mid-September a new phase of the struggle opened when the Quincy imported the first strikebreakers, and by October some 1,200 men had been brought in from the industrial centers of the East and mid-West.[97] During the next few months Calumet and Hecla and its subsidiaries imported about 1,600 men [98] — an effort being made to obtain nationalities different from those in the Copper Country. Late in 1913 all of the important companies were in partial production, and efforts by outsiders to bring about a settlement were meeting with complete failure.

The strike caused something of a sensation in the country at large. Notables — among them Mother Jones, John Mitchell, John L. Lewis, and Clarence Darrow — came to Houghton to fight for labor's cause; [99] letters poured into Congress, and the strike issues were heatedly discussed on the floor; [100] and the State and Federal governments attempted to effect a settlement and launched investigations.[101] But by December the companies could see their way to victory, and late in that year when

Charles Moyer, the President of the Federation, blamed the Citizen's Alliance for a terrible tragedy at a party for strikers' children in which 74 people were killed when an unknown person yelled "*Fire*," Moyer was beaten up by a group of prominent citizens and put on a train for Chicago.[102] On April 14, 1914, the strike was officially ended. Never once had the mine managers deviated from their stand, and it seems probable that they would have been willing to close the properties for years rather than make concessions which could be interpreted as a victory for the Federation. A moral judgment concerning this complex social economic outburst is beyond the scope of this study, but a Catholic priest provided an interesting epitaph for the strike, when he wrote, "The Calumet and Hecla Company cannot shut out progress by sticking its head, like the ostrich into the desert sands of an antiquated and anti-social liberalism." [103] The answer probably is that Father Dietz overestimated the power of the movement toward industrial democracy. Organization was to be a dead issue in Michigan copper for another quarter of a century; in the meantime, paternalism with its evils of worker dependence and community domination continued.

Immediate results of the breaking of the strike and the war labor shortage. During the course of the strike the Copper Country lost some of its finest mining labor — at least 2,000 men left the district for the Iron Country or the West [104] — and the bitterness engendered during the struggle has continued to be a factor in industrial relations of the district to this day.[105] Nonetheless, output and dividend recovery were extremely rapid, in part due to a movement of men into the copper district from the Iron Country, which was adversely affected by the opening of the war in Europe,[106] and by 1915–16 the district reached record outputs of 258 and 267 million pounds of copper. The mining companies adopted an eight-hour day for underground workers and nine hours for surface workers as of January 1, 1914; weekly times were set to hear worker grievances; and community improvements continued to be made.[107] Finally, the State legislature passed a bill resurrecting the old Board of

Mediation, specifically for industrial disputes affecting railroads, mines, and public utilities.[108]

The most significant short-run effect of the breaking of the strike was more indirect and had a bearing upon the second major labor shortage of the period, that of the years 1916 through 1918. The Upper Peninsula of Michigan and the neighboring Minnesota iron range underwent an exceptionally severe labor shortage as a result of manpower requirements for the armed forces, the fact that iron and copper mining were basic war industries, and competitive bidding for labor by the new war factories which sprang up in the Detroit area. Between 1915 and 1918 average wages in Detroit increased by almost 75 per cent, and the *Iron Age* reported that wages in the Lake Superior Iron Country rose by about 123 per cent between September 1, 1915, and October of 1918.[109] In marked contrast Copper Country wages increased by 35 to 45 per cent between 1915 and 1918,[110] and Calumet and Hecla was able to go through 1917, and the first nine months of 1918, with only one over-all increase which amounted to about 5 per cent.[111] Comparative wage figures for 1919 give some indication of what had happened by the end of the War.[112]

Industry	Average Daily Wages All Employees (In Dollars)
Michigan copper	$3.76
Michigan iron	6.38
Minnesota iron	5.59
Montana copper	5.03
Arizona copper	5.62

The explanation seems two-fold: first, the Michigan copper district's ability to stay clear of labor difficulties from 1916 through 1918 and to profit by severe labor troubles in other mining camps; and, second, a rapid introduction of laborsaving devices in 1917 and 1918, such that employment could be allowed to decline substantially in 1918 without a serious curtailment of output. Admittedly the situation by 1919 had become extremely unstable, but the effort to hold the wage rise down during the last year or so of the war was amazingly successful and does much to explain substantial dividends and high output, in spite of fairly rigid government price control.

During 1915, 1916, and most of 1917 the district managed to avoid a *severe* labor shortage. It seems probable that something like the going wage rate (for Upper Peninsula mining) was paid until early 1917 (see Figures 2 and 3 on page 137), and men came into the district from both the iron region and the West. The copper industry recovered more rapidly from the initial shock of the war than did the iron industry, and the flow of men from the Iron Country was still continuing as late as the spring of 1915.[113] During 1916 the great Mesabi iron range of Minnesota was torn by labor controversy with the I.W.W., and by the fall of 1917 Butte was partially closed down by labor difficulties. As a result, mining labor poured into the Michigan copper district, particularly during the summer and fall of 1917,[114] and, although more men were needed, employment in 1916 and 1917 was maintained at about the 1915 level. Each man who arrived was suspected of "radicalism"; the Citizens' Alliance was resurrected to run "agitators" out of the country; [115] and militant anti-unionism by employers, citizens' groups, and "reformed workers" was intensified.[116]

By the spring of 1918, however, the relative wage position of the Copper Country had worsened substantially; the I.W.W. and the Western Federation had gone down to defeat in both Minnesota and the West; and emigration from the copper district began in earnest.[117] The armed forces had taken about 5,000 men from the district,[118] but the main shortage until this time had been in the general run of labor, particularly trammers. Now, the highly skilled men began to leave, many of them for the factories of Detroit,[119] and even a substantial wage increase on October 1, 1918, did not reverse the trend.[120] With the armistice and industrial readjustment in the war factories, there was some relief, and the district ended the period with a temporarily increasing labor supply.

It seems clear that there were two major reasons for the

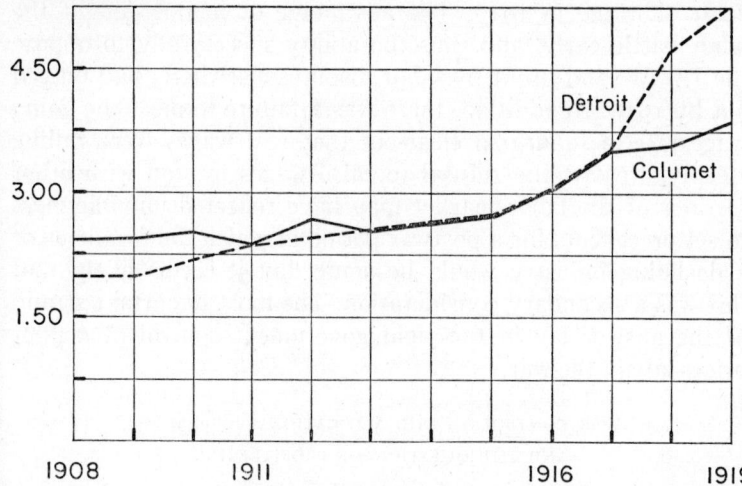

Fig. 2. General Wages at Calumet, Michigan, Compared with Those at Detroit, 1908–1919

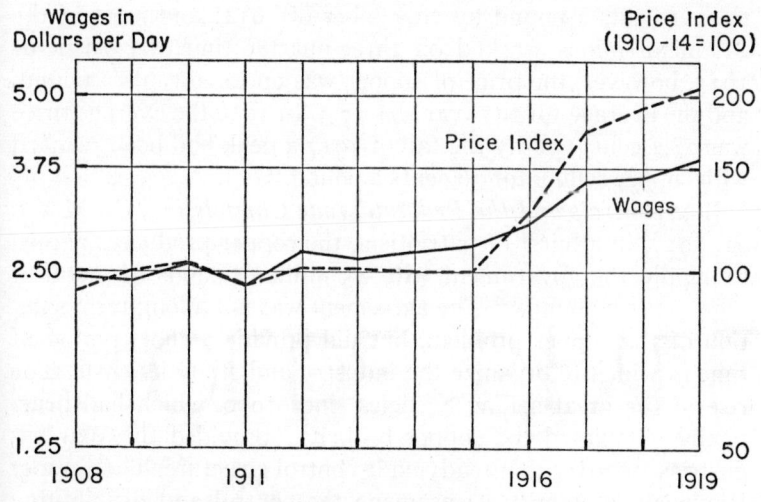

Fig. 3. Wage Trend at Calumet, Michigan, Compared with U. S. Wholesale Price Trend, 1908–1919

Source: Stevenson Corporation, *Industrial Survey of Houghton, Keweenawa, and Baraga Counties* (Hancock, Michigan, probably 1921); Warren and Pearson, pp. 12–13.

acute shortage in 1918. The advantage of having fought the labor battle early, and thus the ability successfully to oppose the I.W.W. and profit by labor disputes elsewhere, had played out by 1918. In addition, there was a failure to meet the going wage rate, a failure so clear-cut that real wages were falling steeply. In part the refusal to raise wages in step with other sections of the labor market may have reflected unwillingness to set precedents for a postwar period in which the problems of a declining industry would be acute, but it seems likely that this was a secondary consideration. The most important strand of the answer lay in the rigid government control of copper prices late in the war.

WAR CONTROLS — THE ALLOCATION PROBLEM — AND THE QUESTION OF PROFITEERING

The first World War began for the domestic copper industry in a fashion similar to the opening months of the Civil War. International lines of trade were disorganized; copper prices fell to 11.3 cents a pound by November of 1914; and most of the Michigan mines worked on three-quarter time. By April of 1915, however, the price of copper was up to 19 cents a pound, and the average for the year was 17.3. In 1916 the average price was 28.2 cents and by the fall of 1917 a peak had been reached with copper selling for 36 cents a pound.[121]

War controls and the Federal Trade Commission. On March 21, 1917, in a burst of patriotism, the copper producers agreed to supply the government with 45 million pounds of metal at 16⅜ cents a pound.[122] The agreement was not a long-term solution of the copper problem, but did provide a short period of time in which to organize the industry and study its costs. The rise of the great selling agencies since 1900, which had practically eliminated the copper broker,[123] provided the War Industries Board with a readymade control structure. The Copper Producers' Committee was made the control and distributing body beneath the War Industries Board, but actual business was done through the two largest selling agencies. The United Metals Selling Company handled the domestic end of the business, while the American Smelting and Refining Company took care of the foreign end, rendering all bills and remitting receipts.[124]

The basic question to be settled was that of the price which producers should receive for the metal, and in July of 1917 the Federal Trade Commission was directed to assist the Price Fixing Committee of the War Industries Board by making continuous cost studies of the United States industry.[125] On September 21, 1917, copper prices were fixed for a four-month period at 23.5 cents a pound (the average for the previous six months had been 28.4). The understanding was that producers would not reduce wages; sales to other parties than the government would be made at prices not higher than 23.5 cents; speculators would be kept out of the market, as far as possible; and every effort would be made to maintain output.[126] The 23.5 cents price was a compromise settlement, the government first offering 18.0. Apparently no duress was used in reaching a final figure, and the ceiling was hailed with much satisfaction by the industry.[127] Four months later, however, small producers were beginning to protest against the level at which the price had been fixed,[128] but the War Industries Board stood firm until July 2, 1918, when an increase to 26 cents a pound was granted on the basis of new cost studies. When the armistice came, the government was anxious to maintain copper production as a precautionary measure, and on November 15, 1918, an agreement was reached with the producers whereby the 26 cent price, wages, production, and allocation machinery were to be continued until January 1, 1919.

As far as the industry as a whole was concerned, the war controls proved quite effective in maintaining output. United States production reached a peak of 1.93 billion pounds in 1916, declined to 1.88 in 1917, and rose again to 1.91 billion in 1918. The falling off in 1917 was primarily the result of labor difficulties in the West,[129] and the conclusion reached by the Federal Trade Commission and the Geological Survey seems sound: "The reduction and pegging of prices by the government did not hinder the maximum production practicable during the war," [130] and even further — higher prices would have encouraged the use of much labor in prospecting to the detriment of highly productive mines.[131] Profits were very high at low cost western properties, and it seems probable that, in light of the small price increase found necessary between September, 1917, and July, 1918, when costs were rising steeply, the original 23.5 cent agreement was unnecessarily high.[132]

Price control and the allocation problem in Michigan. The Michigan copper district was the most marginal section of the industry,[133] and thus is the most significant area to study in considering the effects of the government price control policy, at least from a production viewpoint. Michigan output reached an all-time peak in 1916, was practically maintained during 1917, and fell by about 14 per cent in 1918. It is probably safe to say that a very substantial reduction would have occurred in 1919, if the war had continued and the price of copper had remained frozen at the 26-cent level. Price control made it certain that there would be virtually no labor used in prospecting and the opening up of new mines.[134] Even further, it resulted in almost complete cessation of developmental work at producing properties; after April, 1917, 18 companies stopped opening new ground,[135] and by June of 1918 the managers of the smaller properties were seriously considering complete shutdown.[136] All of these developments represented a desirable allocation of labor in a short-run national crisis. However, if it had been essential to maintain Michigan output for a longer period than was actually the case, fundamental changes in policy would have been necessary. One possibility, which was discussed in the Michigan district, was the taking over of the mines by the government, in order to force an allocation of labor to the richest sections of the richest mines.[137]

What made any solution particularly difficult was the fact that the Upper Peninsula was in the grip of a much more acute labor shortage than that experienced by the western copper fields.[138] Thus, an over-all copper price increase, to make possible heavy wage raises in the Michigan industry, would have been unjustified in the West and perhaps even detrimental to output in the sense of shifting labor to development work. A special price for the Michigan industry would probably have been a satisfactory solution, although it would have raised the ethical problem of cost differences as among producers within the industry, and might have led to special prices for each company. Selective pricing was discussed and rejected by the Price Fixing Committee, in part because its members did not believe in subsidizing units which could not operate in peacetime.[139] Doubtless the administrative problems of such a program would also have been severe, but it would be a mistake to assume that such difficulties were insurmountable — many of them were successfully met two and a half decades later in the second World War. The conclusion is that the government price fixing policy was reasonably successful in maintaining Michigan output and forcing a desirable reallocation of labor, but only because the war was short and the district was in a position in 1916 and 1917 to profit by labor difficulties elsewhere.

The question of war profiteering. The Michigan industry made most of its wartime money during the two-year period of high prices before September of 1917 when the price ceiling was established. Dividends rose from $12.2 million in 1915 to $18.7 million in 1916, $23.9 million in 1917, and then declined to $13.6 million in 1918. These payments represented the highest and most sustained profits in the industry's history, and, using Federal Trade Commission figures for total investment,[140] meant a return of 16 per cent in 1915, 24.5 in 1916, 31.4 in 1917, and 17.9 per cent in 1918. Price control substantially reduced profits which had risen to levels which might well be termed excessive.[141] Prices were pulled down in September, 1917 (from 28.4 to 23.5 cents a pound) to what was still a highly profitable level, and then were held fast against a steeply rising cost trend, with only one mild increase of 2.5 cents a pound in 1918. The Geological Survey report shows average Michigan costs increasing from 9.6 to 18.9 cents a pound between 1915 and 1918, with about 36 per cent of the increase coming in 1918.[142] Figures from Calumet and Hecla reports show a similar trend.

	1915	1916	1917 [a]	8161
		(Cents Per Pound)		
Average price received	18.11	25.48	28.39	24.28
Total operating costs, not including depreciation and depletion	9.33	11.63	13.01	15.71
Gross profit	8.78	13.85	15.38	9.57

[a] Until September Calumet and Hecla sold much of its copper at prices of over 30 cents a

Assuming that it was desirable to maintain Michigan output during the war years and that some variation of the cost-plus principle was not feasible, price control was reasonably effective in holding down Michigan profits during 1918. The only major criticism that might be made is that controls should have been applied several months sooner, and that it might have been wiser policy to start price fixing at a somewhat lower level and to have made advances more frequently. The 26-cent price in 1918 was probably the lowest level consistent with the purpose of maintaining Michigan output. If profits during that year were still considered "high," the matter was one to be rectified by tax policy.

CHAPTER VI

Michigan Copper Mining in Decline
1919-1938

The querulous voice of the white-haired Grand Uncle from Michigan, Calumet and Hecla, jealously guarding the last of his treasure, was insistently heard protesting at the growing influence of foreigners about the court.[1]

— *Alex Skelton*

An examination of the declining phase of Michigan copper mining history is complicated by two highly significant and interrelated developments external to the industry. The first was an obscuring of the internal factors which were bringing about the Michigan contraction by world-wide overinvestment in copper mining and occasional glutting of markets, which weighed heavily upon the price of the metal and resulted in almost continuous national and international attempts at curtailment and price control.[2] The second was a shift from general conditions of business boom to those of depression in the United States after 1929, which greatly intensified the problems connected with the decline of the industry and had even more serious effects in aggravating its impact upon the local community. It is within this complex framework that the next two decades of Michigan copper history unfold.

THE PATTERN OF DECLINE

Although Michigan copper mining contracted substantially during these years, consolidations, carried out in 1923, resulted in expansion of output at Calumet and Hecla until 1929. This development represents an important element in the pattern of decline and tends to obscure the over-all trend.

Declining output in two phases. During the period of the industry's maturity, peacetime output (1905-1912) had fluctuated between 216 and 233 million pounds of copper per annum.

By 1919 there was a drop from the wartime record of 267 million pounds to 178 million, and by 1921 to 92 million.[3] A steady recovery set in thereafter, and by 1929 a postwar peak was reached of 186 million pounds, or about 83 per cent of the average annual production of the years 1905–1912. Depressed business conditions slashed the annual total to 47 million by 1933, but three years later production had risen again to 96 million pounds, or about 43 per cent of the 1905 to 1912 average. United States output fluctuated in a similar fashion so that Michigan's loss of position in the domestic industry was not as pronounced as might have been expected. During the period 1919–1938 the Lake producers accounted for 10.2 per cent of United States output in contrast with 17.4 per cent for the years 1905–1919. The peak year of the period (1929) saw 9.3 per cent of United States production coming from the Michigan properties, as compared with 13.3 per cent for the record year of the previous period (1916).

No new mineral discoveries of any significance were made during these years, although large sums were spent on prospecting, particularly by Calumet and Hecla. Even more serious, a number of the richest lodes were exhausted, and by the early thirties all but four of the companies had been eliminated by closure or consolidation. The mines of two of the survivors (the Quincy and Isle Royale) were in such difficult straits that they were closed down during the depths of the depression and in 1938 produced between them only 11 million pounds of copper. Michigan copper came to be practically synonymous with production from the mines of Calumet and Hecla and Copper Range. Interestingly enough, the impact of consolidation of operating properties was so great that in 1929 the brand name "C. & H." was stamped on more copper than ever before in the company's history — production totaled 124 million pounds in contrast with the previous record of 100 million, established in 1906.[4] The general decline of the industry would have been much more marked except for the output derived from tailings. During the period 1919–1938 the Calumet and Hecla reclamation plants produced over 300 million pounds of copper, or about 12.4 per cent of the Michigan total, and the year 1929 saw over 27 per cent of the output of Calumet and Hecla, and 18 per cent of that of the district, coming from this source.[5]

Rapidly falling employment. Whereas output fell in two jerks, followed by partial recoveries, employment in the industry showed a much more nearly continuous decline (Fig. 6, p. 196). In 1909 the companies had employed over 19,000 men. By 1919 the total was 12,200; in 1929, 7,800; and in 1939, 3,200.[6] The primary reason for a more rapid and more even decline of employment was the fact that the companies increasingly were obliged to use selective mining. This meant that only rock which looked particularly rich was blown loose and that elimination of "poor" material was done as far as possible by sorting underground. It also meant, particularly during the thirties, that only the richest mines were worked. The impact of selective mining is clearly shown by the underground productivity trend at Calumet and Hecla. During the prewar years annual production of copper per underground employee had averaged about 15,000 pounds; by the late twenties 35,000 was not unusual; and in 1936 a record was established of 93,000 pounds.[7]

Dividend payments and market evaluation. As might be expected, the most marked declines were in dividend payments and market evaluation of the companies. During the 20-year period 1919–1938 the industry declared out to stockholders only 40 per cent as much money as during the 14 years 1905–1918.[8] Nothing at all was paid during three years (1921, 1934, and 1935), and, whereas there had been only one year in the previous period when total payments had fallen below $5 million, the period 1919–1938 included only four years when stockholders received more than that amount. As in the case of output, consolidation saved Calumet and Hecla from clear-cut decline until the depression of the thirties. Substantial payments were made during the years 1925–1928, and in 1929 the company disbursed over $9 million, a sum greater than any payment of a single year since the all-time record of 1899.[9] The importance of the reclamation plants in maintaining Calumet and Hecla dividends can scarcely be exaggerated. A conservative estimate from annual reports indicates that the company made profits from tailings amounting to at least $21 million, which represented about 59 per cent of total Calumet and Hecla dividends and 35 per cent of the 20-year total for the district.

In 1938 the market valuation of the stocks of the four producing companies amounted to about $27.5 million as compared with $100 million for Calumet and Hecla alone in 1906, or about the same as the valuation of Calumet and Hecla in the depression year 1921.[10] Depreciation of individual stocks is partially obscured by consolidations. As was the case with both dividends and output, Calumet and Hecla surpassed its record of the previous period. The market value of the company's shares declined from $64 million in 1916 to $28 million in 1921, reached $41 million in 1923 after the consolidation, and then broke all records in 1929 with a total value of $124 million. Stock market value evaporated rapidly after the financial collapse of 1929, and by 1934 the company's shares were worth $13.2 million.

The role of lower copper prices. A mining field cannot stave off decline forever, and it seems certain that the Michigan industry would have contracted substantially during these years in consequence of increasing depth, exhaustion of major deposits, and falling copper content of the general run of rock, even if the sellers' market had continued. But that market ended, and the fact that the general cost and copper price relationship changed substantially was an extremely important factor in speeding up the trend.[11]

The period opened with enormous wartime stocks of copper and an overexpanded industry. World output was temporarily curtailed, but production during the middle twenties was on a par with that of 1918, and by 1928 was running about 40 per cent above the war level.[12] The depression brought about a substantial curtailment, but by 1937 world output had recovered and was about 14 per cent above the 1929 level. Not only was world production of *new* copper increasing enormously during these years, but by the late twenties recovery from scrap had become a highly significant factor on the supply side. The most important development on the demand side was a falling off in the proportion of world copper consumed in the United States. Consumption fell steeply immediately following the war, and it was not until 1929 that the 1918 level was equaled. The decline during the early thirties amounted to over 50 per cent, and in 1937, with world output of new copper running well above the 1929 level, United States consumption was 22 per cent less than that of 1929.

The net effect of these factors was a significant weakening of copper prices when compared with the prewar days, and a substantial shift in the general cost and copper price relationship. During the years 1919–1938 the wholesale price index averaged about 36 per cent more than that of the base period 1910–1914, while copper prices averaged 16 per cent less.[13] A large sector of the world copper industry was able to meet this situation by heavy capital investment in greatly improved plant facilities. Such an alternative was no longer open to Michigan producers.

DECLINE OF MICHIGAN COPPER MINING IN A PERIOD OF GENERAL BUSINESS PROSPERITY, 1919–1929

As might be expected, the problems connected with the decline of an industry, particularly one which depends upon heavy investment in capital goods for the largest sector of its demand, are substantially mitigated when the general economy is going through a period of rapid expansion. Unfortunately it was the middle of the decade before the copper mining industry recovered from the impact of the War, and even then a full measure of prosperity came only to the few large producers who owned vast open-cut properties or mines with very substantial quantities of by-product precious metals.[14]

The threat of overproduction and efforts at control. As of January 1, 1919, world stocks of copper were estimated at about 2.2 billion pounds, or approximately twice the annual average production of new copper during the decade 1911–1920.[15] Producers had increased capacity substantially over the prewar level, and the United States government had forced continued output at full scale for several months following the armistice. Curtailment and control seemed called for, and the largest United States copper interests took charge of the situation. The first step was the formation of Copper Exporters Association, Inc., under authority of the Webb-Pomerene Act.[16] Membership of this organization was made up of the important United States owned companies, and its purpose was to control the foreign market by export quotas, so that the enormous stocks could be gradually liquidated without causing a complete glut.[17] Obviously control of the foreign market was not enough; curtailment was called for, and these same producers shouldered the burden, reducing output substantially in 1919 at both their South American and United States properties. Domestic production fell in that year by about 36 per cent.[18] The depression of 1920–1922, however, made necessary more drastic action, and in the spring of 1921 all but two small members of the Exporters Association shut down completely for a full year. The export quota system and restriction understandings in the United States had effectively eliminated the wartime stocks by 1924, and disagreements between companies with large foreign interests and those primarily concerned with domestic properties ended the career of the Exporters Association that same year.

During 1924 and 1925 swelling output from Chile and Africa held the price of copper down, and by 1926 the formation of another cartel seemed advisable to the industry. Although the largest companies had been making money since 1924, they were equipped with too much plant and may have considered overproduction imminent unless formal controls could be reestablished. Incidentally they were annoyed by the operations of independent brokers on the London metal exchange.[19] In October, 1926, Copper Exporters, Inc., was established, also under authority of the Webb-Pomerene Act, to "stabilize the European market." [20] The new cartel, representing firms which controlled 90 per cent of world output, was empowered by its members to set an "official" price from headquarters in Brussels. Determination of sales quotas was not an announced purpose, but it seems probable that there were understandings as to sharing of the European trade, and each producer was required to furnish the Brussels office complete information on all transactions.[21] A year later the important United States companies formed a producers' association, known as the Copper Institute, as a coöperating body, although its announced purpose was simply to provide channels for sharing information within the industry. For the first two years of the cartel's operations, prices stayed around 13 cents a pound, and then in 1929 rose to 18 and finally 24. In April, 1929, they were stabilized and held for a full year at 17.775 cents, despite the collapse of the stock market and strenuous protests by consumers, particularly abroad.[22]

The Webb-Pomerene Act was based upon the fiction that United States interest groups could be allowed to arrive at a cartel price for sales in foreign markets without affecting free market forces at home. There seems to be little doubt that the result was a substantial amount of coöperation among producers in both the domestic and foreign markets which brought higher domestic prices than were justified in the light of greatly reduced costs in large sectors of the industry [23] and tended to preserve a condition of overinvestment in world copper mining plant.[24]

The Michigan stake in the control system of the twenties. The relative position of the Michigan sector of the industry had worsened so substantially during the period of maturity, 1905–1918, that its voice was a minor, if strident, one in copper councils of the twenties. Calumet and Hecla was the only Lake company to become a member of Copper Exporters Association, Inc., and, although all of the Michigan producers except the Mohawk joined Copper Exporters, Inc., only Calumet and Hecla became a member of the Copper Institute. In so far as the price of copper was kept above a competitive level there is a presumption that all of the Lake companies benefited, and, since Calumet and Hecla was the only one which stood shoulder to shoulder with the large western producers in the curtailment efforts following the war, the rest of the Michigan industry had the additional advantage of operating under the umbrella.[25]

The result was that the Michigan sector of the industry, which was, in general, the most marginal, curtailed much less during the period of declining prices from 1919 to 1922 than did United States producers as a whole. In 1919 output was maintained at the 1918 level at both the Quincy and the Mohawk and reduced by only 10 per cent at the Copper Range mines, while the properties in the Calumet and Hecla interest group curtailed by 27 per cent. Two years later, during the most severe curtailment of United States copper mining history, the Copper Range and Mohawk actually increased output, and the proportion of United States production accounted for by the Michigan companies rose to 19.8 per cent, the highest proportion attained since 1910.[26] It would seem to be a reasonably safe guess that, if events had been left to follow a "natural" course, the Lake producers would have been the worst sufferers in the industry, receiving a blow which, at the least, would have crippled them for all but a year or so of the prosperous twenties.[27]

Throughout these years Calumet and Hecla evidently played the game fairly much according to rules laid down by the giants of the day: Kennecott, Anaconda, and Phelps-Dodge. Rudolph Agassiz of Calumet and Hecla served as president of the Copper and Brass Research Association, as well as on the boards of the various producers' organizations.[28] But increasingly there were disagreements among members of the inner circle, disagreements in which Calumet and Hecla tended to side with the rest of the Michigan industry against the lords of the copper world. Although the United States was still showing a large copper export balance, a situation had arisen in which the Michigan industry had a strong interest in a protective tariff.[29] Apparently there had been a substantial shift in marketing areas for Lake copper during the early twenties, particularly following 1924 when the industry obtained a 35 per cent reduction in railroad freight rates to Detroit. An increasing proportion of the Michigan product was marketed in the mid-West, and very little copper was tied up at the Lake during the winter months.[30] Low-cost Canadian production, which was increasing steadily during these years, also found an outlet in the United States mid-West and began to crowd the Michigan companies in their local markets.[31] As early as 1923 the Copper Range Annual Report called for a protective tariff, and by the spring of 1924 the Michigan industry had organized a full-scale campaign.[32] The rest of the domestic industry (with the single exception of the Calumet and Arizona which was managed by former Michigan men) was indifferent or opposed to the measure, and a bill died in Congress from lack of general support.[33] Alex Skelton has declared that one reason for the breakup of the Exporters Association in 1924 was disagreement over this tariff issue.[34] From that time on, Michigan people were keenly aware of the domestic-foreign cleavage.[35] Copper Exporters, Inc., was an international cartel in which the non-domestic spokesmen became increasingly vocal as the balance of production shifted to the newer producers of Canada, Africa, and Chile. Americans were still in the saddle, but the controlling voices tended to speak more and more often from the viewpoint of properties outside of the United States. Nothing much could be done to change that situation as long as general prosperity continued — the Michigan men were obliged to bide their time.

Adjustment to the new cost-price plateau. In the years following the war the Michigan copper mining industry found itself on a new cost-price plateau. From 1922 to 1926 copper prices averaged 10 per cent less than the 1913 level, while the average price of local labor ran about 50 per cent higher, and railroad freight rates, coal, and other supplies had increased even more substantially.[36] These developments, plus increased costs connected with an aging mining field, were reflected in a lower level of output and dividend payments. The golden age of Michigan copper was clearly past, and the industry set about taking what measures remained to adjust to the new situation and to salvage as much capital as possible from the declining field.[37] An obvious first step was to complete the integration of operations which had been partially blocked in the prewar years. In August, 1923, a consolidation plan was presented to the stockholders of the Calumet and Hecla properties including the

Ahmeek, Allouez, Centennial, Osceola, and Calumet and Hecla. A new company was to be incorporated, known as the "Calumet and Hecla Consolidated Copper Company," with 2.5 million shares of $25 each, approximately half a million of which were to be retained in the company's treasury. The consolidation went through a month later, old Calumet and Hecla shareholders receiving somewhat more than 75 per cent of the shares issued by the new concern.[38] In that same year the Copper Range Company absorbed the Tri-Mountain Mining Company, which had been maintained by court order as an independent operating concern since 1918.[39] These consolidations went far to exhaust the possibilities of integration of operations of properties in the same interest group, the most important exception being the Champion, which continued to operate under joint ownership of the St. Mary's Mineral Land Company and the Copper Range. Very little more than "mopping-up" operations remained — during the next decade Calumet and Hecla and Copper Range were to acquire the great bulk of the outstanding Michigan copper land.

Technological change was significant during the years 1919–1929, but certainly could not be called revolutionary in character. It consisted mainly of a general adoption of changes which had already been introduced at Calumet and Hecla and the adaptation of processes, which had been successfully used on the conglomerate rock, to the special problems of the amygdaloid mines. Underground there were some improvements in the power drill, the Ahmeek introducing a machine which struck about a third more blows per minute,[40] and constant experiments were made with mechanical power shovels and scrapers in an effort to reduce the amount of manual labor required in loading tram cars.[41] Apparently the mechanical loading devices were most effective in the conglomerate workings, and there was a good deal of skepticism as to their value for amygdaloid mines where operations at any one point were on a smaller scale.[42]

On the surface there was a general movement to reduce fuel costs by pulverizing coal and utilizing the exhaust steam from stamps,[43] and in 1928 the United States Bureau of Mines announced successful experiments in adapting the flotation process to the treatment of amygdaloid slimes.[44] During the next two years flotation plants were installed by all of the companies, and savings were reported of 1.3 to 3.0 pounds of copper per ton of rock stamped.[45] Finally, at Calumet and Hecla the smelting plant was completely rebuilt during the early twenties, much larger furnaces being installed,[46] and in 1925 a new railroad system was constructed to rationalize local transportation for all of the newly consolidated mines.[47]

Integration of operations and technological refinements were essential steps in adjusting to the new cost-price relationship, but would have proven utterly insufficient if it had not been possible to adopt a more exploitive, and immediately productive, mining method. Apparently selective mining embodied two different sets of managerial decisions. In the first place, a number of improvements were made in underground organization, which had already begun to be introduced during the period of maturity and would have paid even if the sellers' market had continued. More important, however, was the fact that greater selectivity of one sort or another was the usual mining response to a more unfavorable cost-price relationship: this time the change in the market situation was so drastic and sudden that it seemed to call for unprecedented measures. The contract-wage system for underground work was changed so that premiums were paid for quantity of metal rather than rock mined, or the company reserved the right to choose the location for drill holes; great care was taken in selecting the rock to be broken, and, whenever possible, "poor rock" was sorted out underground.[48]

Whereas rock averaging 15 to 17 pounds of copper per ton was considered worth mining prior to the war, 20 pounds was now set as a low limit.[49] Selective mining meant a faster rate of exploitation of existing mineral bodies, a skimming of the cream, which had to be balanced against lower costs resulting primarily from much higher productivities per man employed. Whereas the district as a whole was getting 11,900 pounds of copper per man-year of labor employed in 1909, and 14,600 in 1919, annual productivity per worker reached 23,800 pounds by 1929.[50] Other factors were operating in the same direction. Increasing dependence upon reclamation output raised over-all productivity substantially since the retreatment plants were small users of labor, and, finally, the aging of the field was constantly reducing the mineral land reserve and cutting down the proportion of the total labor force engaged in development work.

By the late twenties the adjustment had been made, and the Michigan companies were paying out substantial sums of money from a slowly increasing production, which was still well below the prewar level. Some idea of the industry's competitive position at that time can be obtained from a Tariff Commission study of copper mining costs during the years 1928–1930.[51]

TABLE 5

MICHIGAN COSTS COMPARED WITH THOSE OF THE REST OF THE DOMESTIC INDUSTRY, 1928–1930

(Costs in Cents Per Pound of Refined Copper)

	Michigan	Arizona	Other U.S.
Mining labor	4.10	2.82	3.08
Mining supplies	2.39	1.30	1.62
Milling	1.14	2.52	1.91
Smelting	.62	1.17	1.17
Refining	None	.82	.82
Precious metal credit	None	− .84	− 1.12
Other costs (freight, administrative, depreciative, etc.)[a]	1.99	1.94	1.20
Total	10.24	9.73	8.62

[a] Depletion not figured as a cost.

The relative situation was substantially the same as that of the period of maturity; a severe disadvantage, in consequence of higher mining costs and lack of precious metal content, was partially balanced by simpler metallurgical problems. The difference between the two periods was that during the late twenties it was possible to maintain such an equilibrium only at a lower level of output and with a more selective exploitation of the properties.

Partial success in reallocation of labor and capital resources. The years 1919–1929 of Michigan copper mining history provide an example of relatively successful resource reallocation in a "free enterprise system," under conditions of an expanding general economy. It seems probable that between 1918 and 1921 employment in Michigan copper mining fell by 60 per cent or more, and that, even after Calumet and Hecla reopened following the shutdown of 1921–22, the industry was employing only about 55 to 60 per cent as many men as in 1918.[52] In spite of this development, the twenties were considered by local mine managers as a period of labor shortage, and wage differences between Michigan copper, on the one hand, and Lake Superior iron and Western copper, on the other, tended to narrow.

The fall in employment between 1918 and early 1922 amounted to about 7,500 men, yet virtually no unemployment was recorded,[53] and when the mines in the Calumet and Hecla interest group reopened in the spring of 1922, there was a real shortage of labor.[54] The movement to factories in the Detroit area, which had begun as early as 1917, had continued to increase as wages in the Copper Country fell further behind those in Detroit, and had turned into a real exodus as a result of the Calumet and Hecla curtailment of 1919 and shutdown of 1921.[55] Wage increases were granted in 1922, but the competition from Detroit automobile plants continued to be severe, agents from that industry traveling all over the Copper Country recruiting men.[56]

As might be expected, the postwar readjustment period and exodus of Michigan copper workers overturned the unstable relative wage situation which had existed in 1919.[57]

	Average Daily Wages in Dollars All Workers		
Industry	1919	1924	1929
Michigan copper	$3.76	$3.98	$4.03
Michigan iron	6.38	4.43	4.70
Minnesota iron	5.59	4.56	5.10

Until the boom years 1928–29, the Michigan copper mining industry was gradually increasing employment and, in the process, narrowing the wage difference between itself and the neighboring Iron Country.[58] By the end of the decade the differential was beginning to open up again as wages were increased substantially in the Iron Country, and it seems likely that the situation was building up to another exodus of men — copper mining employment in Houghton County showed a mild decline after 1927.[59] One important effect of relative mobility of labor upon the industry's competitive position was that there was no widening of the wage differential compared with the West during this first stage of decline. Data prepared by the Bureau of Labor Statistics show, if anything, a slight narrowing of the differential.[60] Prosperity of the general economy effectively eliminated any possibility of gaining "cheap labor" as a result of a lower level of output and more highly selective mining practices, particularly since the traditional source of low cost labor had been largely blocked by immigration laws.[61]

This first phase of decline of the Michigan copper mining industry saw a certain amount of reallocation of capital as well. For the most part the capital reallocation was not "planned," in that the companies made virtually no investments in new mineral lands or other forms of new enterprise. However, between 1919 and 1929 approximately $48 million was paid out to stockholders, which represented in large part a liquidation of invested capital.[62] During the years immediately following the war there was some talk of the advisability of going into the fabricating end of the business, a step which, in long-run terms, would have represented a "planned" shift. General Manager MacNaughton of Calumet and Hecla predicted in 1921 that the time would come soon for such action,[63] and its advisability was considered at the time of the consolidation in 1923.[64] However, in spite of a general trend toward such a development among other large United States copper mining companies, vertical integration did not take place in the Michigan industry during these years.[65]

DECLINE OF MICHIGAN COPPER MINING IN A PERIOD OF
GENERAL BUSINESS DEPRESSION, 1930–1938

In marked contrast with the twenties, the period 1930–1938 saw years of serious contraction and depression in the national economy. The impact of this development upon Michigan copper mining was so severe that the decline of the industry turned into something approaching a collapse, and the trend toward desirable resource reallocation came to a halt and was replaced by developments which, at times, were actually retrogressive in character. With the onset of the depression the overproduction fears of the world copper mining industry were fully realized, and Michigan developments must be considered in a complex framework of efforts at national and international control.

Intensification of the overproduction problem and new attempts at control. The financial collapse of 1929 and the ensuing depression could not have come at a worse time for world copper producers, who were just beginning to grapple with the most serious threat of overproduction yet experienced. During these years enormous new deposits in Rhodesia and Canada, which had been opened up in the late twenties, began to come into production.[66] The fact that much of the new Canadian output was a by-product of nickel, and political factors tying up rapid exploitation of the new fields with empire building made these sources peculiarly difficult to control. In addition, the economics of the industry was undergoing a fundamental change in consequence of the rise of the United States scrap industry, which had contributed 37 per cent as much copper as domestic primary producers in 1918, to a point where it produced 63 per cent as much in 1929, and substantially more than the primary producers during the worst years of the depression.[67]

Until April, 1930, Copper Exporters, Inc., held fast to the 17.775 price,[68] and the big American trio — Anaconda, Kennecott, and Phelps-Dodge — carried out sizable, but inadequate, reductions at both their United States and South American properties. Most of the rest of the world industry held production about constant in 1930, or, as was the case with the African properties, increased output. During 1931 serious discussions were begun concerning world curtailment, but the problems were so difficult that reduction in 1931 was also hopelessly inadequate, the main curtailment coming from small United States producers out of necessity. In the fall of 1931, however, an international agreement was finally reached to reduce output to 26.5 per cent of capacity, and in March of 1932 a new meeting set the level at 20 per cent of capacity. A few months later the United States Congress cut off the domestic market by tariff action which resulted in the collapse of Copper Exporters, Inc., and two years of cessation of international coöperation.

In 1930 the tariff movement had revived, and the case seemed somewhat more plausible than that of the mid-twenties since imports exceeded exports in 1930 and 1931, although the surplus went to stocks; domestic production still exceeded consumption. Political pressure was very great from the copper producing states,[69] but a measure was not passed by Congress until May of 1932, primarily because of disagreements among the producers, Anaconda and Kennecott having great difficulty coming to a decision concerning the advisability of such a step.[70] In first-class logrolling fashion the copper duty of four cents a pound was tied into an oil-coal-lumber bill and finally pushed through Congress.[71] The duty, although it had a very real effect in shifting lines of trade, did not create a significant differential between the domestic and world price, since the United States maintained an export balance from 1933 through 1938. There was, however, a short period when such a differential did appear. During 1934 and 1935 exports increased substantially, and the export price on electrolytic copper averaged a little more than a cent a pound below the domestic price. (In February, 1935, the difference reached 2.6 cents a pound.)[72] This highly interesting development was a product of legalized combination of producers under the N.R.A.

The domestic copper producers had much difficulty arriving

at a code, largely because of disagreements concerning sales quotas for producer owned fabricators, and it was not until April 21, 1934, that final code approval was obtained.[73] Total annual sales for the primary industry were set at 24.6 per cent of capacity; the "big three" (Anaconda, Kennecott, and Phelps-Dodge) were held to about 20 per cent, while quotas for the rest of the industry varied upward inversely according to capacity.[74] The quotas were on a monthly basis, and each producer was required to file publicly, two days in advance, the price at which sales were made. Finally, there was no limitation on exports which rose in consequence of dumping. The copper code tended to freeze producers in terms of their 1933 relative status, and in the words of Elizabeth May, "If the Copper Code was typical of all codes, there would be but one result: a lower standard of living for the American people." [75] Primary producers were soon obliged to reduce their quotas even further for the benefit of custom smelters and producers of secondary and by-product copper,[76] but with a mild revival in demand after 1933 stocks of refined copper had fallen almost 50 per cent by 1935.[77]

In the meantime the efforts at international coöperation were resumed with the formation of a new cartel. Early in 1935 the South American subsidiaries of Anaconda and Kennecott, the African producers, and several smaller foreign interests came to an agreement to cut production by 240,000 tons a year.[78] This was the first cartel which restricted membership to foreign producers, apparently the only domestic tie-up being an agreement by Kennecott to hold down exports from the United States.[79] No attempt was made to set prices directly, and control was exercised by periodic announcements of changes in production plans, a policy of sales to consumers only, and exchange of information. World copper stocks were lowered, and when European demand revived strongly in 1936 and 1937, largely in consequence of the armaments race, speculators ran away with the market and all restrictions were called off in January, 1937.[80]

Michigan participation in and benefits from the control efforts. It is extremely difficult to judge how much the Michigan industry benefited from the various control devices employed during the years 1930–1938. Certainly conditions within the industry became desperate, and all that can be said with any certainty is that if it had not been for the controls, they would doubtless have been even worse. The *general effect* of the measures was to allocate the restriction burden more in accordance with financial ability to bear it, than inversely according to cost at which copper could be produced. If there is reason to believe that there is not overinvestment in an industry and that a reduction of demand is temporary in character, restricting output on such a basis may be defensible in terms of preserving capital investment and an allocation of labor required in the long run. It seems very doubtful, however, that the copper industry of the early thirties fell in such a category.[81]

Marginal sectors of the industry, such as the Michigan district, were preserved and even showed a net gain in relative importance. In 1929 the Lake companies accounted for 9.3 per cent of United States output, but during the worst years of the depression, 1930–1934, their contribution ran from 10.2 to 12.3 per cent, declining thereafter to a new low of 5.6 per cent by 1937. Developments in 1930, when the cartel adopted the all but incomprehensible policy of holding an umbrella at 17.775 cents a pound, are strikingly similar to those of 1919 and 1921, and show the operations of the control system at their worst. Only two Michigan companies, Calumet and Hecla and the Mohawk, restricted output in that year. Calumet and Hecla curtailed by about 15 per cent, the reduction coming almost entirely from its low-cost reclamation plant,[82] and the curtailment at the Mohawk was probably the result of virtual exhaustion of that property. The rest of the Michigan industry either held output constant or increased it, in such fashion that Lake production fell by only 9 per cent as against a 29 per cent drop in United States output, something more than a 33 per cent fall in United States consumption, and the appearance of an import balance.[83]

Apparently the Michigan people expected to benefit substantially from the tariff and the N.R.A. and were in the vanguard of both movements. As early as September of 1930 the Michigan State Legislature was urging Congress to pass a duty, and when the Phelps-Dodge people and the Lewisohns joined the pro-tariff advocates, the Michigan interests were a strong third in the line-up.[84] Senator Vandenberg of Michigan was one of the leaders of the fight in Congress; [85] people prayed for passage of the measure in Copper Country churches; and when the great day came, there were cheering crowds and torch-light processions.[86] Interest in the N.R.A., was also keen, although only two Lake companies (Calumet and Hecla and Copper Range) were still operating at the time of the passage of the Act. When an association was formed in January, 1934, for the purpose of sponsoring a code, a representative of Calumet and Hecla served as secretary.[87] Initially Calumet and Hecla was allowed a monthly sales quota of about 26 per cent of capacity and Copper Range 36 per cent, as compared with about 20 per cent for each of the "big three." [88] The blessing was a mixed one, however, since the quotas were below current output, and the code made mandatory minimum wages of 37.5 cents an hour for underground men and 32.5 cents an hour for surface workers — a requirement which raised average wages by about 20 per cent at both Calumet and Hecla and Copper Range.[89]

The Michigan industry operates at a loss. The impact of the depression upon the Michigan copper mining industry may have been somewhat alleviated by outside control efforts, but that impact was still disastrous enough. Of the six companies [90] which were producing in 1929, four had shut down completely by 1933, and of those four only two found it possible to reopen their mines when the price of copper revived in 1936–37. That part of the industry which continued to operate showed an out-of-pocket loss for six of the years between 1930 and 1937,[91] and at Calumet and Hecla the drain was so serious that the total excess of cash, government securities, notes and accounts receivable over notes and accounts payable declined from about $7.4 million on December 31, 1929, to a slight negative balance by December 31, 1933.[92] Most of the mines of even Calumet and Hecla and Copper Range had to be shut down, and during the worst years of the depression the Champion and the old Calumet and Hecla conglomerate were the only properties operated in the entire Copper Country.

Between April, 1929, and the fall of 1933 the companies discharged about 5,500 to 6,000 men; Calumet and Hecla alone paid off about 3,600.[93] The bulk of the firing was done in 1932 when employment was just about halved, but even when discharged, the workers in this one-industry district continued to represent a real responsibility for the companies until 1933 when the State and Federal governments assumed the major part of the relief burden. Single men were discharged whenever possible before men with families; [94] work was shared out to as many men as possible, the time on the job allowed to each employee varying with the number of his dependents; [95] and Calumet and Hecla contributed privately to sustain 1,600 cases until January 1, 1933.[96]

With most of the mines shut down and very little money available to invest in new equipment, the possibilities of meeting the problems of the thirties by substantial technological change were practically nonexistent, and almost all of the significant improvements of the period represented the completion of projects planned and often even begun, in the late twenties. In 1930 Calumet and Hecla completed a magnificent boiler and power plant at the Ahmeek mill,[97] and Copper Range (jointly with the Middle West Utilities Company), completed an important hydroelectric development at Victoria, Michigan,[98] which made possible much cheaper power and the introduction of electric crushers to replace stamps in their mills.[99] Finally, experiments carried out by the Michigan College of Mining at Houghton resulted in the development of a successful method for treating the amygdaloid tailings of the Copper Range Company, and a small beginning at reclamation work was made in 1937.[100] Progress along the consolidation line was also confined very largely to the Copper Range interests. In 1931 the company absorbed both the Champion Mining Company and the St. Mary's Mineral Land Company, and in 1934 purchased lands and equipment of the Mohawk and Wolverine companies.[101]

The main weapon relied upon to meet the economic problems

of the day, however, was even more highly selective mining. The course of the depression can practically be charted (with some time lag) from figures on copper return per ton of rock mined.[102]

Year	All Michigan Companies (Pounds Copper per Ton of Rock)
1925–30 average	26.42
1931	33.18
1932	47.60
1933	67.20
1934	68.87
1935	72.95
1936	45.75
1937	42.76
1938	42.28

The extremely high returns of the years 1933–1935 were only obtainable by closure of all but the two most productive mines of the district. At the Champion great emphasis was placed upon hand sorting in the stopes,[103] while at the old Calumet and Hecla conglomerate property the lower levels were allowed to fill with water, and work was confined to the rich shaft pillars and old backs of the long-abandoned higher levels of the mine.[104] Without doubt this shortened the life of the property, and 1938 was the last full year of production from one of the most famous underground copper mines the world has ever seen. Whatever the long-run costs were in terms of loss of metal due to an exploitive mining method, out-of-pocket costs on the small current production were greatly reduced, and annual productivity per man employed at Calumet and Hecla rose from 27,000 pounds of refined copper in 1929 to a record of 47,000 in 1936.[105] Additional factors explaining this substantial rise in labor productivity during the middle thirties were the concentration of the mining force on stoping rather than development work and a substantial amount of selectivity in layoffs such that, as soon as the first impact of the crisis was over, the most productive employees were retained.

Retrogressive labor supply developments and the beginning of a planned capital shift. By June of 1933 there were an estimated 8,800 men unemployed in Houghton County,[106] and in spite of the fact that the basic industry of the district was clearly a declining one, between 1930 and 1934 the population of the county actually increased by about 4,000 persons (8 per cent).[107] In a time of national crisis people returned to their old homes where they were known and could expect help, and where the chances of survival seemed greater in consequence of a rural environment. When the general economy showed signs of recovery in 1936–37, the population trend was reversed, and for the decade 1930–1940 as a whole, Houghton County lost 5,220 people. A migration of 10 per cent of the population in a decade was hopelessly inadequate to counterbalance the decline of the industry (the migration from 1920 to 1930 had amounted to 19,079, or 26 per cent of the 1920 population), and in July of 1940, 37 per cent of the population of the County were still dependent upon some form of public assistance.[108]

As might be expected, the retrogressive development in labor resource allocation is evidenced in relative wage trends.

Average Daily Wages, All Employees[a]
(In Dollars)

	1929	1931	1939
Michigan copper	$4.03	$2.74	$3.31
Michigan iron	4.70	3.82	4.47
Minnesota iron	5.10	3.82	4.85
Arizona copper	5.55	...	5.17
Copper industry	5.27	...	4.63

[a] For the year 1931, see Bureau of Labor Statistics, *Bulletin* 573, p. 3. For 1929 and 1939, see United States Census, volumes on *Mines and Quarries*.

By 1939 the daily wage differential between Michigan copper and Michigan iron, which had been closing during the twenties, opened up again to such an extent that Michigan iron workers were averaging 35 per cent more than Michigan copper workers, in contrast with about 17 per cent in 1929. (The differential stood at 40 per cent in 1931.) In this second phase of decline, 1930–1938, it seems clear that the industry was able to pay lower wages as a result of a reduction of employment opportunities. The differential between Michigan copper and other sections of the labor market might have been even greater if it had not been for the W.P.A. and the N.R.A. The fact that the N.R.A. minimum brought about a 20 per cent increase in the average wage rate has been noted.[109] As for the W.P.A., the pressure of unemployment continued to be so great in the district after 1935 that even as late as July, 1941, copper mining wages were reported near the level of W.P.A. wages.[110] The W.P.A., however meritorious it was in other respects, doubtless slowed down the movement of workers out of the district during the years 1937–1940, although it is conceivable that this effect was partially counterbalanced by the possibility that the W.P.A. minimum may have forced the mining companies to pay higher wages and thus employ fewer men than otherwise would have been the case.

While a trend toward a more desirable labor allocation sloughed down into a depression bog, the movement of capital out of the industry via dividend payments also came to a standstill. Nevertheless, a small beginning was made at a planned shift of capital through investments in new forms of enterprise. In 1931 the Copper Range Company purchased a substantial interest in the C. G. Hussey Company, a Pittsburgh fabricator of various forms of sheet copper,[111] and in 1936 all assets of the concern were acquired by merger agreement.[112] In the meantime, Calumet and Hecla purchased in 1934 an Upper Peninsula gold mining claim, the Ishpeming Gold Mining Company, and commenced exploratory work. The following year options were taken on claims at Goldfield, Nevada, and by 1936 exploratory work was under way by two subsidiaries of Calumet and Hecla — the Eastern Exploration Company and the Goldfield Mining Company — on 88 claims which were owned outright and 106 held under option.[113]

THE IMPACT OF THE DECLINE UPON THE COMMUNITY

A community which has grown up with a mining industry as its economic core often faces the prospect of a more prolonged and agonized decline than that of the industry itself. This is particularly true when the environment is not highly favorable to the development of other forms of enterprise and when the mining industry has followed a policy of discouraging use of labor and land for other industrial purposes. During the period of decline the mining companies are usually able to salvage a substantial amount of capital, via dividend payments and investment of profits elsewhere, but the community investment in homes, public buildings and works, and a settled way of living is not so easily retrievable.[114] Of course, a declining mining industry does not escape unscathed from contraction of the community in which it operates, since such developments react back upon the companies in the form of demands for heavier tax payments from the shrinking assessment base, local crisis conditions when outside forces impede the emigration of workers, and inability to provide a high level of local government services.[115] All of these developments took place in the Michigan copper district.

The Copper Country loses half of its people. Between 1910 and 1940 the population of Houghton County fell by over 40,000 people (46 per cent). Although such a development was highly desirable in terms of labor allocation, falling employment acted as a constant depressant upon the economic life of the community, particularly since the market for virtually all of the goods and services produced, except copper, was in the local area. The mining companies provided the main stream of purchasing power, and between 1919 and 1929 the annual copper mining payroll declined from $14.6 million to $9.8 million, and by 1939 to $3.3 million.[116]

The decline of the industry, and consequent emigration, did not bring about as marked a distortion of the age pattern of the population as might have been expected. The proportion of males from 18 to 44 years old to total population in Houghton County actually increased from 19.1 per cent in 1920 to 21.8 per cent in 1940.[117] Apparently the people with the greatest incentive to move were fairly young couples with large families, which resulted in a decline in the proportion of the population under 21 years of age from 49.2 per cent in 1920 to 35.4 per cent in 1940, and a rise in the proportion above the age of 55 from 13.4 per cent in 1930 to 19.1 per cent in 1940. In the long run a marked distortion would result from such a process, barring the introduction of some new factor, and the County would be left with an "aged population." However, the process seems to have been a fairly slow one. This long-run problem was clearly foreseen as early as 1920, and diversification of industry was proposed as a method of holding experienced miners who were seeking opportunities for their children.[118]

Intense sensitivity to crisis conditions in the general economy. Not only does the community suffer in good times through emigration of its people and a gradual distortion of a normal age pattern, but much more serious developments take place when crisis conditions in the general economy dam up the flow of excess labor out of the declining industry area and even reverse the population trend. This is precisely what took place in Houghton and Keweenaw counties during the depths of the depression.[119] By August, 1934, 66.3 per cent of the families in Keweenaw County and 37.8 per cent in Houghton County were on relief, as compared with a Michigan state average of 12.2 per cent.[120] Harry Hopkins classified the Copper Country as having the highest relief load in the United States.[121] Between March 4, 1933, and June 30, 1939, $16 million of State and Federal relief funds were poured into the two counties,[122] and in July of 1940 there were still 37 per cent of the people of Houghton County dependent upon some form of public assistance.[123]

Between 1907 and 1938 the assessed valuation of all real and personal property in Houghton County declined from $108.3 million to $18.9 million. (Table 17, p. 232.) One of the most interesting features of this evaporation of the tax base was that, after 1920, it was relatively continuous, with nothing more than a mild leveling off from 1925 through 1929 to mark the great American boom. Before World War I dependence upon the mining companies as a tax source was so great that 70 to 75 per cent of total assessments of Houghton County were often assigned to the copper companies. In the late twenties about 50 per cent was usual in Houghton County (Keweenaw still was assessing over 75 per cent to the companies), and by 1935-1937 the proportion had fallen to about 35 per cent.[124] It is little wonder that the Board of Supervisors of Houghton County appeared before the State Social Welfare Commission in August of 1940 to ask the State to assume more of the local welfare burden.[125] At a time when the great majority of local governments in the United States were well on the way to getting back on their financial feet, Copper Country units still found themselves completely unable to cope with current problems.

Difficulty in changing the economic base for the community. In 1940 the male working force of Houghton County totaled 15,277 persons, of whom 3,155 were working on W.P.A. projects, and 2,843 were classified as seeking employment. As for the 9,279 who had private employment, the breakdown was about as follows: [126]

29 per cent	mining
15 per cent	agriculture
5 per cent	logging and allied trades
5 per cent	manufacturing
46 per cent	professional, service, retail and wholesale trade, entertainment, etc.

Although the tourist business was growing and a small proportion of the agricultural and logging products found outside markets, the County was still dependent upon the copper mining industry for its life blood. This dependence had not lessened significantly in spite of 22 years of decline — the process had been one of emigration or unemployment rather than a shift to other forms of local employment. Unquestionably this was very largely because the physical location and environment were not highly favorable to other forms of enterprise. Agricultural possibilities were very limited, due to soil and climatic conditions, and had always served primarily as a part-time employment. Manufacturing possibilities were not particularly bright in consequence of great distance from dense centers of population, high fuel costs, and long winters. In addition there was one other factor which had acted as a barrier to the transition of the economy. In its heyday the mining industry had looked with ill-favor upon efforts to establish manufacturing enterprises in the district, and since the companies owned a very high percentage of the land and had a dominant voice in the community, their displeasure would have been hard to buck. The reasons behind this policy were that industrial employers would have tightened up the labor market, that they might have let unionism slip in through the back door, and that they would have preëmpted land which might some day be valuable for mining purposes.[127] Apparently there was some weakening of this determination to maintain one-industry sway in the years immediately following the first World War,[128] but little came of the drive for diversification at that time. There is no concrete evidence to show that the mining companies "kept manufacturing out" during the twenties and thirties, but many local people believe that the companies were unfavorably inclined toward such a development until very recent years.

CHAPTER VII

World War II and the Future

> . . . Like a hollow ledge
> Holding a little pool
> Left there by the tide
> A little tepid pool
> Dying inward from the edge *
> — *Edna St. Vincent Millay*

Michigan copper mining continued to decline during the War years, in spite of substantial government subsidies, and by 1946 the mines and reclamation plants of the district were producing about the same quantity of copper as they had during the depths of the depression and were accounting for less than 4 per cent of United States output.[1] Decline of the companies as mining enterprises, however, was largely offset by a shift into other stages of the copper industry, and by 1947 the future of Calumet and Hecla, at least, seemed assured as a processor of scrap and a fabricator, if not as a mining venture.

MICHIGAN COPPER MINING ON THE EVE OF UNITED STATES ENTRY INTO THE WAR

Lack of vitality in the industry. The industry never really recovered from the impact of the depression. By 1936 production had climbed back to 96 million pounds, or about half that of 1929, but it then fell off to about 88 million pounds by 1939. Closure of the great conglomerate mine and near-exhaustion of the rich conglomerate tailings were the basic causes of inability to maintain output. Production from the mines of the district

---

* From "Ebb" in *Second April*, published by Harper & Brothers. Copyright, 1921, by Edna St. Vincent Millay.

continued to fall between 1939 and 1941, but a final burst of activity at the Calumet and Hecla reclamation plants pushed total Michigan output up by 5 million pounds. In the United States as a whole production was increasing substantially in response to 11- and 12-cent copper prices, and the Michigan proportion of total U.S. output had fallen by 1941 to a new low of 4.8 per cent. On the eve of United States entry into the War, Calumet and Hecla was accounting for about 65 per cent of the district's total (35 per cent from retreatment of tailings and 30 per cent from mining), while the Copper Range contributed 20 per cent, and the remaining 15 per cent was about equally divided between the highly marginal mines of the Quincy and Isle Royale.[2] Of the four companies, only Calumet and Hecla was paying dividends to stockholders from primary production — Copper Range paid small amounts in 1940 and 1941 from profits made in fabricating.

Labor developments. Mining company employment held at about 3,200 men throughout these years,[3] and unemployment and labor migration continued.[4] In 1939 average wage rates in Michigan copper were about a third less than those paid in Michigan and Minnesota iron, and although there were wage increases between 1939 and 1941, it seems probable that the relative wage situation of the district was worsening until government subsidies were granted in late 1941.[5] In the meantime, a strong movement had developed to organize the workers of the district.

In 1939 the International Union of Mine, Mill, and Smelter Workers, C.I.O., opened an organizational drive and met with greatest success at the smaller properties which were paying substantially lower wages than those prevailing at Calumet and Hecla. The union issue was settled at Copper Range in October of 1939 when the National Labor Relations Board ordered a company union (organized in 1936) disestablished, and held an election which resulted in more than a two-to-one victory for the C.I.O.[6] By early 1941 the Copper Range, Isle Royale, and Quincy were operating under union contracts, but it was not until late 1942, after two N.L.R.B. elections, that Calumet and

Hecla was drawn into the fold. No sooner had elections been held at the smaller properties and the union certified as bargaining agent, than the problem arose of inability of the companies to grant wage increases at current copper prices. The situation came to a head at the Quincy in February, 1941, when the workers voted to strike for higher pay. Since there was recognition by both labor and management that the fundamental issue was whether or not the government was prepared to grant a subsidy, a 90-day truce was worked out, pending Federal action.[7]

Investigations of the industry's potential for war production. By October of 1940 the price of copper had been stabilized by informal agreement between the government and the large United States producers at 11.8 cents a pound, and in April, 1941, the leading companies were requested to hold that price until control machinery could be developed. It was obvious that the Michigan producers, faced by the necessity of increasing wages, could not maintain output — let alone increase it — at the 12-cent price, and as early as the end of 1940 various local business groups were protesting against stabilization.[8] The Quincy strike threat brought the issue to a head, and by the spring of 1941 the United States Tariff Commission and the Copper Price Commission appointed by the Governor of Michigan were engaged in investigations of the wartime production potentialities of the district.[9] Higher wages were considered necessary if employment was to be increased on any long-run basis, and the Michigan Commission concluded that a 40 per cent increase in output within two years could be expected if the industry were paid 15 cents a pound for its copper.[10] In early September the Metals Reserve Company began purchasing the product of the Copper Range, Isle Royale, and Quincy at that price, and a month later signed contracts with the three companies calling for the purchase of their output at average out-of-pocket cost for the first half of 1941, adjusted to allow for a dollar a day wage increase, plus a cent a pound profit. Thus, selective pricing for copper was initiated even before United States entry into the War.

WAR CONTROLS AND THE UNITED STATES
COPPER MINING INDUSTRY

Until February 1, 1942, government controls over the rest of the domestic copper industry were limited to freezing the price at 12 cents a pound and drastically curtailing civilian consumption. In the meantime, a very substantial adjustment had taken place in the supply situation. Between 1939 and 1941 United States output increased by about 32 per cent,[11] and the export balance on unmanufactured copper, which had stood at about 369,000 short tons, shifted to a negative balance of 270,000 short tons.[12] These two developments meant that, as compared with 1939, an additional 869,000 short tons of copper were available to the domestic war economy, or an amount substantially greater than total domestic consumption in 1939.[13] Equally significant, the additional tonnage had been obtained at a cost of only about a cent a pound more than the 1939 average.[14]

The Premium Price Plan. In spite of the substantial increase in the flow of copper into the domestic economy and curtailment of civilian consumption, by early 1942 the metal was one of the most critically short in the war program, and as of February 1 the Premium Price Plan was put into effect in order to increase domestic production of copper, as well as of lead and zinc. The plan, which was administered jointly by the War Production Board and the Office of Price Administration, assigned quotas to each individual mine based upon its 1941 output. Quota production was to be sold at the fixed price of 12 cents a pound, while the government provided a 5-cent a pound premium for all over-quota copper. Originally, mines which had produced more than 14.4 million pounds of copper in 1941 were assigned 100 per cent quotas, which meant that they had to equal their 1941 output before the 5-cent premium could be drawn. Lower quotas were set for mines which had produced less than 14.4 million pounds in 1941, ranging down to zero quotas for those which had produced less than 4.8 million.[15] Thus it was hoped that the anti-inflationary line could be held by stabilizing the market price at 12 cents, while marginal copper would be called out by the 5-cent premium. Flexibility was introduced by a provision that quotas could be revised downward, if such a step seemed advisable in any specific case.

The basic assumption of the plan was that the domestic mines were faced by an easy labor supply situation, such that output could be increased without a substantial rise in average and marginal costs. Quite the opposite situation developed, and provides the fundamental explanation for the fact that, in spite of extremely numerous quota revisions (which were in large part responsible for an increase in the average price — base plus subsidy — for all United States copper of a cent and a half a pound between 1941 and 1944), domestic output increased by only about 15 per cent between 1941 and 1943 and declined substantially thereafter. As early as the summer of 1942 the labor shortage in the West had become serious, all of the mines losing men to high-pay war plants. In September the War Manpower Commission issued a labor-freezing order for Western non-ferrous metals industries; the following month all nonessential gold mining properties were ordered closed; and in late 1942 and 1943 the Army released 5,700 men for copper mining employment.[16] None of these measures was completely effective, since direct controls over the allocation of labor were far from strict. However, with cutbacks in the small arms ammunition program in mid-1943 the need for unfabricated copper was somewhat eased,[17] and continued increases in imports did much to make up for disappointments in the domestic showing.[18]

As an anti-inflationary device and, in consequence, as a method of holding down wartime profits, the Premium Price Plan unquestionably was a success. About four-fifths of the copper mined in this country during the years 1942–1945 was obtained at the 12-cent ceiling,[19] in spite of the fact that average hourly earnings in copper mining and milling increased by about 28 per cent between 1941 and 1944.[20] As a means of allocating critical labor and other resources to obtain maximum output in a war economy, the degree of success of the program is not as easy to determine, and, thus far, has not been adequately treated in the literature. No attempt to pass final judgment can be made in this study, but some of the important questions which should be dealt with in such an investigation seem clear.

The first of these concerns the wisdom of subsidizing copper production in the United States, where the labor situation was extremely tight, and freezing the price at a flat 12 cents a pound for low-cost South American producers. In general, the South American properties were the most productive in the western hemisphere, and full wartime exploitation of them was highly desirable, particularly if actual payment for copper produced (shipment of goods rather than the building up of dollar credits) could have been postponed until after the war. A policy of freezing the Chilean price below the average domestic price, to be justifiable, would have to be based upon one or more of the following premises: that a higher price would not have stimulated production; that machinery for South American expansion could not be made available; or that additional shipping space for the importation of copper could not be provided.

The second question concerns the method used in assigning quotas — that of discriminating among mines in accordance with size of 1941 output. What this amounted to was the favoring of high over low cost producers, and the question might be raised whether such discrimination was justified under the assumption that increasing United States production was the main purpose of the program. An adequate defense would have to assume either that general costs (chiefly wages) had been increasing rapidly during 1941 at *only* the smaller properties, thus rendering them incapable of maintaining 1941 output at the 12-cent price, or that the big producers had been holding output back at an earlier period for market control reasons and were still capable of equaling 1941 production in spite of increased general costs. Alternatively, looking to the future rather than the past, it might have been assumed that wages at the smaller properties were out of line with those at the larger properties and would rise more rapidly as the labor supply was more fully utilized.[21]

However, it seems more probable that this basic provision of the plan was designed with an eye on profits, just as much as on output, and in the belief that the industry was up against a labor allocation problem which could not be solved in a really desirable fashion. The war planners were extremely conscious of the heated charges of profiteering in World War I, and many of them were also concerned about monopoly developments in the postwar period. The large producers were, in general, the low cost operators, and it may have been assumed that patriotic motivation would provide incentive enough for maintenance of their output despite a rising cost trend and heavy excess profits taxes. (In other words, that low cost producers would hold output well past the point of profit maximization during the war period, thus making a subsidy to cover increased cost on current production unnecessary.)

In any case, quota revision tended to become a means of providing for wage increases and, to some degree, for equalization of profits. In spite of the fact that highly productive mines were favored by priorities for equipment and mining labor, the plan often seemed to represent a confession that copper mining wages *in general* were so far out of line with industrial wages and direct allocation controls over labor were so weak that any attempt to discourage production at highly marginal mines would result in an undesirable loss of labor to copper mining as a whole, rather than recapture of such labor by the most productive copper mining operations.[22]

Finally, there is the question of administrative confusion which is closely tied up with that of manpower difficulties. Partial failure of wage stabilization and direct labor allocation measures placed a tremendous burden upon quota revision, which became the basic device for meeting changing cost conditions. Revision was an extremely complicated administrative process which, in the interest of speed, often had to be arbitrary. Even worse, the rules under which it was carried out constantly had to be changed, and it was virtually impossible to keep small producers informed as to their standing. As a result, the industry was unable to lay plans with any sense of security and

WORLD WAR II AND THE FUTURE

was often at a loss in attempting to understand current administrative developments.[23]

Special contracts supplementing the Premium Price Plan. With a few minor exceptions Calumet and Hecla carried on all of its wartime mining operations under the Premium Price Plan. Such was not the case for the rest of the Michigan industry, which operated for much of the war period under special contracts with the Metals Reserve Company. (From 1942 through 1945 about 2 per cent of United States copper was produced under such contracts.) Shortly after the Premium Price Plan became effective in early 1942 the special contracts with the Isle Royale, Copper Range, and Quincy were terminated, and the companies were placed under the industry wide plan with zero quotas. In late 1942 there was union agitation for further wage increases (the smaller companies were still paying substantially less than Calumet and Hecla), and in February of 1943 the War Labor Board ordered a $1.35 increase per shift for miners and $1.25 for semiskilled and unskilled workers. Such increases were out of the question within the framework of the Premium Price Plan, and on March 1, 1943, new Metals Reserve contracts were drawn up for the three companies, effective retroactively to January 1. Costs were forecast on a six-month basis, with no allowance permitted for depreciation and depletion, and a profit per pound was allowed, which was larger, the lower the cost prediction per pound. (Isle Royale received 1.25 cents per pound, and the Copper Range, 1.50.) In 1945 an allowance was made for development work, which applied retroactively, and on August 31 of that year the special contracts expired, throwing the companies back to the Premium Price Plan.

OPERATIONS OF THE MICHIGAN INDUSTRY DURING THE WAR YEARS

Production for the War economy. The Premium Price Plan and the special subsidies of the Metals Reserve Company resulted in stabilization of Michigan mine and reclamation production in 1942 and 1943 at about the 1941 level; and then in falling output — by 9 per cent in 1944 and 29 per cent in 1945.[24] As to production from the mines of the district, Calumet and Hecla was able to show substantial increases in 1943 and 1944 which somewhat more than compensated for gradual declines at the three smaller properties. In the reclamation field the outstanding factor was a decline at Calumet and Hecla after 1941 which was partially balanced in 1944 and 1945 by output from the new Quincy reclamation plant, built with the financial assistance of the Metals Reserve Company.[25] The most significant production development, however, was one quite independent of the various subsidy plans. In late 1942 Calumet and Hecla went into the scrap copper field, directly furnacing pure scrap and treating impure grades by the ammonia leaching process used in the reclamation plants.[26] During the next three years, 54 million pounds of copper were recovered, which amounted to about 23 per cent as much metal as the district's output from mines and reclamation plants. (Including this secondary copper in the industry's total for 1943 and 1944, production reached the highest level attained since 1931.) Calumet and Hecla handled about two-fifths of the scrap on the basis of a treatment charge of $5 per ton, while the remainder was purchased in the scrap markets of the country, to be processed and sold at the 12-cent base price for the metal.[27]

If the intention of the government was to increase the production of Lake copper throughout the war years, the Michigan part of the subsidy program should be counted a failure. Actually it seems probable that such was the intent only at the beginning of the war, and that, as the struggle progressed, stabilization of output was as much as was hoped for. The really important question is not whether the government was successful in attaining this more limited end, but rather whether the costs (largely in terms of the tying up of resources critically needed elsewhere) were not too high. Precise data on what these marginal producers received for their copper are not available. Calumet and Hecla started off in February of 1942 with practically all of its production selling at the 12-cent price. Quota reductions were almost continuous, and by late 1943 a large percentage of the company's output qualified for the additional 5-cent premium. The other mines of the district received 17 cents a pound throughout most of 1942 and then somewhat more than that until the end of the war under the special contracts with Metals Reserve. (An estimate of around 20 cents a pound probably would not be far from the actual figure.) That such prices could not raise output to even the 1935 level when the average price had been 9.5 cents a pound is somewhat startling. Obviously costs must have been rising just as rapidly as price, in part because the industry was in an advanced stage of decline, but also because of labor developments.

The labor and wage problems. As has already been pointed out, Michigan copper mining (particularly the smaller companies) was paying substantially lower wages than those paid in the general mining labor market at the start of the war. Between 1939 and 1944 government administrative decisions, reënforced by emigration of workers, eliminated a good deal of the wage differential [28] which not only accounts for a rapid rise in costs, but makes it necessary to view the Michigan subsidy program as fundamentally a cost-plus technique to provide for wage increases. Between 1939 and 1944 the average daily wage paid at the Isle Royale Copper Company increased by about 80 per cent, while the number of pounds of copper produced per man in an eight-hour shift fell by about 31 per cent.[29] Heavy wage increases, plus the fact that the Michigan district had large-scale unemployment as late as 1941, permitted an increase in mining company employment of about 32 per cent between 1939 and 1943,[30] and the industry did not feel the effects of a severe labor shortage until the summer of 1944, in marked contrast with the experience of western producers.[31] By the fall of 1944 there was a real shortage (with emigration continuing), and employment began to fall off rapidly. Thus, sharply rising labor costs were doubtless an important reason for inability to increase output significantly between 1941 and 1943, and a shortage of labor was an important reason for the declines thereafter.[32] However, the explanation is by no means as simple as that.

The amount of resiliency left in the industry was very slight. In 1943 output was virtually the same as in 1939, in spite of the fact that approximately a third more men were employed,[33] and productivity of underground workers at Calumet and Hecla declined by about 45 per cent in that four-year period.[34] By the summer of 1944 Calumet and Hecla had exhausted its rich conglomerate tailings, and the Copper Range was suffering from falling richness in the Champion mine. Finally, the subsidy program had not made it worth while to carry out development work in the mines, and by 1944 some of the companies were pressed for worth-while stoping ground. Higher subsidies to provide higher wages and more employment might well have meant the tying up of more men with a very small gain in copper production. It even seems probable that, in terms of the critical need for labor in other sections of the war economy, too much labor was allocated to Michigan copper mining as it was. The basic question is whether or not it would have been possible to shift this resource and hold it where productivity was greatest.

When the war ended, the special contracts with Metals Reserve were not renewed by the government, and the three smaller companies were faced with the prospect of returning to the Premium Price Plan, under which they would receive a flat 17 cents a pound for their copper. The Quincy closed down its mining activities the first of September, 1945, and the Copper Range stopped production a few days later after a futile attempt to come to an agreement with the union concerning postwar operations. When the year ended, Calumet and Hecla, the Isle Royale, and the Quincy Reclamation Plant were the only producers of copper in Michigan. Some money had been made during the war years; from 1939 through 1945 an aggregate of $12.8 million was paid out to stockholders, or only about $1.5 million more than was paid in the single year 1929.[35] Dividend payments reached a peak in 1942 of $2.4 million and declined thereafter to $1.2 million by 1945. There could be little doubt as to the effectiveness of the subsidy system in holding down wartime profits.

THE MICHIGAN COPPER COMPANIES FACE THE FUTURE

The general copper situation at the end of the war. Shortly before V-J Day, the Premium Price Plan was extended until June 30, 1946. Dire predictions concerning a postwar copper glut were not realized, and in 1946 domestic consumption was only about a quarter less than that of the peak war year and was bearing so heavily upon the output of the mining industry, which was tied up by strikes, that the government was obliged to draw down its stock pile from 550,000 short tons to 92,000 to meet industrial needs. In April, 1946, a maximum additional premium of 5 cents a pound and special liberalizing provisions for large western producers were added to the Premium Price Plan to enable the industry to meet the general 18.5-cent wage increase, and the plan was extended for another full year. In June the O.P.A. raised the ceiling on copper to 14.4 cents a pound, and when price control ended in late 1946, copper went to 19.5 cents and then to 21.5 in early 1947. The year and a half following the expiration of the Premium Price Plan on June 30, 1947, saw marked fluctuations in the price of the metal. For eleven months the price ruled at the unusually high level of 23.5 cents and then in May, 1949, tumbled down to 16, followed by a gradual recovery to 18.5 by November.

Government stocks of the metal had been virtually exhausted as early as 1947, and, in hope of forestalling a further rise in price, Congress passed and the President signed, in April of 1947, a bill suspending the 4-cent tariff duty until March 31, 1949.[36] The copper picture had altered so substantially during the war years that the ending of tariff protection seemed to be of something more than academic significance. Nineteen-forty-six was the first peacetime year since the Michigan copper industry hit its stride in the 1870's that the United States was clearly a net importer of copper, and by the first half of 1949 domestic production was lagging so far behind consumption that the six-months import deficit totaled some 104,000 short tons. How permanent this development is remains to be seen, but there is every indication of its continuation at very high levels of domestic industrial activity.[37] Tariff suspension will finally expire on June 30, 1950, but — in consequence of reciprocal trade agreements — the new tariff barrier will amount to 2 cents a pound instead of the traditional 4 cents.

As to the domestic industry, the Federal Trade Commission issued a report in early 1947 showing Anaconda, Kennecott, and Phelps-Dodge as in control of 83.5 per cent of known U.S. reserves and with enough fabricating capacity to handle the entire output of their mines. The Commission found evidence of restrictive policies in production [38] and discrimination in distribution, such that independent fabricators were severely handicapped in periods of brisk demand. Such was the postwar copper world which confronted the Michigan industry as it passed a century mark of continuous production.

Michigan mining possibilities of the future. Calumet and Hecla has been the Michigan industry's only significant miner of copper since the ending of the subsidy program,[39] and even its properties were obliged to close for over three months of 1949 following the copper price slump. The stream of Michigan copper has dwindled to a trickle of some three million pounds a month, and even that output seems dependent upon either exceptionally high copper prices or reëstablishment of the subsidy program for marginal producers.

Interest first centered on a bill (H.R. 871, National Resources Development Bill) which would have continued the Premium Price Plan for five years and tied it up with the Thomas-May Strategic and Critical Material Stock Piling Act (Public Law No. 520).[40] Calumet and Hecla and the International Union of Mine, Mill, and Smelter Workers have gone on record as supporting some such measure, basing their case on the desirability of conserving national resources by working out mines which are now open and which would have to be closed permanently if no subsidy were provided.[41] B. D. Noetzel, speaking for the smaller producers of the district, went much further, listing the limitations upon freedom to conduct business imposed by the New Deal and war controls, and concluding, "Where so much of the result of the operations of our mines is controlled by public law and policy, it would seem logical that the Government should assume some measure of responsibility for that result." [42]

It may well be that there is sound reasoning behind a straight conservation case, but such a program would have to be handled with great caution, and, above all, should have a very limited life span. The Department of the Interior has adopted the policy of giving support only to those proposals which would limit subsidies to new exploration and development work, or to saving copper in already existing mines which would be permanently lost if the pumps were stopped. The danger is that, once a peacetime subsidy program is established, political pressure for its extension or permanent retention might well overweigh the public interest. It did not prove possible to reach enough Congressional agreement to pass the bill establishing a new subsidy plan for copper, lead, and zinc before the old program died on June 30, 1947. In its stead a stopgap measure was passed just before Congress adjourned which provided for a two-year extension of the program as a military security measure. On August 8, 1947, the President vetoed the bill, and subsequent proposals have failed of passage in Congress.

In the long run the future of the district as a copper mining center depends upon even more unpredictable factors. The Federal Trade Commission has estimated that world copper resources may last about 50 years, assuming the current rate of consumption and no marked change in technological methods.[43] History has usually made mockery of such predictions, but they promise enough of a chance of a future world copper shortage to justify the Michigan companies in adopting a waiting policy. Exploration has established the fact that large reserves of extremely low content deposits still exist in the district,[44] in addition to the 200 million pounds of developed reserves already available to Calumet and Hecla. Perhaps most interesting of all are an estimated 3.5 billion pounds of copper in low content deposits at the Copper Range White

Pine property in Ontonagon County — development of which is still delayed by the high investment costs involved and extremely difficult metallurgical problems. Exploitation of other low copper content deposits must await either a revolutionary change in technological methods or a period of sustained and even more acute copper shortage than existed immediately following the war. In the meantime, Calumet and Hecla and Copper Range have continued to purchase land,[45] and as of the end of the war Calumet and Hecla owned over 240,000 acres of Upper Peninsula mineral and timber property. The company is counting on timber sales (amounting in 1945 to $714,000) and rental of land to the growing tourist industry to minimize the cost of carrying this investment.

The shift to other forms of enterprise. The most important Lake producers have not been satisfied with basing their future as copper companies on the long-run gamble of Michigan mining potentialities, and the movement to shift to other stages of the copper producing industry has been stepped up to such an extent that, at Calumet and Hecla, it amounts to a major conversion. As of June 1, 1942, the big Lake producer acquired all physical assets of the Wolverine Tube Company of Detroit, a going concern employing about 1,000 workers and alleged to be one of the world's largest producers of seamless non-ferrous tubing for motors, refrigerators, air conditioning equipment, condensers, oil burners, airplanes, and automobiles.[46] In 1944 Calumet and Hecla established a scrap recovery department at its Copper Country works which, by 1946, was producing more copper than came from the company's mines.[47] A year later the Lake Chemical Company was organized under joint ownership of Calumet and Hecla and the Harshaw Chemical Company of Cleveland[48] to produce copper chemicals including patented products useful in petroleum refining, rayon manufacture, and the production of dyes, pigments, and fungicides.[49] In 1946 the company announced that construction was under way on a new eight-million dollar tubing mill at Decatur, Alabama, and three years later the project was completed — six hundred men being employed at the new plant. Finally, production has just commenced at a zinc and lead property developed by the company at Shullsburg, Wisconsin.

Supplementing these programs Calumet and Hecla converted excess plant capacity for the manufacture of detachable drill bits and for a commercial foundry business; took advantage of high metal prices during the war to liquidate much obsolete equipment by a scrap drive which resulted in the shipment of over 25,000 tons of iron and steel to the Republic Steel Company; and in 1946 began exploration for mineral deposits in other sections of the country (presumably the West).[50] Whatever the future of the district as a mining center, Calumet and Hecla, with its diversified new ventures, and Copper Range, with its fabricating plant, railroad, bus lines, and electric power development have high survival possibilities.

THE MICHIGAN COPPER DISTRICT FACES THE FUTURE

The Michigan copper district is not able to face the future with anything like as much confidence as that shown by its major companies.

Local employment prospects. The shift of the large concerns from mining to other stages of the copper manufacturing process seems to promise a severe curtailment of long-run employment opportunities in the district.[51] All of the fabricating plants and new mining enterprises are located elsewhere, and the Calumet and Hecla secondary, chemical, foundry, and drill bit manufacturing departments are all small employers of labor.[52] It seems probable that the copper companies must mine to make a significant contribution to the economic life of the community. Even worse, the prospects for a substantial growth of other kinds of employment are none too hopeful. As the war came to an end, business and other community groups of the district joined together in the preparation of an economic survey, similar to that done two years following the first World War.[53] Besides the copper mining industry, which was employing 3,754 men at the time the report was written, the lumbering products industry was the only other important industrial employer of labor, with a total of 4,174 wage earners. The future of these forest-dependent enterprises may well be good for the next decade, but it seems unlikely that there will be long-run employment in them at anything like such a level. Food products and processing plants, employing 223 workers, and miscellaneous manufacturing plants, employing 641 workers, completed the roster of the basic industries of the two counties, and many of the plants in these two categories were dependent upon local markets.

As might be expected, the mild recession of 1949 hit the district hard. Unemployment in the Upper Peninsula increased from 8,990 in June of 1948 to 15,790 a year later,[54] and the area was declared one of the 32 labor markets in the United States where unemployment was more than 12 per cent.[55] During that month there were 4,490 unemployed in the Copper Country — three-tenths of the working force.[56]

In light of this situation the district is attempting to attract other industries, and as early as 1939 the community received the pledge of the President of Calumet and Hecla to coöperate in such efforts.[57] From the point of view of the mining companies, two classes of industry are most desirable: those which supplement family income by providing employment for women, and those which provide the companies with a revenue on their land holdings without necessitating sale.[58] Apparently there are prospects of attracting garment manufacturers, which would admirably fill the first bill, and an intensive effort is being made to develop a summer tourist and winter sports industry which would fill the second. However, such industries are likely to provide the community with a slim economic base, and it seems probable that what should be hoped for, in order to maintain living standards, is a gradually declining population.[59]

Population developments. There is evidence indicating that, during the war years, emigration from the district continued at an extremely rapid rate. The population of Houghton County was recorded as 47,600 people by the Census of 1940, and by early 1943 estimates from ration coupon issues showed that about 13,500 people had left the County, some of them, it is true, for the armed forces.[60] How many will return in the postwar period remains to be seen, and the population trend in the next decade probably depends primarily upon the degree of prosperity in the general economy. Certainly, the emigration between 1910 and 1944 proceeded in a highly desirable fashion, with the major exception of the depression years, but it seems probable that resistance will constantly increase, since the population is showing a tendency to age, and emigration is acting as a selective process in eliminating those with the least stake in the Copper Country way of life. By the end of the war the workers faced by the most insecure employment future were the 1,700 employees of the three smaller mining companies of the district. Of these workers only 35 per cent were under 45 years of age, and 15 per cent were 60 or over.[61] The pressure required to move such people is likely to be very high, and if events should prove that more emigration is required to maintain reasonable standards of living, their desire to stay in the district will present the Copper Country of the next decade or two with a grave social and economic problem. It might well be said that the Michigan copper industry is dying hard but successfully — while the fate of the community still hangs in the balance.

Epilogue

For purposes of this study the history of Michigan copper mining has been broken down into four periods corresponding, more or less, with a life-cycle pattern of birth, growth, maturity, and decline. Although this was believed to be the most rewarding method of analyzing developments, certain problems and relationships are not well adapted to such an approach. Fortunately the sacrifice price which has been paid is not a high one, and in the remaining pages of this book an effort will be made to repair the damage done and to lay stress on insights which appear more clearly from an analysis which ignores the period-by-period classification.

In considering the history of the Michigan copper mining industry it is apparent that the relative importance of the field at any given time was set by external developments, taking the form of a vast increase in world production and consumption of new copper (some sixty-fold during the century following 1845) and the rise of the great Western camps in the United States, which reduced the Michigan role to one of virtual insignificance even before the district's production had begun to decline. During the 1870's production from the Michigan lodes represented 80 to 90 per cent of United States annual output and was just about in balance with domestic consumption requirements, whereas in the Michigan industry's peak production year (1916) the field accounted for only about 13 per cent of the copper mined in the United States.

The major factors favoring development of the industry. Early and successful development of the Lake Superior copper deposits was favored by two major factors: the metal was always found in a practically pure form which greatly simplified the metallurgical problem, and the deposits were located only a few miles from the Great Lakes waterway to the East. The transportation advantage was an enormously important factor until railroads reached the Western field in the early eighties, and the metallurgical advantage was an almost equally important one until Bessemer converters and electrolytic refineries were introduced in the West in the early nineties, and oil flotation made possible profitable treatment of very low copper content Western sulphide ores a decade or so later. Even after 1910 these factors continued to represent a significant competitive advantage and served to compensate to some degree for worsening mining conditions.

Throughout its history the Michigan industry had a relatively easy supply situation for both capital and labor. The fact that the corporate instrumentality was available from the beginning to tap the stock of speculative capital in the East — particularly at Boston — and the high degree of success attained by a few companies in almost every period of the industry's history do much to explain the relatively easy capital situation. In addition, the Michigan district became a Boston favorite, a socially approved field for speculation. Management was as a rule fairly conservative, and speculative scandals played a very minor role in the industry's history. Both of these secondary factors were in large part the result of the predominance of conservative Boston money, and both tended to maintain the flow of capital when cyclical or other conditions made the going difficult.

Favorable labor supply conditions were in large part the result of the locational factor. The Great Lakes waterway and the fact that the Michigan deposits were the only major copper field east of the Mississippi River created a competitive labor advantage from the beginning. Immigration directly from abroad was heavy and continuous, particularly during the last decade of the industry's growth, and was not curtailed by Federal statute until after the last important deposit had been opened up and maturity had been reached. In addition, the Copper Country, in spite of its northern location, was always a relatively pleasant place to live, particularly when compared with most of the big camps of the West. The rate of exploitation of the deposits was slow enough so that communities developed on a permanent basis, and the mining companies evinced a good deal of interest in the welfare of their workers and in that of the community at large. Benevolent paternalism had serious disadvantages in the stifling of many elements of a democratic way of life and may have eliminated any possibility of changing the economic base of the community when the mining industry began to decline, but it doubtless did a good deal to attract labor, particularly when the need for men to expand the industry was greatest. The ramifications of the paternalistic system have not been fully traced out in this study, and the industry's history still presents an exceptionally fine opportunity for a specialized study with particular emphasis upon employer-employee relationships and the impact of paternalism upon labor costs.

Finally, the development of the industry was aided by a fairly consistent policy of favorable government action. At the local level such action was assured by the dominant voice which the companies had in county government throughout most of the century under consideration. Measures taken at the State and Federal levels were generally in response to legitimate needs of the industry, although on occasion they were so partisan that the question arises of their consistency with the public interest.

The major factors hindering development of the industry. Initially the greatest handicap which the industry had to overcome was the scattered nature of the deposits in a rugged cold country. It was a good 60 miles from the location of the first rich discovery at the northern end of the peninsula to that of the second significant discovery at the southern end, and prospectors tramped every square yard of the intervening territory. Even so, the last important discovery was not made until 32 years after the field was first opened up.[1] Early geological ignorance played in with difficult natural surroundings to handicap the development of the field. Deposits such as these were unknown in the world's mining lore, and geological surprises were plentiful for decades after the first successful mines were established.

Even more significant in the long run were the technical problems presented by the character of the lodes: the fact that they slanted down rapidly, sometimes to depths of over a mile, their low copper content, often as little as one per cent or less; and the variety of rock matrices, some of which were exceptionally hard. All of these conditions put a tremendous premium on technological change (since the technical solution of one year was likely to be obsolete by the next) and increasingly made a large scale of enterprise and heavy capital investment requisites for success. Each major innovation, such as the wire rope and the rock skip, automatic washing equipment, high explosives, the power drill, the steam stamp, regrinding mills, the one-man drill, ammonia leaching, and oil flotation, revolutionized current practices and pumped new life-blood into the field. After the first World War the rate of technological change slowed up significantly and, following 1929, ceased to be an important factor, a situation which, in combination with other developments, made a steep decline in output inevitable.

As might be expected, most of the major technological innovations came from outside the district; that is, they were not local inventions, although they often had to be adapted to special local conditions. In those fields in which local conditions were most unique, this generalization is less true, and it seems probable that substantial new technological ground was broken by the companies in such aspects of the industry as hoisting, milling, and the retreatment of waste sands.

The effect of changes in the price of copper upon the development of the industry. Many of the external factors affecting the development of the industry expressed themselves in the form of changes in the price of copper, and certain generalizations can be made concerning these price changes and the industry's reaction to them.

Throughout the district's history there is a good deal of evidence of a positive lag relationship (usually amounting to a year or two) between rising copper prices and upward swings in output trend, although the initial impact was sometimes a curtailment of output as labor resources were bid away from the productive mines into exploratory and development work.

The correlation, however, is by no means a perfect one, nothing like as clear-cut as that between price rises and unusually high dividend payments which shows up in a marked fashion except in the very early and very late years of the industry's history.

Interestingly enough, there is some evidence of a correlation between new discoveries, or at least their announcement, and initial attempts to work them, and periods of exceptionally high copper prices. Work got under way on the district's three most important lodes during periods of high or rising prices. It is more difficult to come to a definite conclusion concerning a correlation between copper price movements and the adoption of new technology. About the most that can be said is that major changes tended to be initiated during and immediately following periods when prices had been high and earnings substantial.

Price declines, on the other hand, had a much less pronounced effect on the industry's development until after maturity had been reached. During the period of growth, declining copper prices did not result in a reversal of the output trend, although there was often such an effect upon dividend payments. Apparent exceptions to this generalization are significant breaks in the rising output trend in 1887 and 1893–94 which correspond with substantial price declines between 1882 and 1886 and between 1890 and 1894. The major factor operating in the first case, however, was a disastrous fire at the Calumet and Hecla workings in 1887, while the output reaction during the early nineties was perhaps a real exception, although it was in part due to organized restriction. More significant effects of price declines upon output developments show up in the period of maturity, but it is not until the declining phase of the industry's history that the correlation is a clear-cut one. As long as new deposits were being developed and old properties included large acreages of unexploited land, growth of the industry was virtually continuous, irrespective of copper price movements. (There was, as has been pointed out earlier, an effect upon the *rate* of growth.)

APPENDIX

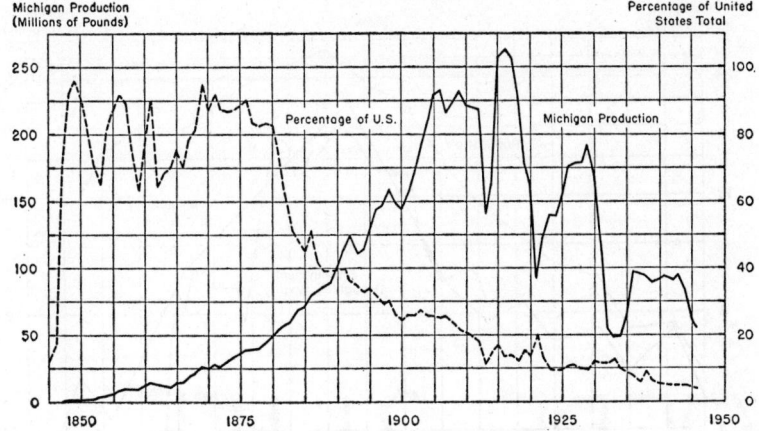

Fig. 4. Michigan Production and Percentage Michigan of
U. S. Total Production

Source: Table 6.

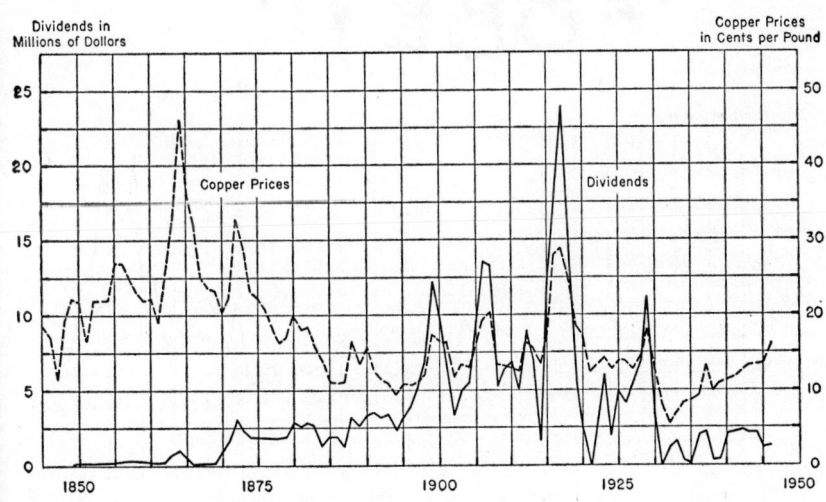

Fig. 5. Michigan Copper Mining Company Dividend Payments
Compared with Average Annual Copper Prices

Source: Tables 8 and 12.

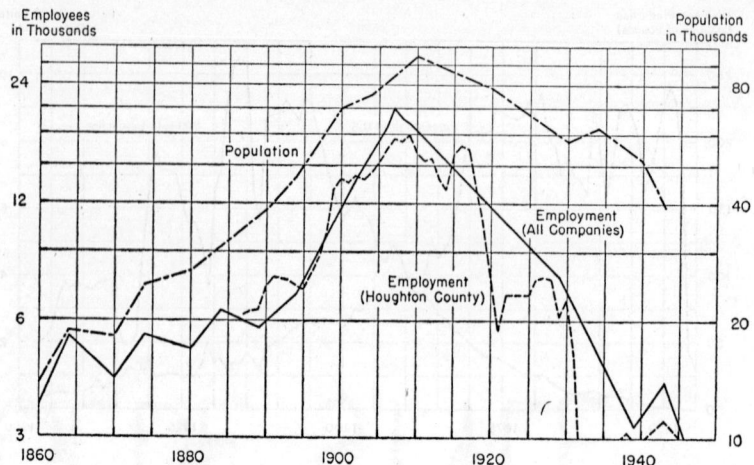

Fig. 6. Population of the Michigan Copper District Compared with Mining Company Employment, 1860–1946

Source: Tables 10 and 14.

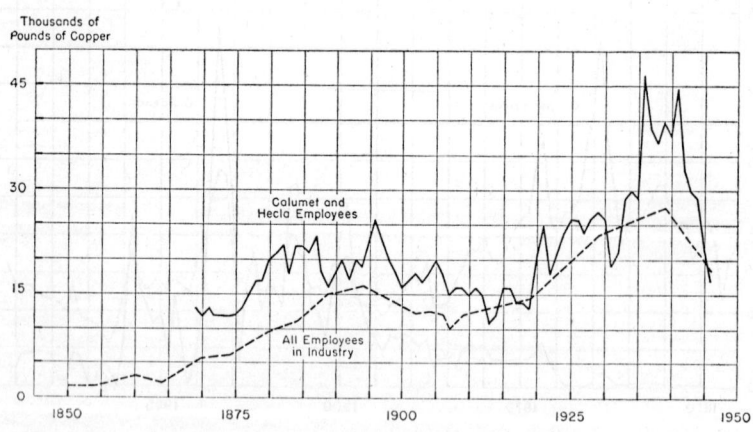

Fig. 7. Production of Copper per Man-Year of Labor Employed in the Michigan Copper Mining Industry, 1850–1946

Source: Table 11.

TABLE 6

WORLD, UNITED STATES, AND MICHIGAN OUTPUT OF NEW COPPER, 1845–1946
(Thousands of Pounds)

Year	World [a]	United States [b]	Michigan [c]	Percentage Michigan of U.S.
1845	98,762	224 [d]	27 [e]	12.1
1846	[a]	336	58	17.3
1847	[a]	672	477	71.0
1848	[a]	1,120	1,033	92.2
1849	[a]	1,568	1,505	96.0
1850	[a]	1,456	1,281	88.0
1851	151,816	2,016	1,745	86.6
1852	[a]	2,464	1,744	70.8
1853	[a]	4,480	2,905	64.8
1854	[a]	5,040	4,075	80.9
1855	[a]	6,720	5,808	86.4
1856	[a]	8,960	8,212	91.7
1857	[a]	10,752	9,531	88.6
1858	[a]	12,320	9,157	74.3
1859	[a]	14,112	8,926	63.3
1860	[a]	16,128	12,069	74.8
1861	229,868	16,800	15,037	89.5
1862	[a]	21,160	13,586	64.2
1863	[a]	19,040	12,985	68.2
1864	[a]	17,920	12,490	69.7
1865	[a]	19,040	14,358	75.4
1866	[a]	19,936	13,749	69.0
Subtotal 1845–1866	3,489,940	202,264	150,758	74.5
1867	[a]	22,400	17,526	78.2
1868	[a]	25,984	20,935	80.6
1869	[a]	28,000	26,625	95.1
1870	[a]	28,224	24,622	87.2
1871	284,748	29,120	26,748	91.9
1872	[a]	28,000	24,553	87.7
1873	[a]	34,720	30,090	86.7
1874	[a]	39,200	34,332	87.6
1875	[a]	40,320	36,039	89.4
1876	[a]	42,560	38,370	90.2
1877	[a]	47,040	39,025	83.0

TABLE 6 (*Continued*)

Year	World[a]	United States[b]	Michigan[c]	Percentage Michigan of U.S.
1878	[a]	48,160	39,691	82.4
1879	337,924	51,520	42,849	83.2
1880	346,696	60,480	49,737	82.2
1881	362,686	71,680	53,573	74.7
1882	404,074	90,646	56,983	62.9
1883	448,614	115,526	59,702	51.7
1884	490,010	144,947	69,353	47.8
Subtotal 1867–1884	5,587,460	948,527	690,753	72.8
1885	506,242	165,876	72,148	43.5
1886	482,176	156,735	79,891	51.0
1887	501,076	180,921	75,472	41.7
1888	589,608	226,361	86,472	38.2
1889	582,036	226,776	88,176	38.9
1890	610,668	259,763	101,410	39.0
1891	633,344	284,122	114,223	40.2
1892	704,500	344,999	123,198	35.7
1893	669,856	329,354	112,605	34.2
1894	706,986	354,188	114,309	32.3
1895	737,926	380,613	129,331	34.0
1896	845,676	460,061	143,524	31.2
1897	909,062	494,078	145,282	29.4
1898	961,808	526,513	158,492	30.1
1899	1,038,672	568,667	147,400	25.9
1900	1,090,878	606,117	145,461	24.0
1901	1,160,018	602,073	156,289	26.0
1902	1,228,872	659,509	170,609	25.9
1903	1,312,960	698,045	192,401	27.6
1904	1,454,432	812,537	208,309	25.6
Subtotal 1885–1904	16,726,796	8,337,308	2,565,002	30.8
1905	1,570,802	888,784	230,288	25.9
1906	1,595,554	916,971	230,525[f]	25.1
1907	1,589,410	847,151	216,007	25.5
1908	1,640,200	956,841	223,540	23.4
1909	1,824,476	1,126,521	233,516	20.7
1910	1,922,636	1,088,237	221,163	20.3

TABLE 6 (Continued)

Year	World[a]	United States[b]	Michigan[c]	Percentage Michigan of U.S.
1911	1,993,014	1,114,764	219,771	19.7
1912	2,205,012	1,249,095	216,793	17.4
1913	2,181,254	1,235,570	139,650	11.3
1914	2,054,090	1,148,431	166,184	14.5
1915	2,330,886	1,488,072	258,103	17.3
1916	2,998,680	2,005,875	266,839	13.3
1917	3,149,186	1,895,434	256,037	13.5
1918	3,158,592	1,910,023	228,174	11.9
Subtotal 1905–1918	30,213,792	17,871,769	3,106,590	17.4
1919	2,191,372	1,212,334	178,366	14.7
1920	2,114,328	1,224,550	161,344	13.2
1921	1,229,266	466,191	92,262	19.8
1922	1,904,774	964,584	121,387	12.6
1923	2,682,998	1,477,740	137,957	9.3
1924	2,987,224	1,606,165	138,160	8.6
1925	3,093,054	1,678,118	154,799	9.2
1926	3,216,512	1,725,276	175,442	10.2
1927	3,348,788	1,649,959	177,538[g]	10.8
1928	3,756,638	1,809,797	178,443	9.9
1929	4,199,764	1,995,110	186,402	9.3
1930	3,530,240	1,410,147	169,382	12.0
1931	3,093,440	1,057,749	118,060	11.2
1932	2,087,680	476,221	54,396	11.4
1933	2,322,880	381,285	46,854	12.3
1934	2,943,360	474,810	48,216	10.2
1935	3,422,720	760,996	64,108	8.4
1936	4,032,000	1,229,031	95,968	7.8
1937	5,252,800	1,683,996	94,928	5.6
1938	4,580,800	1,115,525	93,486	8.4
Subtotal 1919–1938	61,990,638	24,399,584	2,487,498	10.2
1939	4,869,760	1,456,638	87,970	6.0
1940	5,602,240	1,756,172	90,396	5.1
1941	6,048,000	1,932,144	92,880	4.8
1942	6,272,000	2,160,122	91,358	4.2
1943	6,076,000	2,181,636	93,528	4.3

TABLE 6 (*Continued*)

Year	World [a]	United States [b]	Michigan [c]	Percentage Michigan of U.S.
1944	5,686,000	1,945,098	84,842	4.4
1945	4,758,000	1,545,788	60,802	3.9
1946	4,078,000	1,217,474	43,326	3.6
Subtotal 1939–1946	43,391,000	14,195,072	645,102	4.5
Grand Total	161,399,626	65,954,524	9,645,703	14.6

[a] Figures for world output until 1879 are annual averages calculated from total output per decade as reported by Brown and Turnbull. After 1878 the figures refer to smelter output as reported by *The Minerals Yearbook*, various dates. Whenever possible, scrap production has been eliminated from the smelter figures. (For a definition of "smelter output," see note *b*.) World output figures are, at best, reasonably accurate estimates.

[b] Figures for United States output are "smelter production" for the years 1845–1905 and "mine production" thereafter. (Mine production figures first became available in 1906 and reflect more accurately the quantity of metal actually *mined* in any given year.) Smelter production is the output of domestic mines as reported by the companies which smelted the mineral, whereas mine production is output as reported by the mining companies on the basis of smelter reports to them of the copper content of mineral shipped.

There are three major causes of differences between the figures in any given year. First, copper in transit from mine to smelter around the end of a year will be reflected in mine, but not in smelter figures. Second, smelter output is in terms of refined copper produced in any given year, and there may be variations in the quantity of mineral in stock at the smelter. Finally, smelter is likely to be slightly larger than mine production since the mines are not credited for unusually low copper content mineral.

[c] Figures for Michigan output are smelter production for the years 1845–1905 and mine production thereafter.

[d] *Source: The Minerals Yearbook*.

[e] Figures for Michigan output from 1845 through 1905 are from various volumes of *The Minerals Yearbook*.

[f] Michigan figures for the years 1906–1926 are from Hore, pp. 203–220; and Pardee, pp. 30–33.

[g] Michigan figures for the years 1927–1946 are from various volumes of *The Minerals Yearbook*.

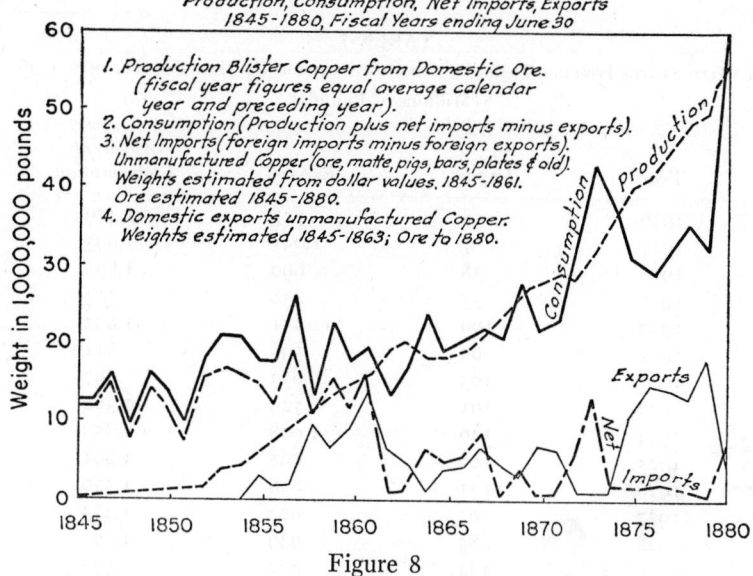

Figure 8

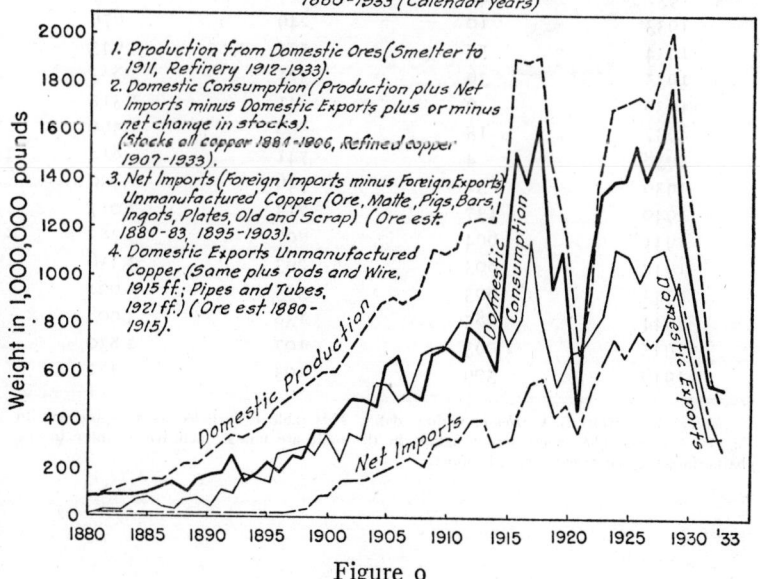

Figure 9

Source: Robert B. Pettengill, "The United States Foreign Trade in Copper, 1790–1932," *American Economic Review*, XXV (1935), 428, 431.

TABLE 7
UNITED STATES FOREIGN TRADE IN AND CONSUMPTION OF NEW COPPER, 1916-1946
(Millions of Pounds)

Year	Imports	Exports	Apparent Consumption
1916	8	717	1,479
1917	7	1,031	1,395
1918	38	690	1,661
1919	35	438	914
1920	109	551	1,053
1921	69	596	611
1922	103	653	897
1923	161	729	1,300
1924	146	1,008	1,355
1925	100	968	1,401
1926	171	856	1,570
1927	102	922	1,423
1928	85	949	1,608
1929	134	822	1,778
1930	86	594	1,265
1931	174	405	902
1932	168	222	519
1933	10	249	679
1934	55	525	645
1935	36	521	883
1936	9	441	1,312
1937	15	590	1,390
1938	4	741	814
1939	32	746	1,430
1940	137	713	2,017
1941	694	207	3,283
1942	803	263	3,356
1943	805	355	3,004
1944	985	138	3,008
1945	1,063	107	2,830
1946	309	105	2,482

Source: *The Minerals Yearbook*, various dates. This table is included as a supplement to Figures 8 and 9. The export-import figures in the table are not as inclusive as those in the charts since they cover only refined copper.

TABLE 8
MICHIGAN OUTPUT OF COPPER AND VALUE OF OUTPUT, 1845–1946

Year	Mine Output[a] (Thousands of Pounds)	Smelter Output[b] (Thousands of Pounds)	Average Price[c] (Cents per Pound)	Estimated Value[d] (Thousands of Dollars)
1845		27	18.5	5
1846		58	17.2	10
1847	Total previous to 1855: 13,419	477	11.5	50
1848		1,033	19.5	200
1849		1,505	22.3	340
1850		1,281	22.0	280
1851		1,745	16.6	290
1852		1,744	22.0	380
1853		2,905	22.0	640
1854		4,075	22.0	900
1855	5,820	5,808	27.0	1,570
1856	7,752	8,212	27.0	2,220
1857	9,708	9,531	25.0	2,380
1858	9,023	9,157	23.0	2,110
1859	9,000	8,926	22.0	1,960
1860	11,792	12,069	22.3[e]	2,690
1861	14,842	15,037	19.1	2,870
1862	13,648	13,586	25.8	3,510
1863	12,812	12,985	32.9	4,270
1864	12,403	12,490	46.3	5,780
1865	14,047	14,358	36.3	5,210
1866	13,240	13,749	31.8	4,370
Subtotal 1845–1866	147,506	150,758	27.9	42,035
1867	16,750	17,526	25.1	4,400
1868	19,795	20,935	23.6	4,940
1869	26,584	26,625	23.4	6,230
1870	24,287	24,622	20.6	5,070
1871	25,707	26,748	22.6	6,050
1872	24,821	24,553	33.0	8,100
1873	29,876	30,090	29.0	8,730
1874	34,267	34,332	23.3	8,000
1875	36,070	36,039	22.5	8,110
1876	38,143	38,370	21.0	8,060
1877	38,880	39,025	18.6	7,260
1878	41,486	39,691	16.5	6,550
1879	42,838	42,849	17.1	7,330
1880	49,601	49,737	20.1	10,000

[203]

TABLE 8 (*Continued*)

Year	Mine Output[a] (Thousands of Pounds)	Smelter Output[b] (Thousands of Pounds)	Average Price[c] (Cents per Pound)	Estimated Value[d] (Thousands of Dollars)
1881	53,872	53,573	18.1	9,700
1882	56,583	56,983	18.5	10,540
1883	59,257	59,702	15.9	9,490
1884	69,328	69,353	13.9	9,640
Subtotal 1867–1884	688,145	690,753	20.1	138,200
1885	72,759	72,148	11.1	8,010
1886	80,260	79,891	11.0	8,790
1887	75,793	75,472	11.3	8,530
1888	86,503	86,472	16.7	14,440
1889	87,414	88,176	13.8	12,170
1890	100,695	101,410	15.8	16,020
1891	114,409	114,223	12.9	14,740
1892	107,540	123,198	11.5	14,170
1893	113,512	112,605	10.8	12,160
1894	114,474	114,309	9.6	10,970
1895	129,676	129,331	10.8	13,970
1896	145,745	143,524	10.9	15,640
1897	142,703	145,282	11.3	16,420
1898	147,966	158,492[f]	12.0	19,020
1899	148,444	147,400	17.6	25,940
1900	142,078	145,461	16.5	24,000
1901	155,617	156,289	16.6	25,940
1902	170,176	170,609	11.9	20,300
1903	192,249	192,401	13.4	25,780
1904	208,279	208,309	13.0	27,080
Subtotal 1885–1904	2,536,292	2,565,002	13.2	334,090
1905	229,120	230,288	15.7	36,160
1906	230,525	229,696	19.6	45,020
1907	216,007	219,132	20.7	45,360
1908	223,540	222,290	13.4	29,787
1909	233,516	227,006	13.3	30,192
1910	221,163	221,463	13.0	28,790
1911	219,771	218,185	12.6	27,490
1912	216,793	231,112	16.6	38,370

TABLE 8 (Continued)

Year	Mine Output[a] (Thousands of Pounds)	Smelter Output[b] (Thousands of Pounds)	Average Price[c] (Cents per Pound)	Estimated Value[d] (Thousands of Dollars)
1913	139,650	155,715	15.7	24,450
1914	166,184	158,010	13.6	21,490
1915	258,103	238,956	17.3	41,340
1916	266,839	269,795	28.2	76,080
1917	256,037	268,508	29.2	78,400
1918	228,174	231,096	24.7	57,080
Subtotal 1905–1918	3,105,422	3,121,252	18.6	580,009
1919	178,366	177,594	18.7[g]	33,210
1920	161,344	153,484	17.5	26,860
1921	92,262	100,918	12.5	12,620
1922	121,387	122,545	13.4	16,420
1923	137,957	137,691	14.4	19,830
1924	138,160	145,333	13.0	18,890
1925	154,799	138,030	14.0	19,320
1926	175,442	174,779	13.8	24,120
1927	177,538	195,135	12.9	25,170
1928	178,443	179,104	14.6	26,150
1929	186,402	185,301	18.1	33,540
1930	169,382	142,986	13.0	18,590
1931	118,060	105,222	8.1	8,520
1932	54,396	63,899	5.6	3,580
1933	46,854	72,341	7.0	5,060
1934	48,216	51,682	8.4	4,340
1935	64,108	73,812	8.6	6,350
1936	95,968	91,105	9.5	8,660
1937	94,928	84,751	13.2	11,190
1938	93,486	75,281	10.0	7,530
Subtotal 1919–1938	2,487,498	2,470,993	13.4	329,950
1939	87,970	89,402	11.0	9,830
1940	90,396	91,486	11.3	10,340
1941	92,880	93,504	11.8	11,030
1942	91,358	94,940	12.5[h]	11,870
1943	93,528	90,996	13.3	12,100
1944	84,842	84,842	13.5	11,450

TABLE 8 (*Continued*)

Year	Mine Output [a] (Thousands of Pounds)	Smelter Output [b] (Thousands of Pounds)	Average Price [c] (Cents per Pound)	Estimated Value [d] (Thousands of Dollars)
1945	60,802	60,802	13.7	8,330
1946	43,326	43,326	16.1	6,875
Subtotal 1939–1946	645,102	649,298	12.6	81,825
Grand Total	9,609,965	9,648,056	15.6	1,506,109

[a] *Source*: For the years 1845–1926, Hore, and Pardee; after 1926, *The Minerals Yearbook*.

[b] *Source:* For the years 1845–1943, *The Minerals Yearbook*; after 1943, "mine" figures have been used, since the Bureau of Mines stopped giving a smelter breakdown by states.

[c] *Source:* For the years 1845–1849, price has been determined by dividing output into gross receipts, as shown by Stevens, *The Copper Handbook*, VI, 1087; for the years 1850–1859, E. D. Gardner, C. H. Johnson, and B. S. Butler, *Copper Mining in North America*, U.S. Bureau of Mines, Bulletin 405 (Washington, 1938), p. 11; for the years 1860–1913 and 1919–1941, various volumes of *The Mineral Industry*; for the years 1914–1918, *The Mines Handbook* (New York, 1922), pp. 40–41; and for the years 1942–1946, *American Metals Market*, January 15, 1947; *The Minerals Yearbook for 1945*; and *Engineering and Mining Journal*, July, 1945, p. 88.

[d] Except for the years 1845–1849, estimated value has been arrived at by multiplying average price by output.

[e] See note c. The quotations are *Engineering and Mining Journal* averages for both spot and future delivery. Since the prices are quotational averages, they may give a distorted picture in periods of rapidly changing prices.

[f] The smelter output figure for 1898 may be an error in the source data, although it is perfectly conceivable that smelter inventories of mineral were substantially reduced at this time.

[g] See note c. All quotations through 1919 are for Lake copper which sold at a premium over other grades. After 1919 the premium ceased to be significant and the quotations are for electrolytic copper.

[h] The government stabilized the market price at 11.8 cents a pound in 1941. The figures given for the years 1942–1946 include subsidy payments (see note c). In consequence of special subsidies, Michigan producers received substantially higher prices than those shown in the table.

TABLE 9

MICHIGAN COPPER MINING COMPANIES CLASSIFIED BY SIZE OF ANNUAL OUTPUT
1845–1945

Number of Companies

Annual Output (millions of pounds)	1845	1850	1855	1860	1865	1870	1875	1880	1885	1890	1895	1900	1905	1910	1915	1920	1925	1930	1935	1940	1945
Less than ½	1	7	22	16	29	18	19	18	15	3	3	3	1	2	2	2	.	.	.	.	.
½ – 1	.	1	.	2	2	3	1	2	.	1	.	2	.	1	.	1	.	.	.	.	.
1 – 2	.	.	1	4	5	2	7	1	2	5	2	2	3	3	4	3	.	.	.	.	.
2 – 3	.	.	1	1	.	1	1	3	3	.	1	.	3	1	2	2	.	.	.	.	.
3 – 4	.	.	.	.	.	.	.	2	2	1	1	1	.	1	2	2	1	1	.	.	.
4 – 5	.	.	.	.	.	.	.	.	.	.	.	2	.	1	.	.	1	1	.	2	.
5 – 7	.	.	.	.	.	.	.	.	.	2	1	.	2	2	3	1	1	.	.	.	1
7 – 10	.	.	.	.	.	.	.	.	.	.	1	.	.	3	3	1	1	.	.	2	.
10 – 15	.	.	.	.	.	1	.	.	.	1	.	2	2	3	2	3	1	3	.	.	.
15 – 20	.	.	.	.	.	.	.	.	.	.	1	1	2	1	1	1	2	1	1	.	.
20 – 25	.	.	.	.	.	.	1	.	.	.	.	.	4	1	2	1	.	1	.	.	.
25 – 50	.	.	.	.	.	.	.	.	1	.	.	.	.	.	.	.	.	.	.	.	.
50 – 75	.	.	.	.	.	.	.	1	.	1	.	1	.	1	1	1	.	.	1	.	1
75 – 100	.	.	.	.	.	.	.	.	.	.	.	.	.	.	.	1	.	.	.	1	.
Over 100	.	.	.	.	.	.	.	.	.	.	.	.	.	.	.	.	.	1	.	.	.
	1	8	24	23	36	25	29	27	24	15	12	14	18	19	22	17	6	7	2	4	4

Sources: For the years 1845–1853, Whitney, p. 304; 1855–1914, Hore, pp. 203–220; 1915–1926, Pardee, pp. 30–32; 1927–1945, reports of the various mining companies. In many of the years before 1900 a small tonnage was listed as coming from "sundry companies." The amount is so small, however, that it can be ignored without doing significant damage to the accuracy of the table. Another source of confusion is that a few of the early companies reported output on a fiscal rather than a calendar year; it has not been possible to make corrections for this factor.

TABLE 10
MICHIGAN COPPER MINING COMPANY EMPLOYMENT, 1850–1946

Year	Total[a]	Houghton[b] County	Calumet and Hecla[c]			Other[d]	Total
			Underground	Mill	Smelter		
1850	706						
1854	2,304						
1860	3,681						
1864	5,447						
1869	4,188		621	134	...	220	975
1870			766	148	...	287	1,201
1871			843	147	...	297	1,287
1872			824	148	...	387	1,359
1873			1,031	162	...	402	1,595
1874	5,453	Not Reported Separately	1,065	165	...	417	1,647
1875			1,114	177	...	489	1,780
1876			984	176	...	447	1,607
1877			951	144	...	436	1,531
1878			969	142	...	414	1,525
1879			872	167	...	487	1,526
1880	4,986		797	190	...	589	1,576
1881			692	194	...	611	1,497
1882			707	219	...	633	1,459
1883			771	233	...	886	1,890
1884	6,296		805	318	...	681	1,804
1885			1,004	419	...	770	2,193
1886			1,199	380	...	820	2,399

Year							
1887		6,221	745	372	...	852	1,969
1888		6,310	1,507	373	245	917	3,042
1889	5,695	6,480	1,745	390	213	872	3,220
1890		7,310	1,888	430	239	889	3,496
1891		7,702	1,790	465	227	913	3,395
1892		7,640	1,891	526	177	903	3,497
1893		7,591	1,797	434	165	915	3,311
1894	6,983	7,343	1,922	422	169	883	3,396
1895		7,249	1,906	449	189	1,067	3,611
1896		8,170	1,884	428	183	1,112	3,607
1897		8,726	2,452	417	172	813	3,854
1898		10,469	2,419	525	204	1,309	4,457
1899		13,051	2,892	601	235	1,527	5,255
1900		13,971	2,750	552	223	1,565	5,090
1901		13,498	2,788	528	203	1,502	5,021
1902	13,887	14,130	2,665	483	188	1,353	4,689
1903	16,452	13,629	2,697	447	203	1,288	4,635
1904		14,321	2,804	488	234	1,239	4,765
1905	18,699	15,355	3,049	538	243	1,256	5,086
1906	21,014	16,506	3,513	557	233	1,431	5,734
1907	20,190	17,509	3,331	576	249	1,474	5,630
1908	19,125	17,224	3,203	485	217	1,389	5,294
1909		17,974	3,103	512	219	1,282	5,116
1910		16,250	2,961	507	232	1,240	4,940
1911		15,361	2,978	521	233	1,227	4,959
1912	16,000	15,554	2,732	526	255	1,262	4,775
1913		13,813	2,012	465	240	1,491	4,208
1914		12,954	2,430	606	388	1,351	4,775

TABLE 10 (*Continued*)

Year	Total[a]	Houghton[b] County	Underground	Mill	Calumet and Hecla[c]		Other[d]	Total
					Smelter			
1915		16,005	2,460	591	536		1,477	5,064
1916		16,520	2,566	664[e]	652		1,616	5,498
1917		16,423	2,759	730	623		1,959	6,071
1918		12,650	2,160	743	505		1,890	5,298
1919	12,235	10,500[f]	1,957	618	468		1,381	4,424
1920		8,500	1,302	493	331		927	3,053
1921		5,700	113	125	207		349	794
1922		7,000	940	433	424		820	2,617
1923		7,000	1,085	442	373		905	2,805
1924		7,000	1,472[g]	591[g]	315[g]		953[g]	3,331[g]
1925		7,054	1,776	682	319		1,057	3,834
1926		7,724	2,045	670	301		1,252	4,268
1927		7,832	2,401	673	228		1,383	4,685
1928		7,724	2,508	689	253		1,507	4,957
1929	7,834	6,258	2,425	698	211		1,501	4,835
1930		6,750	2,191	502	185		1,401	4,279
1931		5,400	1,775	580	190		1,453	3,990
1932		2,716	528	318	150		700	1,696
1933		2,011	426	258	161		445	1,290
1934		2,093	412	251	121		479	1,263
1935		2,286	542	402	133		598	1,675
1936		2,174	638	441	130		592	1,801
1937		2,705	699	516	133		668	2,016
1938		3,125	565	539	136		631	1,871

1939	3,166	3,099	391	469	147	447	1,454
1940		2,997	417	474	137	421	1,449
1941		3,065	450	475	169	450	1,544
1942		3,185	708	487	184	615	1,994
1943	4,178	3,350	822	517	193	721	2,253
1944	3,922	3,160	678	500	191	639	2,008
1945		3,030	638		249	628	2,036
1946	2,589	2,035	688	521			2,150

a Sources for total mining company employment are the following: 1850, 1860, 1870, 1880, 1889, 1902, 1909, 1919, 1929, 1939: U. S. Bureau of the Census, volumes and sections entitled *Mines and Quarries*; 1854, 1864, 1874, 1884, 1904: various volumes, *Census of Michigan*; 1906–1908: various volumes, Commission of Mineral Statistics of the State of Michigan, *Annual Reports*; and 1943, 1944, and 1946, derived by adding the figures reported by the Mine Inspector of Houghton County to those reported by the Mine Inspector of Keweenaw County.

b Annual Reports of the Mine Inspector of Houghton County (1887 to date).

c Prepared for this study by the Personnel Division of the Calumet and Hecla Consolidated Copper Company.

d "Other" includes such employment categories as shops, railroad, fire protection, medical, trucking, etc.

e After 1915 the mill figure includes reclamation employees.

f Houghton County figures for the years 1919–1924 are estimates, since the mine inspector confined his report during those years to underground employees.

g The Calumet and Hecla consolidation went through in 1923, and after that date the figures are for the Calumet and Hecla Consolidated Copper Company.

TABLE 11
POUNDS OF COPPER PRODUCED ANNUALLY PER MICHIGAN
COPPER MINING COMPANY EMPLOYEE, 1850–1946[a]
(In Thousands of Pounds)

Year	All Companies[b]	Houghton County[c]	Calumet and Hecla		
			Underground[d]	Mill[e]	All[f]
1850	1.8	..	..	...	..
1854	1.8	..	..	...	..
1860	3.2	..	..	...	..
1864	2.3	..	..	...	..
1869	...	..	20	92	13
1870	5.8	..	18	95	12
1871	...	..	19	110	13
1872	...	..	20	109	12
1873	...	..	18	116	12
1874	6.3	..	19	122	12
1875	...	..	19	121	12
1876	...	..	22	123	13
1877	...	..	24	157	15
1878	...	..	26	177	17
1879	...	..	30	157	17
1880	9.9	..	40	167	20
1881	...	..	45	162	21
1882	...	..	45	146	22
1883	...	..	43	142	18
1884	11.0	..	50	127	22
1885	...	..	47	113	22
1886	...	..	42	133	21
1887	...	12	62	124	23
1888	...	13	33	135	18
1889	15.3	13	28	125	16
1890	...	13	32	124	18
1891	...	14	36	137	20
1892	...	13	31	110	17
1893	...	15	35	145	20
1894	16.4	15	32	147	19
1895	...	17	41	172	23
1896	...	17	47	209	26
1897	...	16	34	200	23
1898	...	14	36	165	20
1899	...	11	31	149	18
1900	...	10	28	141	16
1901	...	11	30	156	17

TABLE 11 (Continued)

Year	All Companies[b]	Houghton County[c]	Calumet and Hecla Underground[d]	Mill[e]	All[f]
1902	12.3	12	30	168	18
1903	...	13	28	171	17
1904	12.7	13	29	165	18
1905	...	14	31	177	20
1906	12.3	12	28	180	18
1907	10.3	11	25	146	15
1908	11.1	11	26	170	16
1909	12.2	11	26	156	16
1910	...	12	24	142	15
1911	...	12	25	142	16
1912	...	11	25	129	15
1913	...	8	22	97	11
1914	...	10	22	87	12
1915	...	12	29	123	16
1916	...	12	28	116	16
1917	...	12	25	106	14
1918	...	14	27	91	14
1919	14.6	13	22	86	13
1920	...	15	33	117	21
1921	...	13	87	121	25
1922	...	14	30	94	18
1923		Year of Consolidations			
1924	...	..	37	124	24
1925	...	..	36	134	26
1926	...	..	36	156	26
1927	...	..	33	162	24
1928	...	..	36	176	26
1929	23.8	..	37	177	27
1930	...	..	40	211	26
1931	...	..	41	125	19
1932	...	..	61	102	21
1933	...	..	78	129	29
1934	...	..	80	138	30
1935	...	..	67	113	29
1936	...	..	93	178	47
1937	...	..	77	144	39
1938	...	..	85	120	37
1939	27.8	..	74	112	40
1940	...	..	50	106	38
1941	...	..	64	129	45
1942	...	..	40	121	33

TABLE 11 (*Continued*)

| Year | All Companies [b] | Houghton County [c] | Calumet and Hecla | | |
			Underground [d]	Mill [e]	All [f]
1943	22.4	..	41	121	30
1944	21.6	..	55	104	29
1945	...	..	45	75	22
1946	18.3	..	36		17

[a] The calculations are based upon data in Tables 8 and 10; Hore, pp. 206–214; Pardee, pp. 30–32; and annual reports of the Calumet and Hecla Mining Company. The table is of limited usefulness since a very large number of factors affect the trend line. Among the most important are the price of copper; the proportion of underground workers employed at the relatively unproductive task of opening new ground, exploring, or shaft sinking; technological changes; the richness of the general run of rock available at a particular period; and variations in labor supply conditions. In addition, no attempt has been made to make allowance for changes in the length of the working day.

[b] In arriving at these figures Michigan mine output was divided by total number of mining company employees as shown by State and Federal census and other reports.

[c] The number of employees reported by the Houghton County Mine Inspector (usually as of September 30) has been divided into total annual output of the mines lying within the County. After the Calumet and Hecla consolidation of 1923 it was no longer possible to separate out Houghton County production.

[d] Calumet and Hecla employment figures are for December 31 of each year. After 1914 the company's production from tailings was deducted from total output in arriving at output per underground worker.

[e] The number of mill workers was divided into total output from mines and reclamation plants. After 1914 the "mill" category includes reclamation workers.

[f] Besides underground and mill workers the company employed large numbers of men in shops, transportation, construction, etc. The "all" category represents total employment *less* smelter employment. This adjustment was necessary to make the figures after 1888 comparable to those before that date. (Calumet and Hecla built its own smelter in 1888.) Output from scrap treatment is not included in the figures for 1943 through 1946.

TABLE 12
Dividend Payments — All Michigan Copper Mining Companies
(A) Totals for 1845–1946
(In Thousands of Dollars)

Company	Total Amount
Cliff	2,519
Minesota	1,820
National	320
Pewabic	1,000
Quincy	27,353
Franklin	1,240
Central	2,130
Copper Falls	100
Calumet and Hecla [a]	183,871
Ridge	100
Phoenix	20
Atlantic	990
Osceola	18,044
Tamarack	9,420
Kearsarge	160
Wolverine	10,350
Champion	32,171
Trimountain	3,250
Baltic	7,950
Mohawk	17,276
Ahmeek	14,050
Isle Royale	3,681
Allouez	2,850
Copper Range [b]	8,280
Centennial	360
Superior	649
White Pine	33
Grand Total [c]	349,987
Calumet and Hecla Total [c]	200,633
Copper Range Total [d]	33,895

TABLE 12 (*Continued*)

DIVIDEND PAYMENTS — ALL MICHIGAN COPPER MINING COMPANIES. (B) 1849–1866

(In Thousands of Dollars)

Year	Cliff	Minesota	National	Pewabic	Quincy	Franklin	Central	Copper Falls	Total
1849	60	..	..	..	..	..	..	..	60
1850	84	..	..	..	..	..	..	..	84
1851	60	..	..	..	..	..	..	..	60
1852	60	..	..	..	..	..	..	..	60
1853	90	..	..	..	..	..	..	..	90
1854	108	90	..	..	..	..	..	..	198
1855	78	90	..	..	..	..	..	..	168
1856	180	200	..	..	..	..	..	..	380
1857	180	300	..	..	..	..	..	..	480
1858	160	300	..	..	..	..	..	..	460
1859	180	180	..	..	..	..	..	..	360
1860	..	120	..	..	..	..	..	..	120
1861	80	100	80	..	..	..	..	..	260
1862	80	160	80	60	60	..	..	..	440
1863	180	160	..	120	200	60	..	..	720
1864	320	60	80	200	280	100	50	60	1,150
1865	200	..	40	..	160	60	50	..	510
1866	120	..	..	..	..	..	50	..	170
Total	2,220	1,760	280	380	700	220	150	60	5,770

TABLE 12 (Continued)

DIVIDEND PAYMENTS — ALL MICHIGAN COPPER MINING COMPANIES. (C) 1867-1884

(In Thousands of Dollars)

Year	Cliff	Mine-sota	National	Pe-wabic	Quincy	Frank-lin	Central	Copper Falls	Calumet and Hecla	Ridge	Phoenix	Atlantic	Osceola	Total
1867	60	...	...	...	...	...	50	...	...	...	...	...	...	110
1868	...	...	...	...	60	...	40	...	...	...	...	...	...	100
1869	...	...	...	...	40	...	70	...	100	...	...	...	...	210
1870	...	...	...	...	120	...	80	...	500	...	...	...	...	700
1871	100	...	20	20	140	20	50	40	1,250	...	...	...	...	1,640
1872	100	50	20	40	350	40	80	...	2,400	...	...	...	...	3,080
1873	...	...	...	20	100	...	160	...	2,000	50	...	...	...	2,330
1874	...	...	...	...	160	...	160	...	1,600	20	...	...	...	1,940
1875	...	...	...	...	220	...	80	...	1,600	20	...	...	...	1,920
1876	...	10	...	...	160	...	100	...	1,600	...	...	...	...	1,870
1877	...	...	...	...	80	...	140	...	1,600	...	20	...	...	1,840
1878	...	...	...	...	100	...	100	...	1,600	...	...	20	40	1,860
1879	39	...	...	...	40	...	80	...	1,600	...	...	...	60	1,819
1880	...	...	...	...	220	...	100	...	2,500	10	...	40	210	3,080
1881	...	...	...	...	320	...	120	...	2,000	...	...	...	225	2,665
1882	...	...	...	...	520	...	50	...	2,000	...	...	80	200	2,850
1883	...	...	...	...	380	...	60	...	2,000	...	...	80	150	2,670
1884	...	...	...	...	280	80	40	...	800	...	...	40	88	1,328
Total	299	60	40	80	3,290	140	1,560	40	25,150	100	20	260	973	32,012

TABLE 12 (*Continued*)

DIVIDEND PAYMENTS — ALL MICHIGAN COPPER MINING COMPANIES. (D) 1885–1904

(In Thousands of Dollars)

Year	Pewabic	Quincy	Frank-lin	Central	Calumet and Hecla	Atlantic	Osceola	Tama-rack	Kear-sarge	Wolver-ine	Cham-pion	Trimoun-tain	Total
1885	...	180	40	30	1,700	20	...	...	...	...	...	...	1,970
1886	...	240	80	40	1,500	40	...	...	...	...	...	...	1,900
1887	...	200	40	40	1,000	40	50	...	...	...	...	...	1,370
1888	...	360	120	70	2,000	120	150	440	...	...	...	...	3,260
1889	...	280	80	40	1,500	80	50	640	...	...	...	...	2,670
1890	...	320	80	20	2,000	100	225	590	80	...	...	...	3,415
1891	...	450	80	20	2,000	40	150	800	...	...	...	...	3,540
1892	...	350	160	...	2,000	...	150	600	...	...	...	...	3,260
1893	400	300	120	...	2,000	...	100	600	...	...	...	...	3,520
1894	...	400	80	...	1,500	...	...	400	...	...	...	...	2,380
1895	140	600	...	...	2,000	...	100	400	40	...	...	...	3,280
1896	...	1,000	...	...	2,500	...	125	360	...	...	...	...	3,985
1897	...	800	...	...	4,000	40	191	360	40	...	...	...	5,431
1898	...	1,000	...	...	5,000	40	277ᵍ	480	...	60	...	...	6,857
1899	...	950	...	...	10,000	...	558	600	...	210	...	...	12,318
1900	...	900	...	...	7,000	80	571	1,020	...	240	...	...	9,811
1901	...	900	...	...	4,500	80	577	1,200	...	240	...	...	7,497
1902	...	700	...	...	2,500	...	...	...	...	240	...	...	3,440
1903	...	550	...	...	3,500	...	...	...	...	330	300	300	4,980
1904	...	500	...	...	4,000	...	192	90	...	450	200	...	5,432
Total	540	10,980	880	260	62,200	680	3,466	8,580	160	1,770	500	300	90,316

TABLE 12 (*Continued*)
DIVIDEND PAYMENTS — ALL MICHIGAN COPPER MINING COMPANIES. (E) 1905–1918
(In Thousands of Dollars)

Year	Quincy	Calumet and Hecla [a]	Osceola	Wolver-ine	Cham-pion	Baltic	Mo-hawk	Ahmeek	Isle Royale	Allouez	Copper Range [b]	Calumet and Hecla Total [c]	Copper Range Total [d]	Total [e]
1905	600	5,000	385	660	1,000	1,250	...	...	...	...	...	5,000	1,536	9,225 [h]
1906	1,250	7,000	962	1,020	1,200	1,400	500	...	...	...	...	7,000	2,305	13,632 [i]
1907	1,485	6,341	1,250	1,050	1,000	1,000	900	...	...	...	...	6,500	2,305	13,446 [j]
1908	495	1,955	192	600	500	900	250	...	...	...	...	2,000	1,537	5,392 [k]
1909	440	2,478	769	600	800	1,000	300	...	...	...	...	2,700	1,537	6,387
1910	550	2,572	962	600	900	1,000	200	...	...	...	...	2,900	1,537	6,934 [l]
1911	440	2,105	721	540	500	500	175	100	...	...	...	2,400	1,357	5,081
1912	550	3,347	1,202	600	1,100	700	350	900	...	...	...	4,200	788	9,049 [m]
1913	413	2,285	1,010	300	900	200 [n]	500	1,100	150	...	...	3,200	1,084	7,058 [o]
1914	55	755	288	120	...	...	100	300	...	...	...	1,000	...	1,618
1915	880	4,133	769	540	3,100	...	600	1,150	...	100	950	5,000	1,182	12,222
1916	1,760	1,344	1,538	720	6,015	...	1,700	2,500	450	700	1,793	7,500	3,942	18,710 [p]
1917	1,980	5,489	1,923	810	4,480	...	2,050	3,200	900	1,200	1,678	8,500	3,944	23,929 [q]
1918	935	3,699	962	240	1,976	...	1,000	2,000	375	750	1,008	5,500	2,366	13,629 [r]
Total	11,833	48,503	12,933	8,400	23,471	7,950	8,625	11,250	1,875	2,750	5,429	63,400	25,420	146,312 [s]

[219]

TABLE 12 (*Continued*)

DIVIDEND PAYMENTS — ALL MICHIGAN COPPER MINING COMPANIES. (F) 1919–1938

(In Thousands of Dollars)

Year	Quincy	Calumet and Hecla[a]	Osceola	Cham-pion	Trimoun-tain	Mo-hawk	Ahmeek	Isle Royale	Copper Range[b]	Supe-rior	Calumet and Hecla Total[c]	Copper Range Total[d]	Total
1919	440	428	288	1,280	1,300	500	600	150	...	...	1,000	986	5,236[t]
1920	110	318	96	600	...	550	300	...	...	...	500	592	2,004[u]
1921	...	...	...	...	...	...	...	...	...	...	...	...	...
1922	...	599	192	600	...	300	400	150	...	200	1,000	394	2,441
1923	...	3,281[v]	96	700	...	315	1,500	225	...	...	3,703	394	6,117
1924	...	984	...	780	...	...	...	...	...	...	1,003	395	1,764
1925	...	2,940	...	1,140	...	460	...	150	...	249	3,008	395	4,939
1926	...	2,972	...	500	...	575	...	150	...	...	3,008	395	4,197
1927	...	3,982	...	500	...	575	...	150	...	...	4,011	395	5,207
1928	...	4,974	...	1,100	...	690	...	263	...	...	5,014	395	7,027
1929	...	8,950	...	1,000[w]	...	920	...	300	...	...	9,025	790	11,170
1930	...	2,987	...	...	...	460	...	75	...	...	3,008	493	3,522
1931	...	...	...	...	...	112	...	...	...	...	...	...	112
1932	...	...	...	...	...	1,121	...	...	...	...	...	...	1,121
1933	...	...	...	...	...	1,681	...	...	...	...	...	...	1,681
1934	...	...	...	...	...	392	...	...	...	...	...	...	392
1935	...	...	...	...	...	...	...	...	...	...	...	...	...
1936	...	1,504	...	...	...	...	...	...	280	...	1,504	280	1,784
1937	...	2,206	...	...	...	...	...	...	...	...	2,206	...	2,206
1938	...	501	...	...	...	...	...	...	...	...	501	...	501
Total	550	36,626	672	8,200	1,300	8,651	2,800	1,613	280	449	38,491	5,904	61,421[x]

[220]

TABLE 12 (*Continued*)

DIVIDEND PAYMENTS—ALL MICHIGAN COPPER MINING COMPANIES. (G) 1939–1946

(In Thousands of Dollars)

Year	Calumet and Hecla	Isle Royale	Copper Range	Total
1939	501	...	...	501
1940	2,006	...	169	2,175
1941	2,006	...	282	2,288
1942	2,006	...	424	2,430
1943	1,705	...	424	2,129
1944	1,617	74	424	2,115
1945	724	45	424	1,193
1946	827	74	424	1,325
Total	11,392	193	2,571	14,156

Sources: Various volumes, *Mines Register*; B. S. Butler and W. S. Burbank, *The Copper Deposits of Michigan*, U.S. Geological Survey, Professional Paper 144 (Washington, 1929); and reports of the various mining companies.

a During the years 1907–1930 Calumet and Hecla received dividends from other mining companies of the district. The figures shown in this column are total Calumet and Hecla dividends, *minus* dividends from other copper mining companies.

b During the years 1905–1946 Copper Range received dividends from other mining companies of the district and from railroad and other investments. An effort has been made to include in this column only dividends resulting from mining activities directly controlled by the company. The separation in some years is arbitrary, and the dividend total may be somewhat overstated.

c This figure gives total Calumet and Hecla dividends, whether the source was dividends from other companies or its own operations. After 1941 a substantial proportion of the total came from activities other than mining.

d This figure gives total Copper Range dividends, regardless of source.

e The grand total column is designed to reflect dividends from mining activities only. (The total is slightly overstated, particularly after 1941.) The figures

TABLE 12 (*Continued*)

are "net" in the sense that dividends are only counted once; payments to Calumet and Hecla and Copper Range from other companies are only figured in once.

f From 1869 through 1871 there were two mining companies, known as the Calumet and the Hecla. Before they were consolidated in 1871 the Hecla paid $650,000 and the Calumet $300,000. (The payments are lumped under the Calumet and Hecla heading.)

g In 1898 the Osceola consolidated with the Kearsarge and Tamarack, Jr.

h The total includes the following additional payments: Central, $160,000; Atlantic, $50,000; and Tamarack, $120,000.

i The total includes $300,000 paid by the Tamarack.

j The total includes $420,000 paid by the Tamarack.

k The total includes $500,000 paid by the Trimountain.

l The total includes $150,000 paid by the Trimountain.

m The total includes $300,000 paid by the Trimountain.

n In 1915 the Copper Range absorbed the Baltic Mining Company.

o The total includes $200,000 paid by the Trimountain.

p The total includes $90,000 paid by the Centennial and $100,000 paid by the Superior.

q The total includes the following additional payments: Centennial, $90,000; Superior, $100,000; and White Pine, $29,000.

r The total includes the following additional payments: Trimountain, $300,000; Centennial, $180,000; and White Pine, $4,000.

s The grand total for the period 1905-1918 includes the following additional totals: Central, $160,000; Atlantic, $50,000; Tamarack, $840,000; Trimountain, $1,650,000; Centennial, $360,000; Superior, $200,000; and White Pine, $33,000.

t The total includes $150,000 paid by the Wolverine and $100,000 paid by the Allouez.

u The total includes $30,000 paid by the Wolverine.

v In 1923 Calumet and Hecla consolidated with the Ahmeek, Allouez, Centennial, and Osceola.

w In 1931 Copper Range absorbed the Champion.

x The grand total for the period 1919-1938 includes a total of $180,000 paid by the Wolverine and $100,000 paid by the Allouez.

[222]

TABLE 13
Annual High-Low Stock Quotations of Seven Michigan Copper Mining Companies, 1848–1946
(In Dollars Per Share)

Year	Cliff High	Cliff Low	Quincy High	Quincy Low	Franklin High	Franklin Low	Calumet and Hecla High	Calumet and Hecla Low	Osceola High	Osceola Low	Copper Range High	Copper Range Low	Mohawk High	Mohawk Low
1848	81.0	63.0												
1849	105.0	75.0												
1850	105.0	80.0												
1851	125.0	90.0												
1852	124.0	95.5												
1853	195.0	125.0												
1854	153.5	105.0												
1855	182.5	115.0												
1856	275.0	180.0	9.5	8.0										
1857	286.0	170.0	14.0	5.0 ᵃ										
1858	315.0	85.0 ᵇ	20.0	8.5	9.8	4.5								
1859	100.0	56.0	41.0	20.0	31.0	9.3								
1860	69.0	40.0	40.0	27.5	33.0	16.0								
1861	55.0	40.5	34.0	19.3	26.5	10.0								
1862	68.0	42.5	64.5	33.5	49.3	17.8								
1863	100.0	67.5	98.0	61.8	60.1	45.0								
1864	108.0	70.0	112.0	87.0	61.0	40.5								
1865	90.0	48.0	100.3	47.0	54.5	32.0								
1866	60.0	44.0 ᶜ	70.0	37.0 ᶜ	132.0	36.5 ᶜ								
1867	46.0	15.0	37.5	15.0	39.5	8.0								
1868	27.0	12.5	34.0	15.0	16.0	6.3								

[223]

TABLE 13 (Continued)

Year	Cliff High	Low	Quincy High	Low	Franklin High	Low	Calumet and Hecla High	Low	Osceola High	Low	Copper Range High	Low	Mohawk High	Low
1869	23.0	5.3												
1870	11.0	4.0	37.0	18.0	24.0	8.0								
1871	6.5	4.0	32.0	17.0	10.6	2.0								
1872	6.0	1.0	34.0	20.3	6.9	2.5								
1873	Closed		65.0	34.0	15.5	5.0								
1874			53.5	26.0	11.0	3.0	164.0	101.5[d]						
1875			49.0	28.5	7.8	3.5	135.0	61.0						
1876			45.8	34.5	16.0	6.5	165.0	89.3						
1877			49.5	39.5	16.0	9.0	164.5	95.8						
1878			49.8	32.0[e]	14.8	8.0	145.5	119.0	37.0	15.0				
1879			41.8	10.5	8.0	5.0	164.8	139.5	26.0	10.0				
1880			33.5	10.0	31.0	4.0	175.0	160.5	25.0	20.0				
1881			46.0	22.0	50.0	10.8[g]	190.0	162.5	30.0	17.0				
1882			51.5	31.5	18.5	10.3	185.0	174.8	17.0	9.0				
1883			70.0	40.0[h]	17.0	10.0[h]	295.0	170.0[f]	35.0	10.0				
1884			63.5	40.1	15.8	9.0	260.0	200.0	48.0	30.0				
1885			48.0	26.0	11.8	5.8	258.8	201.0	40.0	28.5				
1886			55.0	26.5	13.0	5.3	255.0	231.0[h]	38.0	30.0[h]				
1887			64.5	45.0	17.5	8.5	253.0	230.0	33.0	17.5				
1888			63.0	45.0	15.9	9.8	240.0	124.0	17.3	8.0				
1889			90.0	60.0	23.0	12.3	225.0	135.0	15.0	8.0				
1890			85.0	46.0[i]	17.5	8.3	231.0	210.0	37.0	10.0				
1891			132.5	68.0	28.0	13.0	223.0	175.0	35.3	15.0				
			115.0	85.0	19.0	14.0	324.0	190.0	27.0	17.0				
							299.5	199.0	24.3	7.1				
							323.0	240.0	48.3	23.0				
							280.0	240.0	41.0	26.0				

Year											
1892	145.5	103.0	16.3	11.0	300.0	37.8	23.6				
1893	144.0	80.0	13.5	8.5	320.0	37.5	20.0				
1894	131.0	80.0	15.5	7.5	302.0	28.0	18.0				
1895	170.0	98.0	25.0	9.0	280.0	41.5	20.0				
1896	134.0	104.0	15.0	8.0	335.0	31.5	20.5				
1897	129.0	104.0[j]	26.0	10.0	495.0	42.1	28.0[k]				
1898	150.0	105.0	24.0	10.0	650.0	87.0	38.0				
1899	189.0	125.0	30.0	10.0[m]	860.0	104.3	61.0				
1900	178.0	130.0	18.0	12.0	840.0	79.0	58.5				
1901	187.0	125.0	25.0	11.5	860.0	120.0	72.0	83.0	34.0	58.0	31.0
1902	147.0	100.0	16.0	7.5	650.0	89.8	47.5	65.3	43.5	57.5	34.1[o]
1903	126.5	80.0	14.0	6.8	550.0	79.0	43.0	75.0	37.0[n]	64.8	48.0
1904	124.0	80.0[o]	15.5	7.0[o]	700.0	98.0	53.0[o]	74.5	38.0[o]	85.0	54.5
1905	118.0	95.0	20.1	8.0	720.0	115.0	88.0	85.3	64.0	97.5	37.0
1906	114.0	80.0	26.3	14.5	900.0	151.0	93.0	86.5	66.8	135.5	77.0
1907	148.0	70.0	29.5	6.0	1000.0	181.0	71.0	105.0	44.3	170.0	122.0
1908	100.0	77.0[p]	19.5	6.5	700.0	135.5	77.0	83.9	55.1	75.3	43.0
1909	96.0	84.0	19.0	13.0[q]	695.0	170.0	122.0	86.8	68.5	57.0	36.0
1910	92.0	66.0	22.5	9.0	685.0	166.0	114.0	85.0	57.5	73.0	50.3
1911	76.0	55.0	14.0	5.5	545.0	124.0	81.0	69.8	46.5	57.0	36.0
1912	95.0	72.5	16.5	6.8	615.0	130.5	100.0	66.5	48.5	73.0	50.3
1913	80.0	52.3	9.0	2.5	555.0	107.0	67.3	53.0	32.0	65.0	38.0
1914	68.0	52.0	7.9	2.0	460.0	84.0	64.0	41.0	29.0	49.5	39.0
1915	95.0	50.0	14.3	4.6	630.0	93.5	64.5	65.0	30.3	98.0	46.3
1916	109.5	81.0	13.3	6.0	615.0	105.0	70.0	87.8	55.0	108.0	77.0
1917	94.5	60.0	9.0	4.0	580.0	95.0	53.5	68.0	39.3	98.0	57.0
1918	78.0	59.0[r]	6.0	3.0[r]	470.0	65.0	46.5[r]	51.5	40.0[r]	66.5	51.0[r]
1919	83.0	52.0	6.8	1.3	480.0	73.0	45.0	62.0	39.0	83.0	49.3

TABLE 13 (Continued)

Year	Cliff High	Cliff Low	Quincy High	Quincy Low	Franklin High	Franklin Low	Calumet and Hecla High	Calumet and Hecla Low	Osceola High	Osceola Low	Copper Range High	Copper Range Low	Mohawk High	Mohawk Low
1920			65.0	34.5	5.3	.5	409.0	200.0	58.0	22.5	48.7	25.0	72.0	40.5
1921			46.5	33.5	3.3	1.4	280.0	210.0	32.0	27.5	40.8	27.0	59.0	43.5
1922			50.0	30.0	3.9	1.0	305.0	248.0	38.1	25.0	46.8	35.1	68.0	51.5
1923			50.0	18.0	2.9	.3	20.5	17.1 ˢ			43.8	32.5	71.0	27.0 ᵗ
1924			34.3	14.0	1.0	.4	19.5	13.1			33.7	18.5	34.0	34.0
1925			39.5	19.0	1.3	.4	18.7	12.3			33.0	18.0	41.0	25.5
1926			25.0	15.5	1.3	.3	18.5	13.4			20.0	13.0	46.0	30.0
1927			19.1	13.3			24.4	14.3			21.5	11.9	52.0	37.0
1928			48.8	12.1			47.4	20.1			29.8	14.5	65.0	35.5
1929			51.0	14.8 ᵘ			61.9	25.0			33.0	14.0	64.5	41.0
1930			46.0	6.0			33.4	7.8			16.9	5.3	52.0	14.0
1931			10.8	1.8			11.4	3.0			7.8	1.5 ᵛ	21.0	11.0
1932			3.0	.3			7.9	1.5			3.3	1.1	18.8	9.0
1933			4.5	.3			9.4	2.0			7.0	1.3	Closed	
1934			2.4	.4			6.7	2.8			5.8	3.0		
1935			1.4	.5			6.8	2.5			6.5	3.0 ʷ		
1936			3.5	.5			16.5	6.0			12.8	6.1		
1937			11.8	2.0			20.1	4.0			18.4	4.3		
1938			4.5	1.3 ˣ			10.8	5.3 ˣ			8.0	4.1 ˣ		
1939			2.4	1.6			10.7	4.9			8.3	3.4		
1940			2.0	.8			8.1	4.6			6.8	3.4		
1941			1.5	.5			7.3	4.8			7.3	4.1		
1942			1.6	.6			7.7	5.8			6.0	4.1		
1943			1.8	.7			9.3	6.1			7.9	4.8		

1944	2.5	.7	7.4	6.0	8.8	5.3
1946	4.5	1.3 ʸ	9.5	6.3 ʸ	14.8	6.8 ʸ

Sources: Joseph G. Martin, *A Century of Finance* (Boston: Washington Press, 1898); The Manual of Statistics Company, *The Manual of Statistics — Stock Exchange Handbook* (New York: annual volumes from 1903 to 1917 inclusive); Standard and Poor's Corporation, *Poor's Financial Records* (New York, annual volumes from 1910 to date).

ᵃ Number of Quincy shares increased by stock split from 8,000 to 20,000.
ᵇ Number of Cliff (corporate name: Pittsburgh and Boston) shares increased by stock split from 6,000 to 20,000.
ᶜ In 1866 the various mining companies had the following numbers of shares outstanding: Cliff, 20,000; Quincy, 20,000; and Franklin, 20,000.
ᵈ Number of Calumet and Hecla shares increased by stock split from 50 to 80,000.
ᵉ Number of Quincy shares increased by stock split from 20,000 to 40,000.
ᶠ Number of Calumet and Hecla shares increased by stock split from 80,000 to 100,000.
ᵍ Number of Franklin shares increased by stock split from 20,000 to 40,000.
ʰ In 1882 the various mining companies had the following numbers of shares outstanding: Quincy, 40,000; Franklin, 40,000; Calumet and Hecla, 100,000; and Osceola, 50,000.
ⁱ Number of Quincy shares increased by stock split from 40,000 to 50,000.
ʲ Number of Quincy shares increased by sale of new issue from 50,000 to 100,000.
ᵏ Number of Osceola shares increased by stock exchange from 50,000 to 100,000. Forty-one thousand used to acquire the Kearsarge, Iroquois, and Tamarack, Jr.— 9,000 held in treasury and sold gradually over next decade.
ˡ Number of Franklin shares increased from 40,000 to 80,000 at a cost to old stockholders of $400,000.
ᵐ Number of Franklin shares increased from 80,000 to 100,000 at a cost to old stockholders of $300,000.
ⁿ Number of Copper Range shares increased by exchange from 285,000 to 385,000 when control extended over Trimountain.
ᵒ In 1904 the various mining companies had the following numbers of shares outstanding: Quincy, 100,000; Franklin, 100,000; Calumet and Hecla, 100,000; Osceola, 96,000; Copper Range, 385,000; Mohawk, 100,000.
ᵖ Number of Quincy shares increased by sales to old stockholders from 100,000 to 110,000.
ᵠ Number of Franklin shares outstanding increased from 100,000 to 165,000 by exchange for shares of Rhode Island.
ʳ In 1918 the various mining companies had the following numbers of shares outstanding: Quincy, 110,000; Franklin, 165,000; Calumet and Hecla, 100,000; Osceola, 100,000; Copper Range, 394,310 (gradually sold 9,000 shares after 1904); and Mohawk, 100,000.
ˢ Number of Calumet and Hecla shares increased by exchange from 100,000 to 2,005,502 at time of consolidation with Osceola, Ahmeek, Allouez, and Centennial.
ᵗ Number of Mohawk shares increased by exchange from 100,000 to 115,000 when Wolverine and Michigan absorbed.
ᵘ Number of Quincy shares increased by sale to old shareholders from 110,000 to 200,000 in 1928 and 1929.
ᵛ Number of Copper Range shares outstanding increased by exchange from 394,755 to 542,500 when St. Mary's Mineral Land Company acquired.
ʷ Number of Copper Range shares outstanding increased by exchange to 559,400 when C. G. Hussey acquired.
ˣ In 1938 the various companies had the following numbers of shares outstanding: Quincy, 205,961; Calumet and Hecla, 2,005,000; and Copper Range, 564,950.
ʸ In 1946 the various companies had the following numbers of shares outstanding: Quincy, 150,000; Calumet and Hecla, 2,068,270; and Copper Range, 564,928. (The drop in the number of Quincy shares was due to forfeiture when assessments called.)

TABLE 14
COPPER COUNTRY POPULATION DATA, 1850–1940

	1850	1854	1860	1864	1870	1874	1880	1884
Totals for District:[a]								
No. of people	1,097	6,492	13,821	18,811	18,088	24,445	26,743	30,813
Percentage male	74.9	72.3	66.7	60.0	55.7	58.3	54.7	54.3
Percentage male, age 18–45[b]					25.4		23.9	24.0
Percentage male, age 21–45		55.7		33.1		27.3		
Percentage foreign born			66.9		55.4		48.5	49.2
Houghton County:								
No. of people	708	2,868	9,253	8,224[c]	13,882	19,030	22,473	26,146
Percentage male	72.9	67.2	67.0	59.3	55.8	57.9	54.5	54.2
Percentage male, age 18–45[b]					26.1		24.0	24.1
Percentage male, age 21–45		48.6		33.3	24.4	26.7		
Percentage foreign born			66.9		56.7		48.9	49.0
Keweenaw County:								
No. of people		Keweenaw Separated from Houghton in 1861		5,180	4,206	5,415	4,270	4,667
Percentage male				62.5	55.3	59.8	56.1	54.7
Percentage male, age 18–45[b]					23.2		23.0	23.4
Percentage male, age 21–45				35.3		29.3		
Percentage foreign born					51.0		46.0	50.6

TABLE 14 (Continued)

	1890	1894	1900	1904	1910	1920	1930	1940
Totals for District: [a]								
No. of people	38,283	46,980	69,280	75,171	95,254	78,252	57,927	51,635
Percentage male	55.3	54.2	56.3	54.1	54.1	51.9	53.4	53.0
Percentage male, age 18–45 [b]	26.1	25.1	27.9	26.1		19.1	20.4	22.0
Percentage male, age 21–45								
Percentage foreign born	47.4	45.2	42.8	40.0	38.3	29.5	24.5	19.4
Houghton County:								
No. of people	35,389	44,175	66,063	70,625	88,098	71,930	52,851 [d]	47,631
Percentage male	55.3	54.1	56.1	53.7	53.8	51.8	53.2	52.9
Percentage male, age 18–45 [b]	26.3	25.1	27.9	25.7		19.1	20.3	21.9
Percentage male, age 21–45								
Percentage foreign born	47.5	45.1	42.6	39.4	37.8	29.4	24.3	19.1
Keweenaw County:								
No. of people	2,805	2,894	3,217	4,546	7,156	6,322	5,076	4,004
Percentage male	56.3	54.9	60.2	60.5	58.5	52.9	55.4	55.1
Percentage male, age 18–45 [b]	25.2	24.4	28.8	32.5		19.7	21.2	23.6
Percentage male, age 21–45								
Percentage foreign born	45.8	48.8	46.5	49.2	44.7	30.9	26.6	22.2

Sources: *Census of Michigan,* 1854–1904; United States Bureau of the Census, Volumes on Population.

[a] For the years 1850 through 1864 the totals include data for three counties — Ontonagon, Houghton, and Keweenaw. After 1864 Ontonagon has been dropped since copper mining employment had become insignificant by 1870.

[b] The age group designated here means all males having reached the eighteenth birthday but not yet 45 years of age.

[c] The drop in the Houghton County total in 1864 is due to the separation of Keweenaw from Houghton in 1861.

[d] An investigation of relief cases in 1934 indicated that the population of Houghton County had increased to 57,000 people (Files of the Houghton County Welfare Office). For the 1934 point in Figure 6 above, the increase (from 1930) for the Michigan Copper District was estimated on the assumption that the movement of population in Keweenaw County was proportionate to that in Houghton. Sugar ration book applications indicated that the population of Houghton County had fallen to 36,070 by the summer of 1943 and that of Keweenaw County to 2,917 (*An Invitation to the United States Veterans Administration,* etc., p. 13).

TABLE 15. OUTPUT OF THE CALUMET AND HECLA COPPER MINING
COMPANY PERCENTAGE OF MICHIGAN OUTPUT (1867–1946)

Year	Output in Millions of Pounds	Percentage	Year	Output in Millions of Pounds	Percentage
1867	1.4	8.4	1908	82.5	36.9
1868	5.1	25.8	1909	80.1	34.3
1869	12.3	46.3	1910	72.1	32.6
1870	14.0	57.6	1911	74.1	33.7
1871	16.2 [a]	63.0	1912	67.9	31.3
1872	16.2	65.3	1913	45.0	32.2
1873	18.8	62.9	1914	53.6	32.3
1874	20.1	58.7	1915	72.6 [b]	28.1
1875	21.5	59.6	1916	76.7	28.7
1876	21.7	56.9	1917	77.5	30.3
1877	22.6	58.1	1918	67.9	29.8
1878	25.3	61.0	1919	52.9	29.7
1879	26.3	61.4	1920	57.6	35.7
1880	31.7	63.9	1921	15.2	16.5
1881	31.4	58.3	1922	40.5	33.4
1882	32.1	56.7	1923	62.6 [c]	45.4
1883	33.1	55.9	1924	73.1	52.9
1884	40.5	58.4	1925	91.3	59.0
1885	47.2	64.9	1926	104.3	59.4
1886	50.5	62.9	1927	108.7	61.2
1887	46.0	60.7	1928	121.2	67.9
1888	50.3	58.1	1929	123.8	66.4
1889	48.7	55.7	1930	105.7	62.4
1890	59.9	59.5	1931	72.4	61.3
1891	63.6	55.6	1932	32.4	59.6
1892	57.9	53.8	1933	33.2	70.9
1893	62.8	55.3	1934	32.8	68.0
1894	61.8	54.0	1935	45.4	70.8
1895	77.4	59.7	1936	78.5	81.8
1896	89.3	61.3	1937	74.3	78.3
1897	83.2	58.3	1938	64.9	69.4
1898	86.4	58.4	1939	52.3	59.5
1899	89.6	60.4	1940	50.4	55.8
1900	77.8	54.8	1941	61.5	66.2
1901	82.5	53.0	1942	58.8	64.4
1902	81.2	47.7	1943	62.5	66.8
1903	76.5	39.8	1944	52.1	61.4
1904	80.3	38.6	1945	39.1	64.3
1905	95.1	41.5	1946	31.8	67.3
1906	100.0	43.4			
1907	83.9	38.8	Total	4,611.5	48.7 [d]

Sources: Table 8; Hore, pp. 203–220; Pardee, pp. 30–33; and reports of the Calumet and Hecla Consolidated Copper Company. [a] Before the consolidation of 1871 there were two companies: the Hecla Mining Company and the Calumet Mining Company. [b] After 1915 a substantial part of the company's output came from retreatment of tailings. The aggregate amount from this source was 511.6 million pounds. [c] In 1923 Calumet and Hecla consolidated with the Ahmeek, Osceola, Allouez, and Centennial. [d] Calumet and Hecla produced 48.0 per cent of total Michigan output of the years 1845–1946.

TABLE 16
Freight Rates for Water Transportation of Coal and Copper Between Lake Superior and Lower Lake Ports, 1887–1940
(In Dollars Per Ton)

Year	Coal[a]	Copper	Year	Coal[a]	Copper
1887	.90	2.60	1914	.30	1.35
1888	.70	2.35	1915	.30	1.35
1889	.47	2.25	1916	.30	2.00
1890	.45	2.38	1917	.45	2.00
1891	.43	2.00	1918	.48	2.00
1892	.41	1.40	1919	.425	4.00
1893	.40	1.75	1920	.52	4.00
1894	.40	1.95	1921	.52	5.00
1895	.37	1.66	1922	.45	5.00
1896	.32	1.95	1923	.45	5.00
1897	.30	1.95	1924	.37	4.50
1898	.25	2.00	1925	.36	4.50
1899	.46	2.00	1926	.35	5.00
1900	.44	1.60	1927	.35	4.00
1901	.38	1.65	1928	.35	4.00
1002	.45	1.40	1929	.35	5.00
1903	.53	1.43	1930	.35	5.00
1904	.40	1.45	1931	.35	5.00
1905	.33	1.25	1932	.35	4.00
1906	.35	1.50	1933	.35	4.00
1907	.31	1.40	1934	.37	4.00
1908	.30	1.20	1935	.40	4.00
1909	.31	1.10	1936	.40	4.00
1910	.31	1.50	1937	.45	4.95
1911	.31	1.50	1938	.45	4.75
1912	.30	1.45	1939	.45	3.55
1913	.30	1.40	1940	.40	3.60

Source: U.S. War Department, Corps of Engineers, Office of the District Engineer, Detroit District, "Statistical Report of Lake Commerce Passing Through Canals at Sault Ste. Marie" (Detroit, 1940), mimeographed.

[a] Does not include loading and unloading.

TABLE 17
Equalized Assessed Valuation — All Personal and Real Property of Houghton County, 1900–1946
(Thousands of Dollars)

Year	Valuation	Year	Valuation
1900	98,708	1924	45,634
1901	98,425	1925	40,847
1902	103,716	1926	40,317
1903	93,077	1927	39,005
1904	79,071	1928	38,551
1905	104,811	1929	38,398
1906	108,295	1930	45,045
1907	118,696	1931	40,294
1908	90,207	1932	28,991
1909	97,820	1933	20,037
1910	93,356	1934	19,461
1911	90,005	1935	17,000
1912	92,555	1936	18,839
1913	92,312	1937	19,517
1914	83,583	1938	18,918
1915	85,337	1939	18,238
1916	91,066	1940	16,990
1917	95,552	1941	15,895
1918	91,100	1942	15,974
1919	91,868	1943	15,696
1920	91,878	1944	15,698
1921	64,082	1945	15,239
1922	61,548	1946	14,278
1923	62,531		

Source: Records of the County Clerk of Houghton County, Michigan.

NOTES

BIBLIOGRAPHY

GLOSSARY OF MINING TERMS

Notes

CHAPTER I: Opening the Michigan Lodes, 1845–1866

1. Frank William Taussig, *Principles of Economics* (New York: Macmillan, 1911), II, 93–94.
2. For more detailed accounts of early Indian mining, and exploration by Europeans before 1840, see Michigan College of Mining, *The 1924 Keweenawan* (Rochester, N. Y.: DuBois Press, 1924), unsigned article by James Fisher, pp. 217–288; Angus Murdoch, *Boom Copper* (New York: Macmillan, 1943), pp. 3–26; and John Wills Taylor, "Reservation and Leasing of the Salines, Lead, and Copper Mines of the Public Domain," unpublished Ph.D. dissertation, Department of History, University of Chicago, 1930.
3. *U. S. Statutes at Large*, VII (1854), 591–595, Articles of a Treaty made and concluded at La Pointe, Lake Superior, in the Territory of Wisconsin, between Robert Stuart, Commissioner on the part of the United States and the Chippewa Indians of the Mississippi and Lake Superior by their Chiefs and Headmen, October 4, 1842, proclaimed March 23, 1843.
4. Horace J. Stevens, *The Copper Handbook*, I (Houghton, 1900), 11.
5. *U. S. Statutes at Large*, II (1807), 446.
6. Taylor, dissertation, p. 276.
7. Alfred P. Swineford, *History and Review of the Copper, Iron, Silver, Slate, and Other Material Interests of the South Shore of Lake Superior* (Marquette: The Mining Journal, 1876), p. 23.
8. An Original Shareholder, *A Brief Account of the Lake Superior Copper Companies* (Boston: S. S. Dickinson, 1845), p. 20.
9. *The American Journal of Science and Arts*, 2nd ser., III (1847), 292.
10. A. K. Hamilton Jenkin, *The Cornish Miner: An Account of His Life Above and Underground from Early Times* (London: George Allen and Unwin, Ltd., 1927), p. 88.
11. *Ibid.*, p. 184. (The more obscure mining terms, such as "man-engine," are explained at some length in the glossary, p. 284.)
12. *Report of the Trustees of the Lake Superior Copper Company* (Boston: Beals and Greene, 1845), p. 6.
13. In order to avoid confusion the terms "copper mass," "copper rock," and "copper mineral" should be defined at once. A copper mass is a solid piece of native or pure copper, weighing 100 pounds or more, surrounded by a rock matrix. "Copper rock" is a term used in describing tiny pieces of highly disseminated metal embedded in a rock matrix, which has not yet been sent to the stamp mill for crushing and elimination of waste. Copper mineral is the product of the stamp mill (or a concentrate) before shipment to the smelter for final elimination of nonmetallic materials.
14. L. A. Chase, "Early Copper Mining in Michigan," *Michigan History Magazine*, XXIX (1945), p. 25.
15. John R. St. John, *A True Description of the Lake Superior Country* (New York: Wm. H. Graham, 1846), p. 11.
16. Taylor, dissertation, pp. 285–286.

17. *Ibid.*, p. 307. Also, *U. S. Statutes at Large*, IX, 146, Act approved March 1, 1847.
18. *Ibid.*, IX, 472, Act approved September 26, 1850.
19. J. W. Foster and J. D. Whitney, *Report on the Geology and Topography of a Portion of the Lake Superior Land District in the State of Michigan*, Part I, "Copper Lands" (Washington, 1850).
20. Robert B. Pettengill, "The United States Foreign Trade in Copper: 1790–1932," *American Economic Review*, XXV (1935), 426.
21. For world production of copper, see Table 6, p. 197. Production of individual countries during this period is given in Nicol Brown and Charles C. Turnbull, *A Century of Copper* (London: Effingham Wilson, 1906), p. 8.
22. F. E. Richter, "The Copper-Mining Industry in the United States, 1845–1926," *Quarterly Journal of Economics*, XLIV (1926–27), 250.
23. Brown and Turnbull, p. 10.
24. J. Robert Van Pelt, "Boston and Keweenaw," *Mining and Metallurgy*, XXIX (1948), 377.
25. Amygdaloid is a rock of igneous origin which, in the case of the Michigan copper district, often contains pure metal in the amygdules, or almond-shaped cavities. Conglomerate is a puddingstone rock which, in this case, was cemented together with pure copper metal.
26. Annual Report of the Trustees of the Copper Falls Mining Company for the year 1847.
27. The labor strand of the story is not included in this chapter. It did not seem desirable to break that material down into relatively short chronological periods, and, in consequence, the first half century of the labor and community history is covered in Chapter IV.
28. For annual production data, see Table 8, p. 203.
29. *Hunt's Merchants' Magazine*, XLVI (1862), 379.
30. For employment and population data, see Table 10, p. 208 and Table 14, p. 228.
31. Figures for assessments are from *Hunt's Merchants' Magazine*, LIV (1866), 220. For dividend payments by companies and years, see Table 12, p. 215. None of the companies issued fully paid stock; the amount to be paid in was left to the discretion of the directors.
32. Listed in order of the size of total dividend payments made during this period, the six companies were the Cliff, Minesota, Quincy, Pewabic, National, and Franklin. The Cliff, Minesota, and National were working mainly mass copper deposits while the other three were working the Portage Lake Pewabic amygdaloid lode. (The spelling "Minesota" is alleged to have resulted from a clerical error in a charter application.)
33. The Cliff and Minesota remain to this day the richest mass copper deposits discovered in the world. Very substantial masses have been found from time to time in all of the lodes of the Lake district except the Calumet conglomerate.
34. *The Mining Magazine*, VIII (1857), 176.
35. *Portage Lake Mining Gazette* (hereafter referred to as *P.L.M.G.*), January 20, 1866.
36. Swineford, p. 65.
37. See Table 9, p. 207, for a classification of firms according to size of output.

Annual output figures on individual Michigan copper mining companies are available in R. E. Hore, "Michigan Copper Deposits," *Mineral Resources of Michigan*, Michigan Geological and Biological Survey, Publication 19, Geological Series 16 (Lansing: Wynkoop Hallenbeck Crawford, 1915), pp. 203–220.

38. Swineford, p. 69.
39. Murdoch, p. 119.
40. For data on copper prices, see Fig. 5, p. 195, and Table 8, p. 203.
41. For dividend payments, see Fig. 5, p. 195, and Table 12, p. 215.
42. Richter, "Copper-Mining Industry," p. 245.
43. For a more detailed treatment of the labor supply situation during these years, see pp. 94–96.
44. *P.L.M.G.*, January 11, 1865.
45. E. Rivot, "Visit to the Lake Superior Region in 1854," *The Mining Magazine*, VI (1856), 36.
46. Charles Moore, *The History of Michigan* (Chicago: Lewis Publishing Company, 1915), I, 470.
47. Annual shipments of copper almost tripled between 1853 and 1856. Other developments, among them rising copper prices, partially explain the increase, but the canal was undoubtedly a major factor.
48. Swineford, p. 59.
49. Charles L. Fleischmann, *Portage Mine on Keweenaw Point, Lake Superior —Report of an Examination of the Mine Made During the Summer of 1859* (New York: G. B. Taubner, printer, 1859), p. 9.
50. *The History of the Upper Peninsula of Michigan* (Chicago: Western Historical Company, 1883), p. 254.
51. *P.L.M.G.*, April 26, 1866.
52. *Ibid.*, February 17, 1866.
53. *Annual Report of the Commissioner of Mineral Statistics of the State of Michigan* (Lansing, 1880), pp. 69–70.
54. *P.L.M.G.*, August 19, 1865.
55. *The Mining Magazine*, III (1854), 57; *History of the Upper Peninsula*, p. 267.
56. Annual Report of the Minesota Mining Company for the year 1852.
57. *The Mining Magazine*, IV (1855), 296.
58. For example, see *Acts of the Legislature of the State of Michigan, 1859*, No. 117, p. 310, approved February 12, 1859.
59. *Ibid.*, 1848, Joint Resolution No. 24, p. 448.
60. *Ibid.*, 1857, No. 192, approved February 17, 1857.
61. *Ibid.*, 1863, p. 323, No. 177, Act approved March 20, 1863, and *P.L.M.G.*, March 3, 1864.
62. Documents accompanying the Journal of the House, 1863, State of Michigan, *House Document* 4, p. 1.
63. *P.L.M.G.*, October 8, 1864.
64. *Ibid.*, December 24, 1864.
65. *Ibid.*, March 7, 1863, and March 21, 1863.
66. *Ibid.*, March 3, 1866.
67. *Ibid.*, December 23, 1865, and February 25, 1866. The early express rate was $14.20 per hundred pounds from Chicago. (*Ibid.*, January 6, 1866.)
68. *History of the Upper Peninsula*, p. 167.

NOTES TO CHAPTER I

69. J. C. Hunter, *Yesterday and Today: A History of the Chicago and Northwestern Railroad System* (Chicago, 1910), pp. 57–61.
70. Report of the Central Mining Company for the year 1861.
71. *P.L.M.G.*, February 17, 1866; July 29, 1865.
72. *Ibid.*, December 24, 1864. It is something of a mystery why animals were not more generally used underground at this time. The first horse, working with four men, was supposed to have performed three times the labor of fourteen men. Yet little more is heard of animal haulage until a much later period.
73. *P.L.M.G.*, March 18, 1865. A drift is a horizontal opening in a mine following the direction of the lode. A stope is an excavation above a drift for the removal of paying quantities of copper rock. Keeping openings ahead of stopes means that paying ground has been opened up and made ready for final removal of the copper rock.
74. Foster and Whitney, pp. 146–151.
75. Report of the Central Mining Company for the year 1863.
76. Report of the Minesota Mining Company for the year 1861.
77. *P.L.M.G.*, January 13, 1866.
78. *Ibid.*, September 20, 1866.
79. Foster and Whitney, p. 126.
80. J. D. Whitney, *The Metallic Wealth of the United States* (Philadelphia: Lippincott, Grambo & Company, 1854), p. 278.
81. *The Mining Magazine*, VIII (1857), 287.
82. Whitney, p. 278.
83. A skip is an iron box, open at the top, which runs on wheels in and out of inclined shafts.
84. *Annual Report . . . Mineral Statistics of Michigan*, 1880, p. 17.
85. Report of the Minesota Mining Company for the year 1861; *P.L.M.G.*, June 13, 1863.
86. *P.L.M.G.*, September 20, 1866.
87. Charles T. Jackson, *Report on the Geological and Mineralogical Survey of the Mineral Lands of the United States in the State of Michigan*, 31 Cong., 1 Sess., Senate Executive Document No. 5 (Washington, 1849), p. 434.
88. *P.L.M.G.*, August 2, 1862.
89. *History of the Upper Peninsula*, p. 261.
90. *P.L.M.G.*, November 19, 1864; March 3, 1866. Before going to the mill the larger pieces of rock were usually broken up with sledges until late in the Civil War when large steam hammers, weighing a ton or more, began to be installed in the rock houses of the best equipped companies (*Ibid.*, December 23, 1865; and November 8, 1866).
91. John F. Blandy, "Stamp Mills of Lake Superior," *Transactions of the American Institute of Mining Engineers*, II (1874), 209.
92. *P.L.M.G.*, April 11, 1863.
93. *Ibid.*, November 12, 1864.
94. *Ibid.*, December 23, 1865; June 17, 1865.
95. *Ibid.*, February 3, 1866. Interestingly enough, the same experiment was to be conducted by the Copper Range Company over three-quarters of a century later, with similar, if not so conclusive, results.
96. The hand method of washing mineral to eliminate waste made use of a keeve, or tub; a buddle, or inclined trough; and a tie, or launder.

97. *Report of the Directors of the Eagle Harbor and Waterbury Mining Company* (Detroit Daily Free Press, 1858), p. 24.
98. *P.L.M.G.*, April 8, 1865; Report of the Hancock Mining Company for the year 1865.
99. *P.L.M.G.*, December 13, 1862; February 4, 1865.
100. *The Mining Magazine*, VII (1856).
101. *P.L.M.G.*, May 17, 1866.
102. *Hunt's Merchants' Magazine*, XLIV (1861), 376.
103. James B. Cooper, "Historical Sketch of Smelting and Refining Lake Copper," *Proceedings of the Lake Superior Mining Institute*, VII (1901), 44.
104. *Ibid.*, p. 45.
105. *The Mining Magazine*, I (1853), 298.
106. *History of the Upper Peninsula*, p. 288.
107. *Annual Report . . . Mineral Statistics of Michigan*, 1880, p. 59.
108. *P.L.M.G.*, September 23, 1865; April 11, 1867.
109. The early processes for sulphide ores sound to a mere economist like the darkest sort of alchemy. See A. Snowden Piggot, *The Chemistry and Metallurgy of Copper* (Philadelphia: Lindsay and Blakiston, 1858).
110. A reverberatory furnace is one in which the flame is reflected from the roof on the material treated.
111. Cooper, pp. 44–49.
112. An excellent sketch of early Lake smelting practices is presented in the *Mining Congress Journal*, October, 1931, p. 65.
113. Swineford, p. 34.
114. For an example of an early charter, see *Acts of the Legislature of the State of Michigan, 1848*, No. 74, Act approved March 15, 1848, p. 76.
115. *Ibid.*, 1850, No. 144, Act approved April 8, 1851, p. 179; 1853, No. 41, Act approved February 5, 1853, p. 53.
116. *Ibid.*, 1857, No. 76, Act approved February 5, 1857, p. 188; 1859, No. 62, Act approved February 5, 1859, p. 107.
117. *Ibid.*, 1855, No. 31, Act approved February 8, 1855, p. 44.
118. *Ibid.*, 1857, No. 31, Act approved February 17, 1857, p. 437.
119. *Ibid.*, 1865, No. 202, Act approved March 16, 1865, p. 338.
120. Warren A. Roberts, *State Taxation of Metallic Deposits* (Cambridge: Harvard University Press, 1944), p. 296.
121. *Acts of the Legislature of the State of Michigan*, 1851, No. 144, Act approved April 8, 1851, p. 179.
122. *Ibid.*, 1853, No. 41, Act approved February 5, 1853, p. 53.
123. It is something of a mystery why Boston predominated in the financing of the Michigan copper field. John W. Taylor has implied that the answer lies in early Boston experience as a banking center for Nova Scotia copper mines ("Reservation and Leasing," dissertation, p. 267). Angus Murdoch says that it all began with David Henshaw, Secretary of the Navy under President Tyler, who resigned from the cabinet to promote an early Lake Superior mining venture and interested his Boston friends in the district (*Boom Copper*, pp. 31, 48–49).
124. *The Mining Magazine*, VIII (1857), 67.
125. *Ibid.*, 578; *Annual Report . . . Mineral Statistics of Michigan*, 1880, p. 78.

126. Fisher, unsigned article, p. 244.
127. *The Mining Magazine*, III (1854), 57.
128. Allouez, Hancock, Hulbert, and Huron.
129. Northwestern, National, Mass, Adventure, Aztec, Great Western, and American.
130. For dividend payments by years and companies, see Table 12, p. 215.
131. The companies were the Ridge, Quincy, Knowlton, Pewabic, Franklin, Rockland, and Eagle Harbor.
132. *P.L.M.G.*, May 10, 1866.
133. The Minesota interest group organized the Rockland, Flint Steel, Lake Superior, West Minesota, and Peninsula.
134. *P.L.M.G.*, July 26, 1862.
135. *Ibid.*, June 14, 1866, and May 23, 1863.
136. Pittsburgh and Boston Report for the year 1853; National Mining Company Report for 1857.
137. *P.L.M.G.*, February 4, 1865.
138 Annual Report . . . *Mineral Statistics of Michigan*, 1880, p. 78.
139. *P.L.M.G.*, April 26, 1866.
140. *Ibid.*, December 24, 1864.
141. *Ibid.*, January 27, 1866; December 30, 1865.
142. Annual Report . . . *Mineral Statistics of Michigan*, 1880, p. 78.

CHAPTER II: Michigan Dominates the United States Market, 1867–1884

1. President Johnson in vetoing the Tariff Bill on Copper, February 22, 1869, 40 Cong., *Senate Journal*, pp. 338–340.
2. Lake copper drew a premium of about 1.5 cents a pound over English Standard, also known as Chile bar, because of greater purity. The rest of the difference between the London and New York price is ascribable to the protection afforded the domestic industry by the Civil War tariff, and to the time required for reëstablishment of trade lines. (See U. S. Department of the Interior, *Mineral Resources of the United States, 1883–84* [Washington], p. 350.) For English prices and Lake prices expressed in terms of gold, see Charles Louis Knight, *Secular and Cyclical Movements in the Production and Price of Copper* (Philadelphia: University of Pennsylvania, 1935), pp. 149–150.
3. *P.L.M.G.*, June 2, 1870.
4. For figures on total output, see Fig. 4, p. 195, and Table 8, p. 203. For output by individual companies, see Hore, pp. 203–220.
5. *P.L.M.G.*, May 9, 1867. The *Gazette* goes on to state that the proper method in dull times was to reduce stoping to a minimum and concentrate on opening up new ground. In the discussion which followed the printing of this editorial, there seemed to be a good deal of agreement about the *Gazette* suggestion, as representing rational policy, but skepticism as to its financial practicability.
6. *P.L.M.G.*, July 28, 1870.

7. *Ibid.*, October 27, 1870.
8. *Ibid.*, July 7, 1870.
9. *Ibid.*, July 2, 1874.
10. *E.M.J.*, XXV (1878), 151–152.
11. George R. Agassiz, ed., *Letters and Recollections of Alexander Agassiz, with a Sketch of His Life and Work* (Boston: Houghton Mifflin Company, 1913), p. 75.
12. *P.L.M.G.*, March 7, 1867.
13. *Ibid.*, May 9, 1867.
14. *Ibid.*, May 9, May 23, June 13, and June 20, 1867.
15. *Acts of the Legislature of the State of Michigan, 1869*, No. 32, Act approved March 12, 1869, pp. 4–7.
16. *P.L.M.G.*, September 23, 1869.
17. *Ibid.*, June 3, 1869.
18. D. Houston & Company, *Copper Manual* (New York: D. Houston & Co., 1897), p. 50.
19. *History of the Upper Peninsula*, p. 256.
20. *P.L.M.G.*, March 18, 1869.
21. *Acts of the Legislature of the State of Michigan, 1875*, No. 89, Act approved April 16, 1875, pp. 127–128.
22. *History of the Upper Peninsula*, p. 288.
23. *E.M.J.*, XXXIII (1882), 168.
24. *Ibid.*, p. 196.
25. For Calumet and Hecla output and proportion of Michigan total, see Table 15, p. 230.
26. For dividend payments, see Fig. 5, p. 195, and Table 12, p. 215.
27. Mary Caroline Crawford, *Famous Families of Massachusetts* (Boston: Little, Brown, 1940), p. 254.
28. *P.L.M.G.*, May 4, 1875.
29. For share quotations, see Table 13, p. 223.
30. *Acts of the Legislature of the State of Michigan, 1867*, Joint Resolution 19, approved February 27, 1867, p. 319.
31. *Congressional Globe*, 40 Cong., December 19, 1868, I, 158.
32. *Ibid.*, December 15, 1868, p. 97.
33. *Ibid.*, February 23, 1869, p. 1464; December 19, p. 160; and December 15, 1868, p. 96. For an excellent summary of these debates, see Hoval A. Smith, *American Copper Production* (Miami, Ariz.: Arizona Silver Belt, 1932), pp. 17–45.
34. Passage of the bill was facilitated by personal and party animosity to President Johnson. See F. W. Taussig, *Some Aspects of the Tariff Question* (Cambridge: Harvard University Press, 1931), p. 161.
35. *United States Statutes at Large, 1869*, 40 Cong., 3 Sess., Chapter 45, February 24, 1869, p. 274.
36. *E.M.J.*, XXXII (1881), 87.
37. White and Haskell's *Monthly Metal Report*, reprinted *P.L.M.G.*, March 17, 1870.
38. Files of the Calumet and Hecla Consolidated Copper Company, Boston, Mass., letter from Alexander Agassiz to Naylin Bezin of London, dated September 11, 1874.

39. Report of the Quincy Mining Company for the year 1874.
40. Calumet and Hecla Files, letters dated July 7, 1876; November 4, 1877; March 12, 1878; November 19, 1879.
41. For example, see *E.M.J.*, XX (1875), 569. The statement here was that the company "could easily double its output."
42. For examples of these contracts, see *E.M.J.*, XXV (1878), 318; XXXIV (1882), 145.
43. *Ibid.*, XXXIV (1882), 76. During much of the period manufacturers were organized quite as effectively as the producers. The copper rolling mills had a strong trade association with strictly enforced list prices, and during certain years the brass manufacturers made successful agreements covering prices and production (*E.M.J.*, XXXIV (1882), 79; William G. Lathrop, *The Brass Industry in Connecticut* [Shelton, Connecticut: W. G. Lathrop, 1909], pp. 126–127).
44. For examples, see *P.L.M.G.*, January 26, 1871; July 23, 1874; and *E.M.J.*, XXI (1881), 361.
45. *Ibid.*, XXXIV (1882), 90, and XXXIII (1882), 206.
46. *Report on the Belt Copper Mines* (London: James Wall Co., 1882), p. 21.
47. Calumet and Hecla Files, letter dated May 11, 1874.
48. There continued to be a protective tariff, the Act of 1883, reducing the duty on ingots from 5 to 4 cents a pound.
49. *E.M.J.*, XXXV (1883), 311; Robert B. Pettengill, "United States Foreign Trade in Copper," unpublished Ph.D. dissertation, Department of Economics, Stanford University, 1934, p. 101.
50. *E.M.J.*, XXXVII (1884), 59. A number of buyers under Lake contracts did not hesitate to use cheaper brands and sell all the Lake they could spare (*E.M.J.*, XXXV [1883], 157, 187).
51. Calumet and Hecla Files, letter dated December 15, 1884.
52. *Ibid.*, letter dated August 12, 1884.
53. *Ibid.*, letter dated December 30, 1884.
54. *E.M.J.*, XXXVIII (1884), 80, 433. Such contracts were signed with virtually all of the great copper manufacturing companies of the day — Revere, Coe, Waterbury, Ansonia, Winchester — to name but a few.
55. *Ibid.*, XXXIII (1882), 138.
56. Calumet and Hecla Files, letter dated September 4, 1884.
57. *Ibid.*, letter dated September 3, 1884.
58. *E.M.J.*, XXXIX (1885), 129. The idea occurred to Calumet and Hecla's English broker to sustain the price of Chile bars by open-market purchases, but his suggestion was vetoed by the Boston office (Calumet and Hecla Files, letter dated November 3, 1884).
59. *Ibid.*, letter dated November 28, 1884.
60. *Mineral Resources of the United States, 1883–84*, pp. 353–354; *E.M.J.*, XXXVIII (1884), 405; XXXIX (1885), 17.
61. *Ibid.*, XXXIX (1885), 135.
62. *Ibid.*, XXIII (1877), 158.
63. Smith, p. 16.
64. Taussig, *Some Aspects of the Tariff Question*, p. 167.

65. *Ibid.*, p. 169.
66. *P.L.M.G.*, January 26, 1871.

	Annual Consumption in Millions of Pounds
Navy and other government departments	3
Railroads, locomotive builders, foundries, and machine shops	8
Household — in bathtubs, boilers, kettles, cooking utensils, etc.	10
Sugar machinery, dye-stuffs, distilleries, and chemical apparatus	2
Electroplating, telegraphing, and scientific	1
Shipbuilding, sheathing, etc.	2
	26

67. *P.L.M.G.*, May 7, 1872.
68. Calumet and Hecla Files, letter dated September 26, 1873.
69. Stevens, *The Copper Handbook*, II (1902), 225.
70. *Ibid.*, p. 107.
71. *Ibid.*, p. 258.
72. *E.M.J.*, XVIII (1874), 218.
73. Hore, p. 208.
74. *Annual Report . . . Mineral Statistics of Michigan*, 1882, pp. 60, 83, 100, and 113.
75. H. S. Munroe, "The Losses in Copper Dressing at Lake Superior," *Transactions of the American Institute of Mining Engineers*, VIII (1880), 410.
76. Agassiz, p. 60.
77. *Annual Report . . . Mineral Statistics of Michigan*, 1882, various reports concerning individual companies. Fine copper return on rock stamped is used herein as the measure of richness of mineral bodies. This figure has its limitations in making comparisons over substantial periods of time since it is subject to change due to other factors, such as improvements in mill recovery and more selective mining practices.
78. *Annual Report . . . Mineral Statistics of Michigan*, 1880, p. 134.
79. *Ibid.*, p. 127; *P.L.M.G.*, May 11, 1871; July 6, 1871; March 7, 1872.
80. *Ibid.*, May 11, 1871, December 10, 1874; *E.M.J.*, XVI (1873), 107.
81. *P.L.M.G.*, June 24, 1875.
82. *Ibid.*, July 20, 1875.
83. *Ibid.*, August 20, 1874.
84. *Annual Report . . . Mineral Statistics of Michigan*, 1878–79, p. 174.
85. *P.L.M.G.*, February 19, 1880.
86. *Ibid.*, October 30, 1880; also Table 12, p. 215.
87. *P.L.M.G.*, August 5, 1869.
88. *Ibid.*, April 21, 1870.
89. T. Egleston, "Copper Mining on Lake Superior," *Transactions of the American Institute of Mining Engineers*, VI (1879), 290.
90. *History of the Upper Peninsula*, p. 270.
91. *P.L.M.G.*, October 3, 1878, and August 20, 1874.
92. *Ibid.*, October 28, 1875; March 14, 1878.
93. *Ibid.*, July 6, 1871; June 18, 1874.
94. Swineford, p. 73; *Annual Report . . . Mineral Statistics of Michigan*, 1880, p. 134.
95. *P.L.M.G.*, August 20, 1874.

96. *Ibid.*, May 10, 1877.
97. *History of the Upper Peninsula*, p. 260.
98. T. A. Rickard, *The Copper Mines of Lake Superior* (New York, 1905), pp. 118-119.
99. *P.L.M.G.*, February 19, 1880, and August 20, 1874.
100. Blandy, p. 209.
101. T. Egleston, Comment on article by C. M. Rolker, *Transactions of the American Institute of Mining Engineers*, V (1877), 610. For an interesting contemporary discussion of these problems, see Charles M. Rolker, "The Allouez Mine and Ore Dressing, as Practiced in the Lake Superior Copper District," *E.M.J.*, XXIII (1877), 274-275, 294-296, 314-315, 335-336.
102. Munroe, pp. 410-411.
103. *Ibid.*, p. 431.
104. *P.L.M.G.*, October 15, 1874.
105. Munroe, p. 411.
106. See Table 10, p. 208.
107. For productivity figures, see Fig. 7, p. 196, and Table 11, p. 212.
108. *History of the Upper Peninsula*, p. 254.
109. *First Annual Report of the Commissioner of Mineral Statistics of the State of Michigan for 1877-78* (Marquette: Mining Journal Steam Printing House, 1879), p. 181.
110. *History of the Upper Peninsula*, p. 168.
111. *Ibid.*, p. 254.
112. *E.M.J.*, XXXIII (1882), 168.
113. *P.L.M.G.*, January 20, 1876.
114. *Annual Report . . . Mineral Statistics of Michigan*, 1880, p. 70.
115. *Ibid.*, 1882, p. 61.
116. *P.L.M.G.*, December 10, 1874; also Swineford, p. 60.
117. *History of the Upper Peninsula*, p. 253.
118. *P.L.M.G.*, November 18, 1869; February 28, 1867.
119. *E.M.J.*, XXXII (1882), 168.
120. *P.L.M.G.*, November 25, 1865.
121. *Annual Report . . . Mineral Statistics of Michigan*, 1878-79, pp. 41-42.
122. *Annual Report . . . Mineral Statistics of Michigan*, 1880, p. 121.
123. *P.L.M.G.*, December 11, 1879.
124. *History of the Upper Peninsula*, pp. 254-255.
125. *P.L.M.G.*, October 23, 1873.
126. *E.M.J.*, XXXIII (1882), 168.
127. *History of the Upper Peninsula*, pp. 167-168.
128. *E.M.J.*, XXIII (1877), 396.
129. *Ibid.*, p. 272.
130. *Ibid.*, XXII (1876), 397.
131. *Ibid.*, LVI (1893), 312.

CHAPTER III: The Struggle for Domestic and World Leadership, 1885-1904

1. Reflections of author.
2. Channing Clapp, of Calumet and Hecla, Letters dated March 23, 1886; January 2, 1886; September 18, 1888.

THE STRUGGLE FOR LEADERSHIP 245

3. See Table 8, p. 203.
4. See Table 12, p. 215.
5. Hore, p. 213.
6. Baltic Mining Company, 1897; Champion Mining Company, 1899; and Trimountain Mining Company, 1899.
7. Hore, p. 213.
8. Of the large producers considered in the last chapter, only the Central was obliged to close down during this period as a result of the exhaustion of its mineral body.
9. Although the proportion of Michigan output contributed by Calumet and Hecla declined rapidly after 1899, the great conglomerate mine continued to hold its position as a dividend payer. In 1904 about 74 per cent of the dividends paid in the district came from Calumet and Hecla. See Table 12, p. 215, and Table 15, p. 230.
10. See Table 11, p. 212, and Fig. 7, p. 196. These productivity figures are somewhat misleading as a measure of success of technological change in maintaining worker output in the face of increasing mining difficulties, since from about 1897 to 1901 they are pulled down sharply by heavy employment on development work.
11. Report of the Directors of the Calumet and Hecla Mining Company for the year 1893. Also, *E.M.J.*, LVIII (1894), 348; LXIV (1897), 128.
12. Stevens, *The Copper Handbook for 1904*, V, 278.
13. Report of the Directors of the Quincy Mining Company for the years 1901 and 1903; Rickard, p. 64.
14. *E.M.J.*, XLII (1886), 128. The Tamarack was obliged to introduce this innovation since its property lay over an extension of the conglomerate lode at great depth.
15. *The Copper Handbook*, V, 282.
16. *E.M.J.*, L (1890), 360; LI (1891), 98; LIV (1892), 86.
17. *Ibid.*, L (1890), 360; LI (1891), 215.
18. Rickard, p. 63.
19. In the case of the Calumet and Hecla, where the decline of copper content was most marked, mill productivity (annual output divided by the number of mill workers) increased by about 14 per cent. The contrast with underground developments is very marked. In 1883 underground employment was about 3.3 times as large as mill employment. By 1904 the ratio had risen to about 5.8 to one.
20. *The Copper Handbook*, I, 189.
21. *Ibid.*, V, 284; Rickard, p. 126.
22. *E.M.J.*, XXXVIII (1884), 19; XLII (1886), 209.
23. *Ibid.*, XLIX (1890), 687; LVI (1893), 496.
24. *The Copper Handbook*, V, 634. Compounding means superimposing low pressure above the high-pressure steam cylinders, thus giving maximum power to both the up and down stroke.
25. *The Copper Handbook*, V, 218, 284, 677, 749. Apparently Michigan was late in adopting the Wilfley concentrating tables. Richter speaks of them as a major milling improvement of the early nineties ("Copper-Mining Industry," p. 262).
26. *E.M.J.*, LII (1891), 275.
27. Report of the Directors of the Quincy Mining Company for the year 1903.

28. Three other factors affecting the industry's ability to lengthen its period of vitality will be discussed later in this chapter — consolidation of properties, integration into smelting, and the copper price boom at the turn of the century.

29. The important Michigan lodes were much more scattered than those, for example, at Butte. The Baltic lode lay some twenty-odd miles south of the Calumet lode, in what was virtually a wilderness until several years after the mines had been established.

30. Such seems to have been the case during this period. The high prices of 1888–1890 and 1899–1901 set off development programs lasting a year or two after prices had fallen. Analysis indicates the unlikelihood of this being just an effort to increase output to take advantage of current high prices.

31. For a description of the financial atmosphere of Boston copper circles, see Thomas W. Lawson, *Frenzied Finance* (New York: Ridgway-Thayer, 1905), pp. 226–232.

32. The Tamarack was the only company besides Calumet and Hecla to work the conglomerate lode extensively. There is a presumption that if more companies had been able to buy into the lode, the rate of exploitation would have been more rapid and profits less substantial.

33. In 1896 there were 6,598 shareholders in Lake Superior copper companies; by 1904 the total had reached 22,714. These figures are largely explicable in terms of an increase in the number of companies, but even in the case of such closely held shares as those of the Calumet and Hecla and the Quincy, the number of shareholders increased by about 50 per cent. Whereas about 35 per cent of the shares of Calumet and Hecla had been held under the various family names in 1875 (Shaw-Agassiz-Higginson and Cabot), gradual sale had reduced family holdings to about 14 per cent by 1899 (*The Copper Handbook*, V, 877; *Copper Manual*, p. 339).

34. *E.M.J.*, LI (1891), 149.

35. *Ibid.*, LVI (1893), 648.

36. *The Copper Handbook*, II, 76.

37. *E.M.J.*, LIX (1895), 87.

38. *Ibid.*, LXVIII (1899), 768.

39. *Annual Report . . . Mineral Statistics of Michigan*, 1897–98, p. 141. The merger was effected by increasing the number of Osceola shares from 50,000 to 100,000 — 25,000 of which went to Kearsarge and Iroquois shareholders, and 16,000 to Tamarack Junior shareholders, leaving 9,000 in the Osceola treasury.

40. *The Copper Handbook*, III, 160, 181, 345, 375, 382; V, 873–875.

41. Early Calumet and Hecla dividends played a part in giving these men a successful start in Michigan copper. Horatio Bigelow, the father of Albert, was associated with Shaw in establishing mining on the conglomerate lode, and in 1888 J. W. Clark Company was listed as owning 900 shares of Calumet and Hecla stock.

42. Richter, "Copper-Mining Industry," p. 269. The Michigan mines contributed 25,661,000 pounds of this total and the Montana mines, 60,746,000. In the same year Calumet and Hecla produced about 20 per cent of United States output.

43. The Bigelow-Lewisohn interests established the Isle Royale Consolidated Copper Company in 1899 and reopened the Ahmeek property in 1902.

44. Apparently the connection between the Stanton and Paine interests did not extend to every new enterprise begun by each group. In 1903–04 John Stanton

served on the Board of the Trimountain with William A. Paine as President; Paine served on the Board of the Baltic with Stanton as President; and no member of the Stanton group was on the Board of the Champion. The Phoenix, Mohawk, Wolverine, Atlantic, Winona, and Michigan were considered Stanton mines, but Paine served on the Board of the Mohawk, Atlantic, and Winona.

45. For output of individual companies, see Hore, pp. 208–213.
46. *E.M.J.*, XLII (1886), 129.
47. *Ibid.*, LIV (1892), 182. Also Cooper, p. 46.
48. *E.M.J.*, LII (1891), 171.
49. *Ibid.*, LIX (1895), 123.
50. Cooper, p. 47.
51. *E.M.J.*, LII (1891), 54.
52. *The Copper Handbook*, V, 508.
53. *E.M.J.*, LXVI (1898), 706.
54. *The Copper Handbook*, V, 551.
55. Not only was manufacturing done at the Lake end, but the Lewisohns owned very large refineries for Western ore at Perth Amboy, New Jersey (*Copper Manual*, II, 261).
56. Calumet and Hecla and the Tamarack were owners of very extensive timber land. Deep mining on the conglomerate lode required an enormous amount of timbering (*The Copper Handbook*, I, 174).
57. *The Copper Handbook*, V, 287.
58. The cost savings from owning smelters was fairly substantial. Rickard points out that the ordinary custom charge for smelting in 1904 was about $7.75 per ton and that the Quincy was doing its own furnace work for about $5.25 (Rickard, p. 142).
59. *The Copper Handbook*, I, 194.
60. *Ibid.*, V, 218, 635.
61. See Table 8, p. 203.
62. *Ibid.*
63. *E.M.J.*, LXVIII (1899), 389.
64. *The Mineral Industry in 1900* (New York: The Scientific Publishing Company, 1901), IX, 192.
65. Table 12, p. 215.
66. See Table 13, p. 223.
67. *Mineral Industry*, IX, 191; XI, 167.
68. *Ibid.*, VI, 204; *E.M.J.*, LXIX (1900), 4.
69. Fig. 9, p. 201.
70. *Mineral Industry*, VIII, 179.
71. Calumet and Hecla Files, letter dated April 7, 1885.
72. *Ibid.*, letter dated November 25, 1885.
73. *E.M.J.*, XLI (1886), 452.
74. *Ibid.*, 380; Richter, "Copper-Mining Industry," p. 257.
75. *E.M.J.*, XLII (1886), 84, 103. Calumet and Hecla believed the stoppage at the Anaconda was for the purpose of driving transportation and wage rates down — a sort of girding of loins (Calumet and Hecla Files, letter dated September 1, 1886).
76. *Ibid.*, letter dated December 10, 1886.
77. *Ibid.*, letter dated January 5, 1887.

78. *Ibid.*, letter dated April 16, 1887.
79. *Ibid.*, letter dated May 5, 1887.
80. *Ibid.*, letter dated April 19, 1887.
81. Some idea of the kind of competitive atmosphere which characterized the copper industry of this period can be gleaned from the fact that, for several months, Calumet and Hecla suspected agents of the Anaconda of setting fire to their mine, and Pinkertons were put on the trail of the culprits (Calumet and Hecla Files, letter dated March 16, 1888).
82. *Ibid.*, letter dated January 26, 1886.
83. *Ibid.*, letter dated July 2, 1886.
84. *Ibid.*, letter dated October 25, 1887.
85. E. B. Andrews, "The Late Copper Syndicate," *Quarterly Journal of Economics*, III (1888–89), 509.
86. A copy of this contract is in the Calumet and Hecla incoming "Letters to the President" file for 1888. Also, a letter in the outgoing file dated December 22, 1887, gives further particulars.
87. Andrews, p. 509.
88. *E.M.J.*, XLV (1888), 370. The Anaconda played a lone hand until late in the history of the Syndicate.
89. Calumet and Hecla Files, letter dated November 21, 1888.
90. *Ibid.*, letter dated July 15, 1888.
91. *Ibid.*, letter dated November 21, 1888.
92. *E.M.J.*, XLV (1888), 206.
93. M. A. Abrams, "The French Copper Syndicate," *Journal of Economic and Business History*, IV (1931–32), 419; Andrews, p. 512.
94. *E.M.J.*, XLVII (1889), 61; Richter, "Copper-Mining Industry," p. 258.
95. *E.M.J.*, XLVI (1888), 322–323.
96. Calumet and Hecla Files, letter dated June 15, 1889.
97. Pettengill, dissertation, p. 108.
98. *E.M.J.*, XLVII (1889), 473.
99. Calumet and Hecla Files, letter dated May 18, 1889.
100. *Ibid.*, letters dated July 15, July 25, August 6, and August 9, 1889.
101. *E.M.J.*, XLVIII (1889), 39, 155, 192, 213. The negotiations had actually reached a point where all Lake copper was to be sold through one agency and all other U.S. copper through a second, with production regulated by quotas, exports limited to a set amount, and prices fixed.
102. Calumet and Hecla Files, letters dated October 2 and September 24, 1889.
103. Calumet and Hecla Files, letters dated August 12 and August 21, 1891. By this time, an association of United States producers to hold U.S. above world prices was useless since the Tariff Act of 1890 had reduced the ingot duty to 1.25 cents a pound and that of 1894 placed unmanufactured copper on the free list.
104. Relationships had become very cordial following the breakdown of the Syndicate, and in April of 1890 Haggin had approached Calumet and Hecla, apparently with a merger proposal (Calumet and Hecla Files, letter from Livermore to Haggin, dated April 30, 1890).
105. *Ibid.*, letter dated November 3, 1891.
106. *Ibid.*, letter dated December 10, 1891.
107. *Ibid.*, letter dated December 15, 1891.
108. *Ibid.*, letter dated December 8, 1891, from Livermore to Haggin.

THE STRUGGLE FOR LEADERSHIP 249

109. *Ibid.*, letters dated December 30, 1891, and February 19, March 7, April 21, May 2, and June 13, 1892.
110. *Ibid.*, letter dated June 22, 1892.
111. *Ibid.*, letter dated July 13, 1892, from Livermore to Aldrich.
112. U.S. Department of Commerce and Labor, Bureau of the Census, Special Reports, "Mines and Quarries, 1902," p. 498.
113. Calumet and Hecla Files, box marked "Copper Statistics."
114. *Ibid.*, letters dated September 22 and October 13, 1892.
115. *Ibid.*, letter dated May 16, 1893. Apparently the Rio Tinto was also in on the private agreement (Letter dated June 23, 1893).
116. *Ibid.*, letter to William E. Dodge, dated October 24, 1894.
117. *Ibid.*, letters dated May 17 and May 18, 1895.
118. *Public Laws of the State of Michigan*, No. 225, approved July 1, 1889, pp. 331–332. In spite of this law, the big Lake producer was reported as having closed down three of its smelting furnaces in July of 1892 "as one of the results of the agreement of the copper producers to restrict their production" (*E.M.J.*, LIV [1892], 38).
119. Calumet and Hecla Files, letter dated May 16, 1896.
120. *Ibid.*, letter dated February 25, 1896.
121. *Ibid.*, letters dated February 7 and March 10, 1899.
122. *Ibid.*, letter dated April 28, 1899.
123. Lawson, p. 254.
124. *Ibid.*, p. 283.
125. The Parrot Silver and Copper Company, the Washoe Copper Company, and the Colorado Smelting and Mining Company.
126. Calumet and Hecla Files, letter dated May 19, 1899.
127. This second section of the amalgamation was formally launched in April of 1901 when the Boston and Montana and the Butte and Boston were merged with the other companies. The story of how Bigelow lost control of his Butte properties is a chapter in copper history by itself. According to C. B. Glasscock, Bigelow's private fortune of ten million dollars and his Globe National Bank of Boston had already been wrecked by court fights over apex claims with F. Augustus Heinze when the Standard Oil group took over his Montana interests. (*The War of the Copper Kings* [Indianapolis: Bobbs-Merill, 1935], p. 155.)
128. The companies included were the Anaconda, Boston and Montana, Butte and Boston, Washoe, United Verde, Old Dominion, Arizona, Utah Consolidated, Tamarack, Isle Royale, Arcadian, and Osceola (*Commercial and Financial Chronicle*, LXX [1900], 284).
129. Murdoch, p. 185; *E.M.J.*, LXVI, July 2, 1898.
130. Stevens wrote that Lawson had control of the Trimountain as late as 1902–1903 (*The Copper Handbook*, V, 774).
131. *Copper Manual*, II, 48.
132. Calumet and Hecla Files, letter dated June 5, 1900.
133. *Ibid.*, letters dated April 24, June 11, and July 27, 1900.
134. *Ibid.*, letter dated June 19, 1900.
135. *Ibid.*, letter dated November 28, 1900.
136. *Mineral Industry*, X, 175.
137. Richter, "Copper-Mining Industry," p. 272.
138. Calumet and Hecla Files, letter dated October 14, 1901.

139. *Ibid.*, letters dated November 20, and November 22, 1901.
140. Murdoch, p. 171.
141. Calumet and Hecla Files, letter dated December 13, 1901.
142. *Mines and Quarries in 1902*, pp. 476–477.
143. *The Copper Handbook*, I, 185.
144. *Mineral Industry*, XI, 168.
145. Rickard, p. 63.
146. *Copper Manual*, II, 31–35.
147. James R. Finlay, *The Cost of Mining* (New York: McGraw-Hill, 1909), p. 164.
148. The Osceola got 18.7 pounds per ton in 1904, and the Quincy was down to 1.27 per cent around 1880 (*The Copper Handbook*, V, 632; *Mineral Industry*, VIII, 162).
149. *The Copper Handbook*, V, 250.
150. *Ibid.*, p. 313. The special Census Report of 1902 shows average per cent of copper in ore for western mines as 4.29, and for Michigan mines as 1.43 (*Mines and Quarries in 1902*, p. 483).
151. *E.M.J.*, XLIV (1887), 104, 212, 391; XLV (1888), 311; XLVI (1888), 468, 529; *The Copper Handbook*, V, 280.
152. *The Copper Handbook*, V, 676.
153. Calumet and Hecla Files, letter dated March 7, 1892.
154. *Ibid.*, letter from Agassiz to Livermore, dated April 30, 1894.
155. *Ibid.*, letter dated October 4, 1895.
156. *Ibid.*, for examples see: letters dated February 19, and June 24, 1897; June 9, and June 20, 1898; May 9, and June 24, 1899; and February 4, 1902.
157. *Mines and Quarries in 1902*, p. 479.
158. Calumet and Hecla Files, letter dated January 27, 1900.
159. *Copper Manual*, II, 35.
160. *Mines and Quarries in 1902*, p. 478.
161. Anaconda and the Boston and Montana had electrolytic refineries and Bessemer converters in operation at their Montana works by 1893 (Pettengill, dissertation, pp. 147, 167).
162. Richter, "Copper-Mining Industry," p. 260.

CHAPTER IV: Labor and the Community to 1904

1. The Michigan District around 1900. Rickard, p. 20.
2. The Michigan District around 1900. Murdoch, p. 158.
3. *Mines and Quarries in 1902*, p. 475.
4. An eight-hour day for miners became law in Montana in 1901, in Utah in 1898, and in Colorado in 1899 (*E.M.J.*, LXV [1898], 276; LXVII [1899], 389; Robert G. Raymer, *A History of Copper Mining in Montana* [Chicago: Lewis Publishing Co., 1930], pp. 71–72). The Western miner had much more political power than did his Michigan counterpart, in part because of constant political jockeying among the mine owners and operators. For numerous examples, see Glasscock, *The War of the Copper Kings*.
5. *The Mineral Industry in 1893*, II, 244.
6. Murdoch, p. 151.

LABOR AND THE COMMUNITY TO 1904

7. James Fisher, "Michigan's Cornish People," *Michigan History Magazine*, XXIX (1945), 379.
8. Jackson Report, p. 436.
9. Jenkin, p. 326.
10. Fleischmann, pp. 21–22.
11. Report of the Amygdaloid Mining Company for the year 1863.
12. *P.L.M.G.*, July 11, 1863.
13. *Ibid.*, October 15, 1864.
14. *Ibid.*, February 4, 1865, and December 3, 1864.
15. *History of the Upper Peninsula*, pp. 253, 323, 517. (Ontonagon, 254; Keweenaw, 119; Houghton, 460.)
16. *P.L.M.G.*, May 16, 1863; June 27, 1863.
17. *Ibid.*, June 27, 1863; January 11, 1865.
18. *Ibid.*, September 10, 1864; May 13, 1865.
19. *Ibid.*, December 3, 1864.
20. For examples, see *P.L.M.G.*, April 19, 1866; Report of the Central Mining Company for the year 1864, and that for the year 1865.
21. Swineford, p. 70.
22. *Ibid.*, p. 72.
23. Jenkin, pp. 137–140.
24. *The Mining Magazine*, I (1853), 294.
25. *P.L.M.G.*, October 4, 1862, and Report of the National Mining Company for 1862.
26. Horace Greeley, Letter in the *Weekly Tribune*, July 17, 1874, p. 1; also, St. John, p. 110.
27. *The Mining Magazine*, I (1853), 294; III (1854), 426.
28. Swineford, p. 65; *The Mining Magazine*, IV (1855), 188. Here was a speculative incentive for the *working classes* of the district.
29. *P.L.M.G.*, September 20, 1866.
30. *Ibid.*, April 22, 1865.
31. Report of the Central Mining Company for the year 1865.
32. *P.L.M.G.*, May 5, 1865.
33. *Ibid.*, May 17, 1866.
34. *The Mining Magazine*, I (1853), 294.
35. *P.L.M.G.*, August 19, 1865.
36. Horace Greeley, Letter in the *Weekly Tribune*, p. 1, col. 3. The hours of work for underground men are not portal to portal, but rather time spent at the working surface.
37. *The Mining Magazine*, I (1853), 294.
38. *P.L.M.G.*, September 30, 1865; May 3, 1866.
39. Emerson David Fite, *Social and Industrial Conditions in the North during the Civil War* (New York: Macmillan, 1910), p. 200. Also, Aldrich Report, IV, 1568–1569.
40. *P.L.M.G.*, various months, 1866.
41. *Ibid.*, March 18, 1865.
42. St. John, pp. 82–83.
43. *History of the Upper Peninsula*, p. 135.
44. In 1853 with surface rates about $28 a month and underground rates $34, board and lodging were around $9 (*The Mining Magazine*, I [1853], 295).

45. The Cliff had a population of 1,443 in 1860 (Report of the Pittsburgh and Boston Mining Company for 1860).
46. *P.L.M.G.*, August 2, 1862.
47. Jenkin, p. 141.
48. *The Mining Magazine*, I (1853), 294.
49. *P.L.M.G.*, September 24, 1864.
50. *Ibid.*
51. Annual Report of the Minesota Mining Company for the year 1852.
52. *The Mining Magazine*, I (1853), 294.
53. *P.L.M.G.*, February 7, 1863.
54. State of Michigan, *House Documents*, 1865, Testimony of Samuel W. Hill, House Document No. 10, Relative to the Organization of Four Additional Townships in Keweenaw County.
55. Fite, p. 184.
56. *P.L.M.G.*, April 26, 1866.
57. United States Censuses of 1870 and of 1880.
58. Jenkin, p. 322.
59. *P.L.M.G.*, August 14, 1873; *E.M.J.*, XVI (1873), 107.
60. United States Census of 1900, "Population," p. 760.
61. Egleston, "Copper Mining on Lake Superior," p. 280.
62. The Michigan Census of 1874 gives some interesting data on wages for day laborers in various sections of the state. Houghton County figures were $2.00 a day without board and $1.50 with board which was on a par with rates prevailing in Wayne County. Corresponding figures for the state as a whole were $1.68 and $1.19 (pp. 687–688).
63. Tiger Mining District, Arizona, in 1882; Globe District, Arizona, in 1881; and Colorado in 1881.
64. *E.M.J.*, LII (1891), 542; LVI (1893), 611–612; LIX (1895), 542.
65. Census of the State of Michigan for 1894, p. 570.
66. *E.M.J.*, LVIII (1894), 62; LXI (1896), 381; and *Mines and Quarries in 1902*, pp. 400, 474.
67. *History of the Upper Peninsula*, p. 299.
68. *P.L.M.G.*, June 13, 1878.
69. *Ibid.*, March 21, 1867; *History of the Upper Peninsula*, p. 257.
70. *E.M.J.*, XVI (1873), 107.
71. *P.L.M.G.*, October 1, 1874.
72. *Ibid.*, August 26, 1875.
73. Census of the State of Michigan for 1874, p. 405. Certain categories stand out:

Wood choppers	291
Farmers	133
Smelting works	75
Hunters	60
Store clerks	53
Merchants	46
Butchers	32

74. *P.L.M.G.*, August 10, 1876.
75. Calculating what this policy meant in terms of additional cost to the companies would be all but impossible. Interest on the money invested in land and

THE INDUSTRY AND MATURITY 253

housing would both be important factors. Much of the out-of-pocket expenditure was made by the industry in a period of youthful vigor and paid returns in lower labor rates long after mining maturity had been reached.

76. Report of the Directors of the Calumet and Hecla Mining Company for the year 1895. In 1904 Calumet and Hecla owned 1,200 houses and about 1,000 plots of land upon which employees had built houses (*The Copper Handbook*, V, 283).
77. *Ibid.*, I, 158.
78. Murdoch, pp. 153–155.
79. *Ibid.*, p. 153.
80. Calumet and Hecla Files, letter dated August 20, 1901.
81. *Ibid.*, letter dated June 7, 1894, from the Superintendent of Railroads to Alexander Agassiz.
82. Report of the Directors of the Central Mining Company for 1872.
83. *P. L. M. G.*, May 9, and May 16, 1872.
84. *Ibid.*, May 30, 1872.
85. *Ibid.*, June 27, 1872.
86. *Ibid.*, January 15, 1874.
87. Calumet and Hecla Files, letter dated January 5, 1874.
88. Calumet and Hecla Files, letters dated March 29, June 8, June 10, June 13, June 22, 1887.
89. *Ibid.*, letter dated June 13, 1887.
90. *Ibid.*, letters dated July 17, and July 22, 1890.
91. *Ibid.*, letter dated February 9, 1891.
92. As early as 1891 the directors of Calumet and Hecla commented upon personnel difficulties due to a large increase in the number of non-English speaking workers. Too much can be made of the point, but productivity of labor began to fall at about the time this new stream of immigration reached its peak.
93. *E.M.J.*, XLIX (1890), 503, 713, 719; L (1890), 14, 107.
94. *Ibid.*, LXXVII (1904), 303, 497.
95. Reports of the Directors of the Calumet and Hecla Mining Company for the years 1893 and 1894; *E.M.J.*, LIII (1892), 648; LIV (1892), 253; LVI (1893), 196; LVIII (1894), 326; LX (1896), 430; and LXIV (1897), 646. The extent of the "status-nationality" rift is shown by the fact that when the Finnish trammers struck at Calumet and Hecla in August, 1893, 600 of the Cornish miners acted as deputy sheriffs to maintain order and protect company property.
96. Murdoch wrote an extremely interesting chapter on this problem of a benevolent paternalism in the Copper Country (*Boom Copper*, pp. 151–159). The workers received very substantial material advantages, and the disadvantages were mainly intangibles. Certainly the situation did not represent "a democratic way of life" and ultimately made the transition to a different order of things more costly and bitter.
97. Calumet and Hecla Files, letter dated May 15, 1900.
98. *Ibid.*, letter dated August 21, 1901.

CHAPTER V: The Industry and Maturity, 1905–1918

1. Reflection of the author.
2. See Fig. 4, p. 195, and Table 8, p. 203.

3. See Fig. 4, p. 195, and Table 6, p. 197.

4. For output of individual companies during the years 1905–1914, see Hore, pp. 213–215; and for the period 1915–1918, see F. G. Pardee, Part I: "Metallic Minerals," Michigan, Department of Conservation, *Mineral Resources of Michigan*, Geological Survey Division, Publication 37, Geological Series 31 (Lansing, 1928), pp. 30–31.

5. The decline would have been even more marked if it had not been for important technological improvements which made possible low cost treatment of tailings (accumulated waste sands from the mills) beginning in 1915. By 1918 Calumet and Hecla was recovering over nine million pounds of copper annually from this source.

6. The Champion was the only one of the Baltic Range mines which showed large increases. Both the Baltic and the Trimountain were already declining.

7. For dividend payments, see Fig. 5, p. 195, and Table 12, p. 215.

8. In arriving at these percentages dividends received from other mining companies have been deducted from the Calumet and Hecla total. The company began buying shares in the Bigelow properties in 1905.

9. See Table 7, p. 202.

10. See Fig. 9, p. 201.

11. *The Mineral Industry in 1905*, XLV, 147.

12. For copper prices see Table 8. Too much can be made of a comparison of average copper prices in the two periods, since there were also substantial differences in wholesale prices and general costs. Using the period 1883–1904 as a base for both copper prices and wholesale prices (summing annual averages and dividing by the number of years), corresponding averages for the period 1905–1918 show a rise in copper prices of 38 per cent and for wholesale prices of 25 per cent. Such results can hardly be called conclusive. Nonetheless it is in such periods of lagging general costs that real money is made in a basic industry. (The wholesale price index used is that of Warren and Pearson.)

13. Taking the peak 1907 figure in every case, the shares of the various important companies were valued as follows:

Calumet and Hecla	$100,000,000.
Copper Range	40,950,000.
Osceola	18,100,000.
Quincy	14,800,000.
Tamarack	10,200,000.
Total	$184,050,000.

14. *Appraisal of Mining Properties of Michigan by the State Board of Tax Commissioners* (Lansing, 1911). The old specific tax on output had been repealed in 1891, and for a number of years the industry had been subject to the general property tax — valuation being determined by the average price of the outstanding shares of each company as shown on a set date of each year by the Boston Stock Exchange. The assessment figure was then adjusted to provide for different classes of mines: dividend paying, operating but not dividend paying, and nonoperating. Finlay rejected the stock market system as a reflection of speculators' hopes rather than taxable value; declared that companies which had paid no dividends during the previous five years had no taxable value; and based his assessment on the future value of a series of dividends, reduced to present value by the annuity method. Average costs were determined for

each company; ore reserves were estimated; and 14 cents was chosen as a conservative estimate of average copper prices for the next ten years. His assessments ran as much as 50 per cent below current market evaluations of most companies. (Higher market judgments as to the future price of copper may account for some of the difference. Finlay's estimate of 14 cents proved much too conservative.)

15. See p. 70; Calumet and Hecla was a major exception.
16. *Appraisal of Mining Properties*, p. 26.
17. *E.M.J.*, CIII (1917), 13. Calumet and Hecla invested heavily in other mines of the district following 1905, but the funds used were not new stock market money, and the investments did not result in the establishment of a large number of new mines.
18. The porphyry mines were very low copper content deposits, usually lying near the surface and thus subject to mining by cutting off the overlay and removing the ore with power shovels. They are also known as "open-cut mines."
19. Production data for the porphyry mines from H. A. C. Jenison, "Costs of American Copper Production, 1909–1920," *E.M.J.*, CXIII (1922), 442–445.
20. *Ibid.*, p. 443. All costs are included except Federal Income Tax, Excess Profits Tax, and depletion. Precious metal content is credited to costs. Other studies indicate that the difference in 1917–18 may have been overstated. A Federal Trade Commission Report, which included a charge for depletion, showed Michigan costs in 1918 as 17.6, the porphyry mines 14.9, and the industry average as 16.2. However, the only difference seems to be one of degree (Cost Reports of the Federal Trade Commission, *Copper* [Washington, 1919], pp. 13, 17).
21. The wholesale price index is included as a very general measure of the cost trend for mining supplies, etc. Admittedly, its usefulness for that purpose is very limited, but the fact that it corresponds with the Michigan wage trend through 1916 gives it an added significance. (See Fig. 3, p. 137.)
22. *Public Acts of the State of Michigan*, No. 105, Act approved May 10, 1905, pp. 153–154.
23. Richter, "Copper-Mining Industry," p. 688. Coöperation of any sort with Bigelow controlled properties seemed to be out of the question. In 1905 Calumet and Hecla invested $8.6 million in cash and notes in these holdings (William H. Weed, *The Mines Handbook*, XIV [New York: Stevens Copper Handbook Company, 1920], 759).
24. *Bigelow v. Calumet and Hecla Mining Company*, CC Mich. 155 F, April 12, 1907, pp. 869–881.
25. Calumet and Hecla, Osceola, Quincy, Tamarack, and Wolverine.
26. *Bigelow v. Calumet and Hecla*, CC Mich. 167 F, October 3, 1908, pp. 704–720; *Bigelow v. Calumet and Hecla*, Federal Register 167, Circuit Court of Appeals, February 18, 1909, pp. 721–741.
27. *E.M.J.*, LXXXVII (1909), 514.
28. Calumet and Hecla, Osceola, Ahmeek, Allouez, Tamarack, Centennial, Seneca, Laurium, La Salle, and Superior. (Total production in 1910: 124 million pounds, or 56 per cent of the district's output.)
29. *E.M.J.*, XCI (1911), 117, 733, 785. An even more inclusive consolidation had taken place at Butte in 1910.
30. *Ibid.*, p. 746.

31. *Ibid.*, p. 733. There is an interesting parallel here between financial opposition to a cost reducing merger and labor opposition to important technological improvements, which were being introduced at the same time.

32. *The Mineral Industry in 1912*, XXI, 162.

33. *The Mines Handbook*, XIII, 829.

34. *E.M.J.*, XCIII (1912), 530–531 and 534. Merger is particularly important for milling, since it is all but impossible to get correct estimates of copper content of rock by sampling before milling.

35. Report of the Directors of the Calumet and Hecla Mining Company for the year 1917.

36.

Percentage of Calumet and Hecla Control	Company	Output (In pounds)
100	Calumet and Hecla	67,988,357
49.5	Ahmeek	24,851,235
34.0	Osceola	15,191,647
22.0	Isle Royale	15,442,508
41.0	Allouez	7,071,218
46.0	Centennial	2,492,857
50.0	White Pine	3,273,680
51.0	La Salle	1,832,665
50.0	Superior	1,676,446

In addition, Calumet and Hecla had practically complete ownership of the Frontenac, organized in 1906 to hold the Central and other mineral lands totaling over 22,000 acres, and the Manitou, organized in 1906 to hold 38,693 acres of old mineral lands.

37. During the period 1905–1918 Calumet and Hecla dividends totaled $64.4 million, about 25 per cent of which had come from dividends of companies in which shares were held.

38. Copper Range Report for the year 1911.

39. *Michigan Reports*, March, 1918, pp. 58–75, *Paine v. Saulsbury*. Full integration of the Baltic lode mines was made particularly difficult since the St. Mary's Mineral Land Company owned 50 per cent of the Champion stock. Copper Range owned the other 50 per cent.

40. *The Mines Handbook*, XIV, 820.

41. Y. S. Leong and others, *Technology, Employment, and Output per Man in Copper Mining*, Works Project Admin., National Research Project, Report No. E-12 (Philadelphia, 1940), p. 109.

42. The light drill was particularly useful for overhead work.

43. Report of the Directors of the Quincy Mining Company for the year 1912.

44. *Strike in the Copper Mining District of Michigan*, 63 Cong., 2 Sess., Senate Document 381 (Washington, 1914), p. 28.

45. See Table 11, p. 212.

46. The Calumet and Hecla annual reports of this period give average cost data (no allowance for depletion) for Calumet and Hecla, Ahmeek, Allouez, Osceola, and Isle Royale. Cost reduction at the Champion mine was most startling — cost per pound dropped to .063 in 1915 or a cent and a half a pound below the previous record — that of 1910. Part of the explanation in this case was more highly selective mining.

47. In part the lag in adopting power tramming was due to unwillingness of mine managers to experiment with a technique which required changing mining plans and concentrating stoping.

48. *Conditions in Copper Mines of Michigan,* hearings before House subcommittee, 63 Cong. (1914), part III, p. 1336.

49. Claude T. Rice, "The Baltic Method of Mining," *E.M.J.*, XCIII (1912), 847.

50. Calumet and Hecla Reports for 1917 and 1918. An improved storage battery locomotive became available in 1916 (Leong, p. 124).

51. Calumet and Hecla completed its Chilean Mill regrinding plant in 1909.

52. C. H. Benedict, "Developments in Lake Superior Milling," *E.M.J.*, CVIII (1919), 7.

53. *The Mines Handbook,* XIII, 908. The Quincy had Hardinge grinders in operation by 1916; the Mohawk began introducing them in 1912.

54. C. H. Benedict, "Calumet and Hecla Reclamation Plant," *Proceedings of the Lake Superior Mining Institute* (Ishpeming, 1925), XXIV, 71. Leaching means to dissolve copper out of sands, the solvent used in this case being a water solution of ammonium carbonate. See also C. H. Benedict and H. C. Kenny, "Ammonia Leaching of Calumet and Hecla Tailings," *Transactions of the American Institute of Mining and Metallurgical Engineers* (New York, 1924), LXX, 595.

55. *Ibid.*

56. Slimes are exceedingly small particles of rock and mineral, held in suspension in water.

57. Leong, p. 171. Froth flotation employs the principle of separating mineral particles from waste by causing them to become attached to air bubbles rising to the surface of a solution. The mineral particles are then scooped off mechanically (*E.M.J.*, CVII [1919], 50–51).

58. The most serious mill losses had always been from the finely disseminated conglomerate rock, and successful efforts at retreatment during this period were only made on the rich conglomerate sands. The Calumet and Hecla plant consisted of a dredge, a shore pumping station, a regrinding plant, a leaching plant, and a flotation plant.

59. *The Mines Handbook,* XIII, 945.

60. *Appraisal of Mining Properties,* p. 166.

61. United States Census of 1910, *Mines and Quarries in 1909* (Washington, 1913), XI, 49, 101, and 111.

62. This pay level works out to just about the rates Finlay gave for the period 1901–1907 when the shifts are divided by nine hours for a Michigan day and eight hours for a Butte day.

63. For population data see Table 14, p. 228.

64. The phrase "labor shortage" is not too meaningful, and all that is meant by it, at this stage of the discussion, is that the mine managers made frequent complaints of inability to hire men at wages the companies were willing to pay.

65. The shortage after 1910 is rather surprising since the presumption is that an industry which suddenly stops growing will have a period of abundant labor supply.

66. *Senate Document* 381, 63 Cong., 2 Sess., p. 11.

67. Copper and iron wages were obtained from various sections of the United States Census of 1910. Daily figures were obtained by dividing total wage payments by average number of employees and the resultant annual figure by 312. The Detroit figure appeared in the report of a New York engineering firm which did an economic survey of the Michigan copper district around 1920 (The Stevenson Corporation, *Industrial Survey of Houghton, Keweenaw and Baraga Counties*, Hancock: Chambers of Commerce of Houghton, Hancock, Calumet, and Lake Linden, no date).

68. Rice, "Copper Mining at Lake Superior," *E.M.J.*, XCIV (1912), 127.

69. *Ibid.*, 418.

70. The question arises as to why there was not an immediate wage increase. The answer is not altogether clear, but it seems possible that the operators had become used to immigration as a labor source and expected large numbers of new men at any moment.

71. A report by the Immigration Commission in 1911 showed average Michigan copper wages as $2.31 per day; Michigan iron, $2.36; and Minnesota iron, $2.38. The iron companies went over to an eight-hour day for underground men in 1912 which made the hourly wage difference a significant one (*Reports of the Immigration Commission*, 61 Cong., 2 Sess., Senate Document 633, 1911, Part 17, pp. 165, 516, and 552).

72. *E.M.J.*, XCVII (1914), 61–62.

73. *Senate Document* 381, 63 Cong., 2 Sess., p. 7.

74. Paul F. Brissenden, *The I.W.W. — a Study of American Syndicalism* (New York: Columbia University, 1919), pp. 149–151.

75. In 1910 Western Federation leaders at Butte were complaining about the "unfair advantage" of Michigan companies over those at Butte (*E.M.J.*, XC [1910], 440).

76. *Senate Document* 381, 63 Cong., 2 Sess., p. 40. It seems fairly certain that, on the eve of the strike, the Federation did not represent a majority of the district's copper mining employees.

77. On the basis of a sample of 5,632 workers, the Immigration Commission concluded that over 80 per cent of the workers in the industry were foreign born (*Senate Document* 633, 61 Cong., 2 Sess., p. 87).

78. G. R. Taylor, "The Clash in the Copper Country," *The Survey*, XXXI (1913), 128; Innis Ward, "The Reasons Why the Copper Miners Struck," *The Outlook*, CVI (1914), 248.

79. In Michigan the men were underground 10 to 11 hours a shift, including an hour off for lunch, for five days a week — while on Saturday a shorter day was required, particularly for miners. In Butte, the men were underground $8\frac{1}{2}$ hours plus the time required to return to the surface, which usually meant about nine hours with a half hour off for lunch. In actual working time, most Michigan mines were probably doing well to get an average of $8\frac{1}{2}$ hours a day, or about an hour more than the Montana mines (*Senate Document* 381, 63 Cong., 2 Sess., p. 10).

80. *Ibid.*

81. For the year ending June 30, 1913, Calumet and Hecla and its subsidiaries paid miners an average wage of $3.28 a day, whereas the rest of the companies paid average wages of $2.74. Corresponding figures for trammers were $2.75 and $2.40 (*Senate Document* 381, 63 Cong., 2 Sess., pp. 13, 15).

82. The report was published by a local businessmen's group which strongly favored the employers. The figures were attacked by the Union with vigor, but it seems probable that differences between Michigan and Montana costs of living were substantial, particularly for rent and fuel (Copper Country Commercial Club, *Strike Investigation* [Chicago, 1913], p. 31; *The Miners' Bulletin*, August 14, 1913). The *Bulletin* was a local newspaper set up by the Union, which was published in Hancock and appeared about 30 times during the period August to November, 1913.

83. *Acts of the Legislature of the State of Michigan*, No. 163, Act approved April 25, 1911, pp. 263–267. The first inspection act had been passed in 1887, but had provided for appointment of the Inspectors by the County Boards of Supervisors.

84. *Ibid.*, No. 10, Act approved May 20, 1912, pp. 20–39.

85. *Ibid.*, No. 59, Act approved April 11, 1913, pp. 83–84.

86. For an interesting article showing the full extent of the benevolent paternalism the union faced, see Claude T. Rice, "Labor Conditions at Calumet and Hecla," *E.M.J.*, XCII (1911), 1235–1239.

87. The State Legislature recognized this feature of the new device, and passed an act in 1912 which required drill operators to be no more than 150 feet from other workers (*Acts*, No. 220, approved May 7, 1913, p. 437).

88. *Conditions in Copper Mines of Michigan*, testimony of lawyer for Calumet and Hecla, Hearings, p. 1347.

89. Taylor, "Clash in the Copper Country," p. 135; *The Mines Handbook*, p. 247.

90. *Senate Document* 381, 63 Cong., 2 Sess., pp. 135–136.

91. *Acts of the Legislature of the State of Michigan*, No. 173, Act approved April 26, 1911, pp. 29–30.

92. *Ibid.*, No. 254, Act approved May 1, 1911, pp. 435–436.

93. *Senate Document* 381, 63 Cong., 2 Sess., p. 8.

94. *Ibid.*, p. 73.

95. *Ibid.*, p. 8.

96. *Ibid.*, p. 122.

97. *Ibid.*, p. 66.

98. *Conditions in Copper Mines of Michigan*, Hearings, p. 1483.

99. *The Miners' Bulletin*, September 9 and 27, August 9 and 23, 1913.

100. *The Congressional Record*, 63 Cong., 2 Sess., LI, 1501–1503; 1567–1569; 1693–1694; 2395–2399; 2400–2409.

101. The union saw the handwriting on the wall and was anxious to have mediation. Various attempts by the governor and the Department of Labor were rejected by the companies (*Senate Document* 381, 63 Cong., 2 Sess., pp. 167–180). An interesting sidelight on the strike was an article by Frank W. Taussig, in which he declared that company ability to pay, as shown by dividends, was not relevant to a discussion of whether or not wages should be increased (*The Survey*, February 14, 1914, pp. 612–613).

102. Murdoch, pp. 224–228; *The Survey*, January 3, 1914, XXXI, 368.

103. Father Peter E. Dietz, "A Catholic View of the Copper Miners' Strike," *The Survey*, January 31, 1914, XXXI, 522.

104. Copper . . . Club, *Strike Investigation*, p. 59.

105. In April, 1914, the *E.M.J.* commented upon a general movement in the Upper Peninsula of Michigan to get rid of the Finnish Socialists as an undesirable class of labor (XCVII [1914], 793).

106. Walter E. Hopper, "The Michigan Copper Industry in 1914," *Michigan Geological and Biological Survey*, Publication 19, Geological Series 16, Lansing, 1915, p. 166.

107. *E.M.J.*, XCVII (1914), 61–62; Reports of the Directors of the Quincy Mining Company for 1915 and 1916; Report of the Directors of the Mohawk Mining Company for 1914.

108. Acts of the Legislature of the State of Michigan, No. 230, Act approved May 14, 1915, pp. 387–392.

109. *The Iron Age*, October 3, 1918, p. 847.

110. The evidence indicating the development of an extremely substantial differential seems conclusive — just how much the Michigan increase amounted to would be difficult to say since it is probable that the smaller companies were obliged to increase wages more rapidly than was Calumet and Hecla. The Quincy reports show a 45 per cent increase between 1915 and September of 1918.

111. Calumet and Hecla Annual Reports for 1917 and 1918.

112. United States Census of 1920, *Mines and Quarries in 1919* (Washington, 1922), XI, various pages. In an inflationary period such as the War years, the Michigan worker had one compensating advantage: some of his living costs, such as housing, were stabilized against the general price trend by the tradition of company provision of housing services, etc., at a nominal fee.

113. *E.M.J.*, XCIX (1915), 880.

114. *Ibid.*, CIV (1917), 277, 450, and 856.

115. *Ibid.*, p. 277.

116. A strike attempt by I.W.W. members was easily broken up in July, 1917 (*E.M.J.*, CIV [1917], 321). Since the strike of 1913 the Copper Country had become a very unhealthy place for union men (*E.M.J.*, XCIX [1915], 425 and 632).

117. *Ibid.*, CV (1918), 939.

118. *Ibid.*, CVI (1918), 683.

119. *Ibid.*, pp. 42 and 237.

120. *Ibid.*, p. 683. An examination of the *Mining Gazette* during these years shows the shortage reaching a peak from March through August, 1918.

121. For annual averages, see Table 8, p. 203. For monthly high-low quotations, see *The Mines Handbook*, XIII, 218–220.

122. William B. Dana Co., *The Financial Review for 1917* (New York, 1918), pp. 90–91.

123. W. R. Ingalls, "How the Metals Are Sold — Copper," *E.M.J.*, XCIII (1912), 889. By 1912 practically all U.S. copper was sold direct to manufacturers by five big agencies and Calumet and Hecla. (The Quincy and the Stanton mines sold their own metal.) The big agencies were the United Metals Selling Company, the American Smelting and Refining Company, Phelps-Dodge, American Metal Company, and L. Vogelstein.

124. *E.M.J.*, CV (1918), 56.

125. Cost Reports, Federal Trade Commission, p. 7. The original report for 1917 was not made public, but one of the most interesting facets of the Commission's approach was to ignore depletion costs as calculated for the income tax and to adopt a method based upon actual cost of mineral land divided by tons of ore

in reserve plus tons mined. Depreciation cost as presented by the companies was accepted at face value (*Ibid.*, pp. 10–11).

126. *Mineral Resources of the United States in 1917*, p. 784.

127. Lewis Kennedy Morse, "The Price-Fixing of Copper," *Quarterly Journal of Economics*, XXXIII (1918–19), 93. *The Engineering and Mining Journal* reported that the price was satisfactory even to the small Lake producers who were on the margin of the industry with average costs of about 20 cents a pound (CIV [1917], 620).

128. *Ibid.*, CIII (1918), 56 and 1016.

129. Morse, p. 90.

130. Cost Reports, Federal Trade Commission, p. 21.

131. *Mineral Resources of the United States in 1917*, p. 733.

132. The western producers have been bitterly criticized for profiteering. (For example, see Harvey O'Connor, *The Guggenheims: The Making of an American Dynasty* [New York: Covici-Friede, 1937], pp. 377–379.) According to Alex Skelton, stabilization did have a very marked effect — profits of the western porphyrys declined a third in 1917 and by about another third in 1918 ("Copper," *International Control in the Non-Ferrous Metals* [New York: Macmillan, 1937], p. 403).

133. The concept of a field as a "marginal" section of an industry is a dangerous one since there were very real cost differences as between firms within the Michigan industry; however, it is probably a close enough representation of the actual facts to be useful in considering the war allocation problem.

134. The state of maturity of the industry probably made this much certain, even without price control. The high prices of 1916 did not set off such a movement.

135. *E.M.J.*, CVII (1919), 50–51.

136. *Ibid.*, CV (1918), 1107.

137. An attempt was made to hold labor in the district by government decree but proved completely ineffective (*E.M.J.*, CVI [1918], 466–467).

138. Miners' wages in western copper fields increased by from 34 to 54 per cent between 1915 and 1918.

	Sept., 1915	Sept., 1916	Sept., 1917	Sept., 1918
Butte	$3.83	$4.42	$5.50	$5.50
Arizona	4.10	5.32	5.60	5.50
Utah	3.25	3.50	4.50	5.00

(*Monthly Labor Review*, 1919, VIII, 177–179.)

139. *Premium Price Plan for Copper, Lead, and Zinc*, report of Senate subcommittee, 79 Cong., 2 Sess. (Washington, 1946), pp. 74–75.

140. The Federal Trade Commission set the Michigan investment in 1918 at about $76.3 million. It is not completely clear from the report how this figure was arrived at, but it probably represented investment by the existing companies in mineral lands at cost price, less an allowance for depletion. As of 1918, the Commission showed the Michigan district earning (not paying) 21.26 per cent, the porphyry coppers 33.98, and the rest of the industry 25.82. The Trade Commission included depletion and depreciation as costs in making these estimates (pp. 18–19).

141. The Federal Income and Excess Profits taxes were a relatively minor factor in reducing profit levels. In 1917 Calumet and Hecla declared $8.5 million

out of earnings, retained $3.6 million as a reserve for depletion and depreciation, and paid $979,000 in income and excess profits taxes. It seems probable that more of the burden of holding profits down should have been carried by taxation.

142. Costs were increasing all along the line. The price of coal delivered at Lake Superior ports doubled between 1916 and January of 1918 (*E.M.J.*, January 12, 1918, p. 56), and railroad freight rates on copper to New York were increased by about 25 per cent in June, 1918, and another 7 per cent in October (from information compiled for this study by the Duluth, South Shore and Atlantic Railroad Company, Marquette, Michigan).

CHAPTER VI: Michigan Copper Mining in Decline, 1919–1938

1. Alex Skelton, commenting on the copper situation during the mid-twenties ("Copper," *International Control in the Non-Ferrous Metals*), p. 459.
2. Initially the causal relationship was from wartime overinvestment to efforts at control. Later, the two factors interacted as the control tended to preserve conditions of overinvestment in the world industry.
3. See Table 8, p. 203, and Fig. 4, p. 195.
4. For production of individual companies during the years 1919–1926, see Pardee, pp. 31, 32. For the years 1927–1938, see various volumes of *The Mines Register* (New York: Atlas Publishing Company).
5. For Calumet and Hecla production from tailings, see Annual Reports of the Directors of the Calumet and Hecla Consolidated Mining Company.
6. See Table 10, p. 208.
7. See Table 11, p. 212.
8. For dividend payments by years, see Table 12, p. 215.
9. In this connection, it should be remembered that Calumet and Hecla invested heavily in other mines throughout the years 1905–1918.
10. In all comparisons of market valuation, the highest figure quoted in each year has been used.
11. Whether or not relatively low copper prices prolonged the life of the industry is a different question. It might be contended that lower prices slowed down the rate of exploitation, but this ignores the factor of selective mining, which was a consequence of a worsening price-cost relationship, and reduced the life of the available mineral bodies.
12. For annual figures on world output by countries, see U.S. Department of the Interior, *Mineral Resources of the United States*, various annual volumes; also Table 6, p. 197.
13. The period 1910–1914 was used as a base for both copper prices and the wholesale price index (Warren and Pearson), and annual average figures were summed and divided by the total number of years. If the entire period, 1905–1918, is used as a base, the results are even more conclusive. The comparison is significant in so far as the wholesale price index may be taken as a measure of general mining costs.
14. There was much talk during this period of the great "economies of scale" which were being discovered by the western producers. It seems probable that these represented, in large part, new technology and organizational methods, but it is also probable that lower copper prices were shaking the big western companies out of prewar psychology of contentment with things as they were.

15. U.S. Temporary National Economic Committee, *Investigation of Concentration of Economic Power*, Hearings on Cartels, 76 Cong., Part 25 (Washington, 1940), p. 13117. Of the total, 839 million pounds were held by producers, 630 million by governments, and 808 million lay in the form of scrap on the European battle fields.

16. The Webb-Pomerene Act permitted domestic producers to act in combination in the export trade without fear of prosecution under the Sherman Anti-Trust Act, as long as the domestic price was not affected.

17. Some of the stocks were carried by an extremely neat financial arrangement. Bonds were issued to the public with the copper as security — the result being that producers received an advance payment of 10 cents a pound on 400 million pounds of copper hanging over the domestic market (*E.M.J.*, CXI [1921], 374-375).

18. See Table 6, p. 197. The two major foreign owned properties (Rio Tinto and Katanga) increased output in 1919 (Skelton, p. 418).

19. Elizabeth S. May, "The Copper Industry in the United States," *International Control in the Non-Ferrous Metals*, p. 561; Skelton, p. 438.

20. As a result of consolidations and purchases, two interest groups — Anaconda and Guggenheim-Kennecott — were clearly dominant in world copper by this date (C. P. Fuller, "The Copper Cartel," *Harvard Business Review*, VI [1928], 327).

21. *Ibid.*, p. 323. Also Pettengill, "United States Foreign Trade in Copper, 1790-1932," p. 436.

22. It seems clear that the cartel leaders did not intend to push the price as high as 24 cents in 1929. However, their control system had so reduced manufacturers' stocks that they were unable to increase output fast enough to hold the price down against an upsurge of demand.

23. May, p. 544. It is difficult to arrive at an idea of what would have happened without controls during the years 1919-1923. Certainly the disorganization of the industry would have been terrific, which does not mean that such an adjustment would *necessarily* have been undesirable.

24. Hearings on Cartels, testimony of Arthur Notman, consulting engineer, p. 13547. There is some question, however, if the condition of overinvestment would have corrected itself in any short period of time under a "freely competitive situation," since the production balance was shifting rapidly during these years from the United States to enormous new fields in Chile and Africa, and political factors, usually connected with empire building and defense, were often overruling purely economic considerations.

25. It is interesting to note the reversal of position from an earlier day, 1878-1880, when an umbrella held by Michigan producers was exploited by the newly established western mines.

26. It might be argued that such would have been the case even without the cartel, in that costs of curtailing output at deep underground properties are relatively high and there is no real evidence to show that (around price) the marginal cost curve of "low-cost" producers (in this case western open-cut mines) is rising more rapidly than that of "high-cost" producers. Ignoring for a moment the future cost idea, the argument concerning the slope of marginal cost curves probably does not apply in this case since the price fall was extremely substantial (from 24.7 cents in 1918 to 12.5 in 1921) and the difference in output reaction very

great. The argument concerning future cost of a scale of current output remains as a possible qualification to any conclusion reached concerning the effects of cartel action. Again, however, it should be held in mind that the really important future cost differences arise when it is a question of complete shutdown, not of partial curtailment.

27. The most serious effect might have been on the labor supply situation. As will be shown later in this section, the district's labor force was unusually mobile in this period as a result of exceptional employment opportunities in the new Detroit industrial area. Even the partial shutdown of 1921 resulted in a tight labor situation for the remaining years of the decade. Total shutdown for several years might have been catastrophic.

28. *E.M.J.*, CXII (1921), 345.

29. Besides the special interest presented hereafter, the Michigan producers were doubtless thinking in terms of dumping, although such a position was never taken publicly. For the most detailed statement of their case, see F. Paine, "Will a Tariff on Copper Help or Injure the United States?" *E.M.J.*, CXVII (1924), 796–799.

30. *The Mineral Industry, Its Statistics, Technology, and Trade* (New York: McGraw-Hill), XXXVII, 141. *E.M.J.*, CXVIII (1924), 350, 622; CXX (1925), 345. The rise of the Detroit automobile industry may have been the underlying reason for the shift.

31. Skelton, p. 424. This implies that the domestic copper market was by no means "perfect." Two factors which were probably increasing the competition for specific customers were, first, the elimination of the broker and direct sales to fabricators, and, second, a growing tendency for producers to integrate into the fabricating end of the business, following the example set by Anaconda in 1922.

32. *E.M.J.*, CXVII (1924), 445, 576, 661, 796–799; CXVIII (1924), 870.

33. Somewhat higher copper prices by late 1924 also served to knock the props out from under the tariff campaign (*E.M.J.*, CXIX [1925], 380).

34. Skelton, p. 425.

35. *Ibid.*, p. 459.

36. Average daily wages in Michigan copper mining were running about $4.00 in 1924 as compared with about $2.36 in 1913. For the 1924 figure, see United States Bureau of Labor Statistics, *Bulletin* 573, January, 1933, p. 3. For other cost comparisons, see Skelton, p. 429; *E.M.J.*, CIX (1920), 1382, and CX (1920), 497.

37. With the possible exception of the years 1928 and 1929, the companies were no longer able to make enough money to cover depletion costs, and the dividends paid out during the twenties should be thought of primarily as a salvaging of capital. Even the Mohawk, which was the lowest cost Michigan producer, was not meeting depletion costs in 1925 (*The Mineral Industry*, XXIV, 202).

38. *E.M.J.*, CXVI (1923), 251; *Mines Register for 1936*, p. 192.

39. *Mines Register for 1940*, p. 204.

40. *E.M.J.*, CXIX (1925), 455; Quincy Report for 1925.

41. *E.M.J.*, CIX (1920), 625; CXX (1925), 465; U.S. Bureau of Mines, *Mining Methods and Practices in the Michigan Copper Mines* (Washington, 1929), p. 154.

42. Quincy Report for 1925; *Mining Congress Journal*, October, 1931, p. 35.

43. *E.M.J.*, CXIV (1922), 785; *The Mineral Industry*, XXXIII, 190; and Copper Range Report for 1921.

44. *E.M.J.*, CXXV (1928), 1065.
45. Quincy Report for 1928; Copper Range Report for 1929; and Mohawk Report for 1929.
46. *Mining Congress Journal*, October, 1931, p. 66.
47. *Ibid.*, p. 50.
48. For comments upon this change in mining method, see *E.M.J.*, CXIV (1922), 785; CXVI (1923), 648; CXVII (1924), 66 and 818.
49. *Mineral Industry*, XXXIII, 191. At the Mohawk the copper yield of rock stamped was running about 15 pounds per ton stamped in the years 1911–1913, while by 1927–1929 the average was around 30. *Some* of the increase can be accounted for by improvements in mineral treatment (Annual Reports of the Mohawk Mining Company).
50. See Table 11, p. 212.
51. Various sections of the *Report of the United States Tariff Commission*, No. 29, Washington, 1932, in accordance with Senate Resolution No. 434, dated February 5, 1931.
52. These estimates are based on the data presented in Table 10, p. 208. It seems probable that about 14,000 men were employed by the industry in 1918, and perhaps 8,000 by late 1922.
53. The Records of the Superintendent of the Poor of Houghton County show 158 men unemployed in 1921.
54. *E.M.J.*, CXIV (1922), 652, 1107.
55. *Ibid.*, CVII (1919), 676, 852.
56. *Ibid.*, CXIV (1922), 119.
57. Data for the 1919 and 1929 figures were taken from the United States Census Reports, volumes entitled *Mines and Quarries*. The source for the 1924 figures is Bureau of Labor Statistics, *Bulletin* 573, January, 1933, p. 3.
58. It is interesting to note that Calumet and Hecla was advertising for workers in the Iron Country in 1926 (*E.M.J.*, August 7, 1926, p. 229). Data on average daily wages which were furnished by one of the mining companies for this study show a rise from $4.04 in 1923 to $4.62 in 1929 with leveling offs in 1925 and 1928.
59. See Table 10, p. 208.
60. *Monthly Labor Review*, October, 1938, p. 866. The figures shown in this article are for miners' wages only.
61. The industry was extremely interested in the immigration question and was able to get a small number of English and German workers after 1923 when the immigration law was amended to permit entry of certain classes of skilled labor (*E.M.J.*, CXVII [1924], 224; CXVIII [1924], 68 and 746). Sault Ste. Marie was the port of entry for foreign workers heading for the Copper Country, and in 1924 the *E.M.J.* reported that the Michigan copper industry had lost its permit to import German workers in consequence of opposition by trade unions at Sault Ste. Marie (CXVII [1924], 535).
62. For dividend payments by companies and years, see Table 12, p. 215.
63. *E.M.J.*, CXI (1921). The idea seemed to be that fabricating was more profitable than mining.
64. *Ibid.*, CXVI (1923), 251.
65. The reasons why such a development did not take place are not altogether clear. The Stevenson Corporation in its economic survey of the district about 1920 declared that the companies feared they would be boycotted from the raw

material market if they went into fabricating (*Industrial Survey of Houghton, etc.*, p. 91). As for the rest of the domestic industry: Anaconda purchased the American Brass Company in 1922, the Detroit Copper and Brass Rolling Mills in 1927, and incorporated the Anaconda Wire and Cable Company in 1929. Kennecott acquired a large fabricator in 1929 — the Chase Company — and in 1930 Phelps-Dodge obtained a majority interest in the Nichols Copper Company (May, pp. 548–550).

66. Skelton, p. 343.

67. May, p. 463; Hearings on Cartels, p. 557; Skelton, p. 386. Skelton says that the steady increase in world stocks of mined copper is pushing the primary industry into a marginal role (pp. 384–386).

68. Stabilization of copper prices against the general trend of business conditions was bad policy from almost any viewpoint. The reasons behind it are not altogether clear, although it seems probable that the big producers were attempting to protect fabricators, in which they held large interests, who were heavily stocked with high-price copper (Skelton, p. 441).

69. In April, 1932, the governors of 12 states, including Michigan, petitioned Congress for a tariff (*Commercial and Financial Chronicle*, April 9, 1932, p. 2619).

70. It is difficult to understand why these companies did not put up more opposition to the tariff since their South American properties were to be the greatest sufferers. Apparently a combination of factors was involved — a belief that they could find adequate European markets for South American copper, labor and local government pressure from their domestic fields, and the knowledge that bankruptcy of large domestic competitors would be more likely to result in elimination of debt burden than a cessation of output (May, p. 578).

71. Skelton, p. 479.

72. *Mineral Industry for 1939*, p. 92.

73. United States National Recovery Administration, *Codes of Fair Competition*, Washington, 1934, Vol. IX, approved code No. 401.

74. May, p. 586.

75. *Ibid.*, p. 588.

76. *Commercial and Financial Chronicle*, October 6, 1934, p. 2143; November 10, 1934, p. 2906.

77. May, p. 589.

78. *Mineral Industry*, XLIV, 113.

79. Adelaide Walters, "The International Copper Cartel," *Southern Economic Journal*, XI (1944), 138.

80. *Business Week*, October 22, 1938, p. 39.

81. Unless, of course, the wartime shortage of copper is to be taken as evidence of "underinvestment" in the industry. In a world ridden by wars and trade cycles the problem of sensible resource allocation becomes inordinately complex.

82. Throughout the worst years of the depression Calumet and Hecla kept the reclamation plants closed and worked the richest sections of the conglomerate mine. Cost data contained in annual reports indicate that the reclamation plants were the lower cost units. Apparently in terms of future cost — both to maintain underground workings and to preserve labor — it was considered desirable to work the mine, even at a loss. Closure of the reclamation plants should probably be thought of as a speculation on the future price of copper, similar to an inven-

tory problem. The company also carried heavy inventories of refined copper during these years.

83. For consumption and import-export figures, see Table 7, p. 202.
84. For the most lucid expression of the Michigan case, see a series of articles by Benjamin D. Noetzel: "The Right to Live," *Evening Copper Journal*, Hancock, Mich., February 26, 1932; "The Social Significance of a Tariff on Copper," Houghton *Mining Gazette*, February 7, 1932; "Does American Copper Need a Protective Tariff," Houghton *Mining Gazette*, January 24, 1932.

A representative of Calumet and Hecla spoke for both Calumet and Hecla and Phelps-Dodge before the Tariff Commission in November, 1931 (*E.M.J.*, November 9, 1931, p. 429).

85. *Congressional Record*, Senate, 72 Cong., 1 Sess., pp. 7527, 10975.
86. Ira B. Joralemon, *Romantic Copper — Its Lure and Lore* (New York: Appleton-Century, 1936), p. 66.
87. May, p. 584.
88. *Ibid.*, p. 587. Calumet and Hecla capacity was set at 100 million pounds and Copper Range at 35 million. Their mine production in 1929 had been, respectively, 90.3 million and 23.8 million.
89. Various company reports for 1934.
90. Calumet and Hecla, Copper Range (Champion), Mohawk, Seneca, Isle Royale, and Quincy.
91. "Michigan Copper Survey," p. 25. Profits were shown for the years 1935–1937.
92. Calumet and Hecla annual reports. If copper on hand is counted as a current asset, the decline was nothing like as severe, since the quantity carried increased enormously and was valued at cost, including depreciation and depletion.
93. For employment figures upon which these estimates are based, see Table 10, p. 208.
94. Calumet and Hecla Report for 1931.
95. *E.M.J.*, CXXXIII (1932), 406; Copper Range Report for 1932.
96. Spencer R. Gordon and Associates, "Public Relief in Three Michigan Counties" (unpublished study at the University of Michigan, 1940), p. 151.
97. Calumet and Hecla Report for 1930.
98. Copper Range Report for 1930.
99. *E.M.J.*, CXXXIV (1933), 43.
100. Copper Range Report for 1937.
101. *The Mines Register for 1940*, p. 204. In 1937 Copper Range interests purchased the Calumet and Hecla stockholdings in the Isle Royale Company and reopened the mine.
102. "Michigan Copper Survey," p. 20.
103. *E.M.J.*, CXXXV (1934), 275.
104. Calumet and Hecla annual reports.
105. See Table 11, p. 212.
106. Gordon, p. 149.
107. Houghton County Steering Committee, *An Invitation to the U.S. Veterans Administration to Locate the Upper Peninsula 500-Bed General Veterans Hospital in Houghton, Michigan* (Houghton, May 8, 1945), p. 47.
108. Gordon, p. 197.

109. Calumet and Hecla and Copper Range reports for 1934. In other sections of the industry the minimum was set as indicated below.

	Hourly Rate	
	Surface	Underground
Michigan	32.5 cents	37.5 cents
Southwestern	30.0	45.0
Northwestern	40.0	47.5

110. "Michigan Copper Survey," p. 16.
111. *E.M.J.*, CXXXII (1931), 424.
112. Not only did this represent, in the long run, a shift to a different form of enterprise, but in the short run it probably represented a further attempt to save capital invested in the mines by providing a fabricating outlet for copper.
113. Calumet and Hecla reports.
114. This is, of course, a cost which never fully appears in the price of the product, although a good deal of it is usually met and written off by the companies years before in their expenditures for community betterment.
115. Occasionally there may be temporary advantages, such as short periods of extremely cheap labor.
116. United States Census data.
117. All figures were obtained from published reports of the United States Bureau of the Census except that for males, age 18–44, in 1940, which was provided by the Bureau for this study.
118. Statement of James MacNaughton of Calumet and Hecla, *E.M.J.*, CIX (1920), 1375; *Industrial Survey of Houghton*, etc., p. 39.
119. For the reversal of the trend in 1934, see Fig. 6, p. 196.
120. Gordon, p. 156.
121. *The Milwaukee Journal*, July 15, 1934, p. 5. In describing depression conditions — which, without question, were very bad — care must be taken to avoid giving a "rural slums" picture. If a man had to be unemployed, it may well be that Houghton County was a fairly wise choice of location. Housing continued to be fairly good; gardening was always possible; and it must not be forgotten that community equipment had been laid down for a much larger number of people. For a brighter side of the depression days, see Murdoch, pp. 236–237.
122. Furnished from files by the Houghton County Welfare Board.
123. Gordon, p. 197.
124. "Michigan Copper Survey," pp. 21–22.
125. *Statement, Statistics, and other Pertinent Material Bearing on the Welfare and Relief Problem in Houghton County, Submitted on Behalf of the Board of Supervisors of Houghton County to the State Social Welfare Commission, August 29, 1940.*
126. United States Census of 1940, *Population*, Volume II, Part III, p. 809.
127. *Industrial Survey of Houghton*, etc., p. 16.
128. Statement of James MacNaughton of Calumet and Hecla, *E.M.J.*, CIX (1920), 1375.

CHAPTER VII: World War II and the Future

1. For output figures, see Fig. 4, p. 195, and Table 8, p. 203.
2. Production of individual companies during these years was taken from company reports.

3. See Fig. 6, p. 196, and Table 10, p. 208.

4. In 1940 Phelps-Dodge sent an employment agent to Calumet, and 200 workers took jobs and left for Jerome (*Report of Proceedings of the National War Labor Board Hearings at Denver, Colorado*, March, 1943, p. 31).

5. The 1939 comparison was made from data in the United States Census Report, *Mines and Quarries in 1939*. The Census of 1939 showed Michigan copper workers receiving about 30 per cent less than the average wage in U.S. copper mining, whereas by August of 1941 the differential was about 37 per cent (U.S. Department of Labor, Bureau of Labor Statistics, *Wage Structure of the Non-Ferrous Metals Industry*, Bulletin No. 729 [Washington, 1943], p. 11).

6. *Mining Gazette*, December 2, 1939.

7. *Premium Price Plan*, etc., pp. 75–76.

8. *E.M.J.*, CXLI (1940), 84.

9. *Ibid.*, CXLII (1941), 80.

10. Report of the Copper Range Company for 1941; *Premium Price Plan*, etc., p. 40.

11. See Table 6, p. 197.

12. See Table 7, p. 202.

13. *Ibid.*

14. The most significant difference between World War I experience and that of World War II was not, as is generally assumed, the Premium Price Plan, but rather the contrasting developments which took place before the plan was applied. As in so many sectors of our economy, there was substantial unused capacity available in copper mining (due to the depression), and an enormous increase in output was possible with very little increase in price. Such had not been the case in the years immediately preceding our entry into the first World War.

15. U.S. War Production Board, *Wartime Production Achievements and the Reconversion Outlook* (Washington, October 9, 1945), p. 53.

16. U.S. Department of the Interior, Bureau of Mines, *Minerals Yearbook for 1943*, p. 138; *Premium Price Plan*, etc., pp. 49–50.

17. *Minerals Yearbook for 1943*, pp. 134–135.

18. There is the possibility that the phrase "disappointments in the domestic showing" is an ill-chosen one. As will be indicated later in this section, the most advantageous place to obtain copper was abroad; and the situation as it developed in late 1943 may have reflected an easing of the shipping shortage which permitted a desirable letup in attempts to get more copper from higher cost domestic sources.

19. *E.M.J.*, CXLVI (1945), 88. Earnings of the major copper companies were stabilized or falling in 1942 and 1943 and declining rapidly thereafter.

20. Social Security Board, "Employment, Payrolls, Hours and Earnings in Copper Mining." This is a continuous study distributed from time to time in mimeographed form.

21. Another factor may also enter: discrimination against large producers might be justified if it could be shown that they were much more highly mechanized (required proportionally less labor) and that wages were the cost item which was expected to rise in the immediate future.

22. *Survey of the Nation's Critical and Strategic Minerals and Metals Program*, preliminary report of Senate subcommittee, 78 Cong., 2 Sess. (Washington, 1944), pp. 12–13. According to the President of the International Union of Mine, Mill

and Smelter Workers, by the end of the war, 25 per cent of domestic output was being produced by mines receiving premiums while these same mines employed over 50 per cent of the labor in the industry (U.S. Congress, Senate, Hearings before the Subcommittee on Mining and Minerals Industry of the Special Committee to Study and Survey Problems of Small Business Enterprise [held at Helena, Montana, August, 1945], p. 8335).

23. *Survey of the Nation's Critical and Strategic Minerals* . . . ,p. 16.

24. Table 8, p. 203, and Fig. 4, p. 195.

25. The Quincy reclamation plant was an ideal war project. Labor requirements were small and technical assistance and excess equipment were furnished by Calumet and Hecla. Most of the capital was put up by the Metals Reserve Company, and the Quincy received 17 cents a pound for the product, 4 cents a pound of the 17 being deducted to liquidate the loan (*E.M.J.*, CXLIII [1942], 147; CXLV [1944], 74–78; CXLVII(2) [1946], 126).

26. Calumet and Hecla was the only company in the United States equipped to treat some of the wartime scrap. (Copper-coated steel scrap from bullet jackets, known as gilding metal, had to be treated by the ammonia leaching method.)

27. For a discussion of this scrap program, see *E.M.J.*, CXLVII(2) (1946), 138; and Calumet and Hecla Annual Reports for 1944 and 1945.

28. Between 1939 and 1944 average wages in the copper mining industry increased by about 50 per cent, while average wages in the Michigan section of the industry rose by 80 per cent or more. The absolute differential probably continued to be about the same, but percentage-wise it decreased substantially.

29. Hearings at Helena, Montana, p. 8377.

30. Table 10, p. 208.

31. *Mining Congress Journal*, February, 1947, p. 65. Apparently the labor situation never became as tight in the Michigan district as in the West. *The Engineering and Mining Journal* was highly critical of the War Labor Board decision increasing Michigan wages in 1943 (*E.M.J.*, CXLIV [1943], 120). It is probably true that there was no *immediate* necessity for such an increase in terms of labor allocation requirements.

32. By 1944 the companies were complaining of inability to maintain output because of labor shortage (Copper Range Report for 1944; Calumet and Hecla Report for 1944; *E.M.J.*, CXLV [1944], 118, and CXLVI [1945], 141).

33. Doubtless part of the explanation lies in a deterioration of the quality of labor.

34. See Table 11, p. 212.

35. See Table 12, p. 215.

36. It is rather interesting that the industry lost its protection at just the moment when it would have resulted in higher copper prices. Even more startling is the fact that Michigan and other producers who had been calling for retention of the tariff as late as October of 1946 came out favoring a temporary suspension in the spring of 1947. Fear of competition from other metals (mainly aluminum) was one factor in the policy shift. Also it seems probable that there was a deal made with certain fabricating interests exchanging support for tariff suspension for support of a long-run subsidy program (*E.M.J.*, CXLVII(2) [1946], 109, and April, 1947, p. 138; *American Metals Market*, April 17, 1947, and March 14, 1947).

37. The preliminary report of the Federal Trade Commission was reprinted in *American Metals Market*, beginning with the March 22, 1947 issue. The Com-

mission estimates world copper prices as 111 million tons in sight at prices of 15 cents a pound, about 26 per cent of which were in the United States.

38. There is an implication in the report that there may have been restriction in 1946 which took the form of intentional delay in settling labor disputes.

39. The Isle Royale continued to mine small quantities of copper until the price break of 1949.

40. When the President signed the Stockpiling Bill in July, 1946, he protested against the provision which interested marginal producers most — that, whenever possible, purchases for the stockpile would be made from domestic producers. The bill to extend the Premium Price Plan provided, in extremely vague terms, that conservation payments should be made when market price did not justify the development of marginal domestic resources, and that the materials so produced should be stockpiled and only released in times of severe copper shortage or national emergency.

41. An address by A. E. Peterman before the Michigan Congressional delegation on February 7, 1946, Washington, D. C.

42. Hearings at Helena, Montana, p. 8377.

43. *American Metals Market*, March 22, 1947.

44. *E.M.J.*, CXLVII(2) (1946), 111.

45. *Ibid.*, CXL (1939), 82; Calumet and Hecla Report for 1944; *E.M.J.*, CXLII (1941), 90. Copper Range purchased the Lake Copper Company, and Calumet and Hecla the Ojibway and Keweenaw Copper Companies.

46. *Mining Gazette*, June 12, 1946; Calumet and Hecla Report for 1942.

47. For a detailed account of the development of this program, see Calumet and Hecla Report for 1944.

48. The arrangement was that Calumet and Hecla would handle production at its Upper Michigan plants while the Harshaw Company marketed the products.

49. Calumet and Hecla Report for 1945.

50. *E.M.J.*, CXLIII (1942), 84; CXLVII(2) (1946), 11.

51. In August, 1949, the Department of Labor estimated that the ratio of permanent jobs to available workers was as unfavorable as 1 to 30 (*Daily Mining Gazette*, August 27, 1949).

52. The largest of these is the secondary copper department which employed about 108 men in late 1946 (*E.M.J.*, CXLVII[2] [1946], 111).

53. The survey is called *Report on Economic Surveys in Houghton and Keweenaw Counties*, by the Copper Country Committee for Economic Development, August 18, 1945.

54. *Daily Mining Gazette*, July 28, 1949.

55. *Ibid.*, August 27, 1949.

56. *Ibid.*, August 16, 1949.

57. *E.M.J.*, CXL (1939), 80.

58. The companies are unwilling to give up their land permanently to other industries, offering instead leases to desirable industrial and other tenants.

59. Since the end of the war the population of the district has increased markedly; it is too soon to say how permanent this reversal of the trend will be. Today there is a mild flurry of excitement over reports of 13 uranium strikes in the Upper Peninsula (*Daily Mining Gazette*, December 31, 1949).

60. *An Invitation to the United States Veterans Administration*, etc., p. 47.

61. Files of the Houghton County Welfare Board.

EPILOGUE

1. Relative slowness in exploitation did have certain advantages in the "orderliness" of the development of the field; an adequate transportation system, a substantial labor force, and much technical and geological experience had been acquired before some of the most important discoveries were made. In addition, new mines were usually able to shift labor and other resources from old mines which had passed their peak.

Bibliography

BOOKS

Agassiz, George R., ed. *Letters and Recollections of Alexander Agassiz, with a Sketch of His Life and Work.* Boston: Houghton Mifflin Company, 1913.

Ashley, Ossian D. *The Copper Mines of Lake Superior.* Hyde Park, Mass.: Norfolk County Gazette Press, 1873.

Brissenden, Paul F. *The I.W.W. — a Study of American Syndicalism.* New York: Columbia University Press, 1919.

Brown, Nicol and Charles C. Turnbull. *A Century of Copper.* London: Effingham Wilson, 1906.

Copper Handbook, The. See Stevens.

Copper Manual. See Houston.

Crawford, Mary C. *Famous Families of Massachusetts.* Boston: Little, Brown & Company, 1930.

Finlay, James R. *The Cost of Mining.* New York: McGraw-Hill Book Company, 1909.

Fite, Emerson David. *Social and Industrial Conditions in the North during the Civil War.* New York: Macmillan Company, 1910.

Glasscock, Carl Burgess. *The War of the Copper Kings.* Indianapolis: Bobbs-Merrill Company, 1935.

History of the Upper Peninsula of Michigan, The. Chicago: Western Historical Company, 1883.

Houston, D., & Co. *Copper Manual.* Vols. I and II. New York: D. Houston & Co., 1897 and 1899.

Hunter, J. C. *Yesterday and Today: A History of the Chicago and Northwestern Railroad System.* Chicago: 1910.

International Geological Congress. Washington, 1933. *Copper Resources of the World,* Vols. I and II. Menasha, Wis.: George Banta Publishing Company, 1936.

Jamison, James K. *This Ontonagon County*. Ontonagon: The Ontonagon Herald Company, 1939.

Jenkin, A. K. Hamilton. *The Cornish Miner: An Account of His Life Above and Underground from Early Times*. London: George Allen & Unwin, Ltd., 1927.

Joralemon, Ira B. *Romantic Copper — Its Lure and Lore*. New York: D. Appleton Century Company, 1936.

Knight, Charles Louis. *Secular and Cyclical Movements in the Production and Price of Copper*. Philadelphia: University of Pennsylvania Press, 1935.

Lathrop, William G. *The Brass Industry in Connecticut*. Shelton, Conn.: W. G. Lathrop, 1909.

Lawson, Thomas W. *Frenzied Finance*. New York: The Ridgway-Thayer Company, 1905.

Manual of Statistics Company. *The Manual of Statistics — Stock Exchange Handbook*. New York: Annual volumes from 1903 to 1917, inclusive.

Martin, John B. *Call It North County: The Story of Upper Michigan*. New York: Alfred A. Knopf, 1944.

Martin, Joseph G. *A Century of Finance: History of the Boston Stock and Money Markets, 1798–1897*. Boston: Washington Press, 1898.

May, Elizabeth S. "The Copper Industry in the United States," *International Control in the Non-Ferrous Metals*. Coypright by The Bureau of International Research, Harvard University and Radcliffe College. New York: Macmillan Company, 1937. Pp. 537–590.

Mines Handbook, The. See Weed.

The Mines Register (Successor to *The Mines Handbook* and *The Copper Handbook*). New York: Atlas Publishing Company.

Moore, Charles. *The History of Michigan*. Chicago: Lewis Publishing Company, 1915.

Murdoch, Angus. *Boom Copper: The Story of the First United States Mining Boom*. New York: Macmillan Company, 1943.

O'Connor, Harvey. *The Guggenheims: The Making of an American Dynasty*. New York: Covici-Friede, 1937.

Parsons, A. B. *The Porphyry Coppers*. New York: American Institute of Mining and Metallurgical Engineers, 1933.

Piggot, A. Snowden. *The Chemistry and Metallurgy of Copper*. Philadelphia: Lindsay and Blakiston, 1858.

Raymer, Robert G. *A History of Copper Mining in Montana*. Chicago: Lewis Publishing Company, 1930.

Rickard, T. A. *The Copper Mines of Lake Superior*. New York: The Engineering and Mining Journal, 1905.

Roberts, Warren A. *State Taxation of Metallic Deposits*. Harvard Economic Studies. Cambridge: Harvard University Press, 1944.

St. John, John R. *A True Description of the Lake Superior Country*. New York: W. H. Graham, 1846.

Skelton, Alex. "Copper," *International Control in the Non-Ferrous Metals*. Copyright by The Bureau of International Research, Harvard University and Radcliffe College. New York: The Macmillan Company, 1937. Pp. 363–536.

Smith, Hoval A. *American Copper Production and History of a Copper Tariff and Other Copper Tariff Details*. Published by the Arizona Copper Tariff Commission. Miami, Ariz.: Arizona Silver Belt, 1932.

Standard and Poor's Corporation. *Poor's Financial Record*. New York: Annual volumes from 1910 to date.

Stevens, Horace J. *The Copper Handbook*. Houghton, Michigan: Vols. I–XI, 1900–1912–13. *See also* Weed, William H., *The Mines Handbook*, and *The Mines Register*.

Swineford, Alfred P. *History and Review of the Copper, Iron, Silver, Slate, and Other Material Interests of the South Shore of Lake Superior*. Marquette: The Mining Journal, 1876.

Taussig, Frank W. *Principles of Economics*. New York: Macmillan Company, 1911.

Taussig, Frank W. Some Aspects of the Tariff Question. "Copper," pp. 161–170. Harvard Economic Studies. Cambridge: Harvard University Press, 1918.

The Mineral Industry, Its Statistics, Technology, and Trade. Annual Review Since 1892. New York: McGraw-Hill Book Company, 1911–, various dates. (1893–1910, Scientific Publishing Company.)

Warren, George F. and Frank A. Pearson. *Prices*. New York: J. Wiley, 1934.

Weed, William H. *The Mines Handbook: an Enlargement of the Copper Handbook*. New York: Stevens Copper Handbook Company, Vols. XI–XXI, 1912–13–1942.

Whitney, J. D. *The Metallic Wealth of the United States*. Philadelphia: Lippincott, Grambo & Company, 1854.

PERIODICALS

Abrams, M. A. "The French Copper Syndicate," *Journal of Economic and Business History*, IV (1931–32). 409–428.

Agassiz, George R., et al. "The Operations of the Calumet and Hecla Consolidated Copper Company," *The Mining Congress Journal*, October, 1931, pp. 468–565.

Andrews, E. B. "The Late Copper Syndicate," *Quarterly Journal of Economics*, III (1888–89), 508–516.

Benedict, C. H. "Calumet and Hecla Reclamation Plant," *Proceedings of the Lake Superior Mining Institute*, XXIV (1925), 68–88.

——— "Developments in Lake Superior Milling," *Engineering and Mining Journal*, CVIII (1919), 5–10.

Benedict, C. H. and H. C. Kenny. "Ammonia Leaching of Calumet and Hecla Tailings," *Transactions of the American Institute of Mining and Metallurgical Engineers*, LXX (1924), 595–610.

Blandy, John F. "Stamp Mills of Lake Superior," *Transactions of the American Institute of Mining Engineers*, II (1874), 208–215.

Chase, L. A. "Early Copper Mining in Michigan," *Michigan History Magazine*, XXIX (1945), 22–30.

Chase, L. A. "Early Days of Michigan Mining," *Michigan History Magazine*, XXIX (1945), 166–179.

Chase, L. A. "Michigan Copper Mines," *Michigan History Magazine*, XXIX (1945), 479–488.

Clarke, Robert E. "Notes from the Copper Region," *Harpers New Monthly Magazine*, March and April, 1853, pp. 433–448, 577–588.

Commercial and Financial Chronicle. New York, July, 1865, to date.

Cooper, James B. "Historical Sketch of Smelting and Refining Lake Copper," *Proceedings of the Lake Superior Mining Institute*, VII (1901), 44–49.

Daily Mining Gazette. Houghton, Michigan. (Successor to the *Portage Lake Mining Gazette.* Used extensively for recent developments.)

Dietz, Father Peter E. "A Catholic View of the Copper Miners' Strike," *The Survey*, XXXI (January 31, 1914), 521–522.

Egleston, T. Comments on article by C. M. Rolker, *Transactions of the American Institute of Mining Engineers*, V (1877), p. 610.

Egleston, T. "Copper Mining on Lake Superior," *Transactions of the American Institute of Mining Engineers*, VI (1879), 275–312.

Engineering and Mining Journal, 1864 to present. Vols. I–CXLVIII. (Weekly until 1930, bimonthly 1930 and 1931, monthly thereafter. New York. The majority of the issues contain material bearing on the history of the Michigan copper mining industry. Articles of special importance are listed separately in this bibliography.)

Fisher, James. "Michigan's Cornish People," *Michigan History Magazine*, XXIX (1945), 377–385.

―――― Unsigned article in *The 1924 Keweenawan*. Rochester, N. Y.: Du Bois Press, 1924, pp. 217–288.

Fuller, Carlton P. "The Copper Cartel," *Harvard Business Review*, VI (April, 1928), 322–328.

Ingalls, W. R. "How the Metals Are Sold — Copper," *Engineering and Mining Journal*, XCIII (1912), 887–890, 939–942.

Jenison, H. A. C. "Costs of American Copper Production, 1909–1920," *Engineering and Mining Journal*, CXIII (1922), 442–445.

Miners' Bulletin. A newspaper printed by the Western Federation of Miners. Hancock, Michigan. August to November, 1913.

Mining Congress Journal, October, 1931.

Mining Magazine. New York, monthly, 1853–1857. (Most of the issues contain material bearing on the history of the Michigan copper mining industry.)

Morse, Lewis K. "The Price-Fixing of Copper," *Quarterly Journal of Economics,* XXXII (November, 1918), 71–106.

Munroe, H. S. "The Losses in Copper Dressing at Lake Superior," *Transactions of the American Institute of Mining Engineers,* VIII (1880), 409–451.

Noetzel, Benjamin D. "Does American Copper Need a Protective Tariff," *The Mining Gazette.* Houghton, Michigan, January 24, 1932.

——— "The Right to Live," *Evening Copper Journal.* Hancock, Michigan, February 26, 1932.

——— "The Social Significance of a Tariff on Copper," *The Mining Gazette.* Houghton, Michigan, February 7, 1932.

Paine, F. W. "Will a Tariff on Copper Help or Injure the United States?" *Engineering and Mining Journal,* CXVII (1924), 796–799.

Pettengill, Robert B. "The United States Foreign Trade in Copper: 1790–1932," *American Economic Review,* XXV (1935), 426–441.

Portage Lake Mining Gazette. Houghton, Michigan. Weekly, 1858–1885. (Most of the issues are available at the Michigan College of Mining and Technology, Houghton, Michigan.)

Rice, Claude T. "The Baltic Method of Mining," *Engineering and Mining Journal,* XCIII (1912), 843–847, 897–902, 947–951.

——— "Copper Mining at Lake Superior," *Engineering and Mining Journal,* XCIV (1912), 119–124, 171–175, 217–220, 267–270, 307–310, 365–368, 405–407.

——— "Labor Conditions at Calumet and Hecla," *Engineering and Mining Journal,* XCII (1911), 1235–1239.

Richter, F. E. "The Amalgamated Copper Company: A Closed Chapter in Corporate Finance," *Quarterly Journal of Economics,* XXX (1915–1916), 387–407.

── "The Copper-Mining Industry in the United States, 1845–1926," *Quarterly Journal of Economics*, XLIV (1926–27), 236–291, 684–717.

Rivot, E. "Visit to the Lake Superior Region in 1854," *The Mining Magazine*, VI (1856), 28–37, 97–106, 207–212, 414–418.

Rolker, Charles M. "The Allouez Mine and Ore Dressing, as Practiced in the Lake Superior Copper District," *Engineering and Mining Journal*, XXIII (1877), 274–275, 294–296, 314–315, 335–336.

Taylor, G. R. "The Clash in the Copper Country," The Survey, XXXI (1913), 127–135, 145–149.

Van Pelt, J. Robert. "Boston and Keweenaw," Mining and Metallurgy, XXIX (1948), 370–378.

Walters, Adelaide. "The International Copper Cartel," *Southern Economic Journal*, XI (1944), 133–156.

Ward, Innis. "The Reasons Why the Copper Miners Struck," *Outlook*, CVI (January 31, 1914), 274–251.

REPORTS

Annual Report of the Commissioner of Mineral Statistics of the State of Michigan, 1877–1909.

Annual Reports of the Mine Inspector of Houghton County, 1887 to date. (Available at the County Clerk's Office, Houghton, Michigan.)

Appraisal of Mining Properties of Michigan by the State Board of Tax Commissioners. Lansing, Mich.: Wynkoop Hallenbeck Crawford Company, 1911.

Bainbridge, Seymour, and Rathbone (Mining Engineers). *Report of the Belt Copper Mines*. London: James Wall Co., 1882.

Broughton, Samuel H. *Remarks on the Mining Interests and Details of the Geology of Ontonagon County, December, 1859*. Philadelphia: King and Baird, Printers, 1863.

Copper Country Commercial Club. *Strike Investigation*. Chicago: M. A. Donohue & Company, 1913.

Copper Country Committee for Economic Development. *Report on Economic Surveys in Houghton and Keweenaw Counties of Michigan.* Houghton, August 18, 1945.

Fleischmann, Charles L. *Portage Mine on Keweenaw Point, Lake Superior — Report of an Examination of the Mine Made During the Summer of 1859.* New York: G. B. Taubner, printer, 1859.

Houghton County Steering Committee. *An Invitation to the United States Veterans Administration to Locate the Upper Peninsula 500-Bed General Veterans Hospital in Houghton, Michigan.* Houghton, Michigan, May, 1945.

An Original Shareholder. *A Brief Account of the Lake Superior Copper Companies.* Boston: S. N. Dickinson Co., 1845.

Reports of the various mining companies. (The Keweenaw Historical Collection at Houghton, Michigan, and the Geological Files of the Calumet and Hecla Consolidated Copper Company at Calumet, Michigan, contain large collections of mining company reports dating back to 1845.)

Statement, Statistics, and Other Pertinent Material Bearing on the Welfare and Relief Problem in Houghton County, Submitted on Behalf of the Board of Supervisors of Houghton County to the State Social Welfare Commission. August 29, 1940.

Stevenson Corporation. *Industrial Survey of Houghton, Keweenaw, and Baraga Counties.* Hancock, Michigan: Chambers of Commerce of Houghton, Hancock, Calumet, and Lake Linden, no date (probably 1921).

GOVERNMENT PUBLICATIONS

Aldrich, Nelson W. *Report on Wholesale Prices, Wages, and Transportation.* 52 Cong., 2 Sess., Senate Report No. 1934. 4 parts. Washington, 1893.

Butler, B. S., Burbank, W. S., et al. *The Copper Deposits of Michigan,* U. S. Geological Survey, Professional Paper 144. Washington, 1929.

Foster, John W. and J. D. Whitney. *Report on the Geology and Topography of a Portion of the Lake Superior Land District in the State of Michigan.* Part I, "Copper Lands." Washington, 1850.

Gardner, Eugene D., et al. *Copper Mining in North America.* United States Bureau of Mines, Bulletin No. 405. Washington, 1938.

Hopper, Walter E. "The Michigan Copper Industry in 1914," *Mineral Resources of Michigan.* Michigan Geological and Biological Survey, Publication 19, Geological Series 16. Lansing, Mich., 1915.

Hore, R. E. "Michigan Copper Deposits," *Mineral Resources of Michigan.* Michigan Geological and Biological Survey, Publication 19, Geological Series 16. Lansing: Wynkoop Hallenbeck Crawford Company, 1915. Pp. 21–161 and pp. 203–220.

Jackson, Charles T. *Report on the Geological and Mineralogical Survey of the Mineral Lands of the United States in the State of Michigan.* 31 Cong., 1 Sess., Senate Executive Documents. Washington, 1849.

Leong, Y. S., et al. *Technology, Employment, and Output Per Man in Copper Mining.* Report No. E-12, Works Projects Administration, National Research Project. Philadelphia, 1940.

Michigan, Secretary of State. *Census of Michigan.* (First volume published in 1854; discontinued in 1904.)

Pardee, F. G. Part I: "Metallic Minerals," *Mineral Resources of Michigan.* Michigan, Department of Conservation. Michigan Geological Survey Division, Publication 37, Geological Series 31. Lansing, 1928. Pp. 5–58.

Public Acts of the State of Michigan. Compiled by the Secretary of State of Michigan. Lansing, various dates, 1845 to date.

U.S. Bureau of the Census. Volumes on *Population.*

U.S. Bureau of Mines. *Mining Methods and Practices in the Michigan Copper Mines.* Washington, 1929.

——— Volumes on *Mines and Quarries and the Mineral Industry.*

U.S. Congress, House. Committee on Mines and Mining. *Conditions in Copper Mines of Michigan.* Hearings before subcommittee pursuant to House Resolution 387. 63 Cong. 7 parts. 1914.

——— *Report of the Tariff Commission, appointed under Act of Congress, Approved May 15, 1882.* Misc. House Document Six. 47 Cong., 2 Sess. Washington, 1883.

U.S. Congress, Senate. Committee on Education and Labor. *Strike in the Copper Mining District of Michigan.* Senate Document No. 381. Report of the Department of Labor. 63 Cong., 2 Sess. Washington, 1914.

——— *Hearings before the Subcommittee on Mining and Minerals Industry of the Special Committee to Study and Survey Problems of Small Business Enterprise* [held at Helena, Montana, August, 1945]. 79 Cong., 1 Sess. Washington, 1945.

——— Reports of the Immigration Commission. Senate Document No. 633, Part 17. *Copper Mining and Smelting.* 61 Cong., 2 Sess. Washington, 1911.

——— Special Committee to Study and Survey Problems of American Small Business. *Survey of the Nation's Critical and Strategic Minerals and Metals Program,* Preliminary Report of the Subcommittee on Mining and Minerals Industry. Senate Subcommittee Print No. 6. 78 Cong., 2 Sess. Washington, 1944.

——— Special Committee to Study and Survey Problems of American Small Business. *Premium Price Plan for Copper, Lead, and Zinc,* Report of the Subcommittee on Mining and Minerals Industry. Senate Subcommittee, Print No. 8. 79 Cong., 2 Sess. Washington, 1946.

U.S. Department of the Interior, Bureau of Mines. *The Minerals Yearbook,* sections on copper. (Before 1932 this series was called *Mineral Resources of the United States;* the first volume was published in 1883.) Washington, annual.

U.S. Department of Labor, Bureau of Labor Statistics. *Wage Structure of the Non-Ferrous Metals Industry.* Bulletin No. 729. Washington, 1943.

U.S. Department of Labor, Bureau of Labor Statistics. *Wages in the Non-Ferrous Metals Industry — June, 1943.* Bulletin No. 765. Washington, 1944.

U.S. Federal Trade Commission. Cost Reports. *Copper.* Washington, 1919.

——— *Report on the Copper Industry — Summary.* Washington, March 11, 1947.

——— *Report on the Copper Industry*. Part I, *The Copper Industry of the United States and International Cartels*. Washington, 1947. Part II, *Control by the Three Dominant Companies*. Not yet available.

U.S. National Recovery Administration. *Codes of Fair Competition*. Vol. IX, approved code No. 401. Washington, 1934.

U.S. National War Labor Board. *Report of Proceedings of the National War Labor Board Hearings at Denver, Colorado*, March, 1943.

U.S. Social Security Board. "Employment, Payrolls, Hours and Earnings in Copper Mining." Continuous study distributed from time to time in mimeographed form.

U.S. Tariff Commission. *Report to the United States Senate on Copper*. Report No. 29. Washington, 1932.

U.S. Temporary National Economic Committee. Investigation of Concentration of Economic Power, Hearings, 76 Cong., Part 25, *Cartels*, Washington, 1940.

U.S. War Department, Corps of Engineers, Office of the District Engineer, Detroit District. "Statistical Report of Lake Commerce Passing Through Canals at Sault Ste. Marie." Detroit, 1940 (mimeographed).

U.S. War Production Board. *Wartime Production Achievements and the Reconversion Outlook*. Report of the Chairman, October 9, 1945. Washington, 1945.

UNPUBLISHED MATERIAL

Gordon, Spencer R., and Associates. "Public Relief in Three Michigan Counties." University of Michigan, 1940 (mimeographed).

Michigan Council of Defense. "Michigan Copper Survey, August, 1941," prepared for the Honorable Murray D. Van Wagoner, Governor of Michigan (mimeographed).

Pettengill, Robert B. "United States Foreign Trade in Copper." Ph.D. dissertation, Department of Economics, Stanford University, 1934.

Taylor, John Wills. "Reservation and Leasing of the Salines, Lead and Copper Mines of the Public Domain." Ph.D. dissertation, Department of History, University of Chicago, 1930.

Glossary of Mining Terms

AIR-BLAST. A violent blast due to the escape of air compressed by the settling of the upper workings of a deep mine.

AMYGDALOID. A rock of igneous origin which, in the case of the Michigan copper district, sometimes contains pure metal in the amygdules — or almond-shaped cavities.

BARREL WORK. Copper in small masses, detached from its rock matrices at the rock house, and shipped in barrels direct to the smelter.

BUDDLE. Inclined trough used in the process of washing to eliminate waste materials.

CONCENTRATE. The concentrated ore or metal after elimination of gangue rock — at Lake Superior the product of the mills, before smelting.

CONGLOMERATE. A pudding-stone rock which, in the case of the Michigan copper district, was often cemented together with pure copper metal.

DISSEMINATED. Ore or metal found scattered through a gangue of valueless rock.

DRIFT. A horizontal opening in a mine, following the direction of the lode or vein.

ELECTROLYTIC COPPER. Copper gained from impure metal by electrical decomposition and redeposit, whereby the copper is taken from an impure bar and redeposited in a pure form at the opposite pole of the battery, while other metals are precipitated to the bottom of the tank in which the work is done.

GANGUE. The particles of rock matter adhering to disseminated ores or native metal; the gangue rock is mechanically united with the ore or metal.

HORSE WHIM. A windlass operated by horsepower.

JIG. A machine for concentrating ore or mineral by means of oscillatory or vibrating motion, aided by jets of water, separation of the mineral from the gangue being effected by greater specific gravity of the former.

GLOSSARY OF MINING TERMS

KIBBLE. A bucket used for hoisting material in a shaft.

KEEVE. A tub used in the process of washing to eliminate waste material.

MAN-CAR. A skip-truck having tiers of circus seats, used for carrying miners to and from work in mines operating inclined shafts.

MAN-ENGINE. An appliance for raising and lowering miners in deep shafts. Consists essentially of two long beams, worked in counterbalance and having platforms at short intervals. (The men step back and forth.)

MASS. A solid piece of native or pure copper, weighing 100 pounds or more, embedded in a rock matrix.

MINERAL. The product of the stamp mill, or a concentrate, ready to be shipped to the smelter for final elimination of nonmetallic materials.

OPEN-CUT. A mine worked as a quarry without underground openings.

REVERBERATORY FURNACE. A smelting furnace in which the flame from the grate is reflected back on the charge of ore or mineral by the roof.

SANDS. Tailings (refuse matter) from the stamp mills.

SKIP. An iron box, open at the top, running on four wheels and hauled by a cable. Used in inclined shafts for hoisting rock and lowering timber and other mining supplies.

SLAG. The vitreous refuse matter from a smelting furnace.

SLIME. Exceedingly small particles of rock and mineral held in suspension in water.

STOPE. The excavation above a drift, or the pay rock remaining above a drift.

TAILINGS. Refuse matter from a stamp mill.

TIE. A launder or sluice used in the washing of mineral to eliminate waste.

TRAM CAR. A car running underground on light T-rails, used for carrying rock from the stopes and other openings to the shafts.

(The source for most of these definitions is Horace J. Stevens, *The Copper Handbook* [Houghton, Michigan, 1904], IV, 72–96.)

INDEX

INDEX

INDEX

Adams properties, 42
Administration, of mines, 36–38; problems, 141; confusion, 176
Adventure Mine, 66, 70
Africa, production from, 148, 151, 158
Agassiz, Alexander, 41, 44, 50, 115; on Calumet and Hecla lode, 57; on railroads, 60–61; on expenses, 91; on strikes, 113, 114
Agassiz, Rudolph, 150
Age distribution in mining companies, 106, 166–167
Agent (superintendent at mine), functions and duties, 35–36
Aging of mining fields, 154
Agriculture, growth, 168
Ahmeek Mine, Bigelow interest, 73; production increases, 117; Calumet and Hecla holdings, 123, 152; improvements, 152, 162
Air blasts, 90
Aldrich, Senator Nelson W., 82, 101
Allouez Mine, 55, 56, 110; depths, 56; transportation, 61; control, 71, 152; production increases, 117
Amalgamated Copper Company, 76, 85–89
American Federation of Labor, 130
American Producers' Association (1892), 83
American Smelting and Refining Company, 139
Amygdaloid Mine, depths, 56; nationality of employees, 95, 97; Calumet and Hecla ownership, 122, 124
Amygdaloid rock, deposits, 8; shift to, 25; mining, 55; yield, 90; adaptation of conglomerate processes, 152
Anaconda Copper Company, 77, 80, 85, 150; attitude on associations, 81–85; production, 83, 157, 158; depths,
90; by-products, 92; contraction of reserves, 182
Anti-trust agitation, 89
Anti-trust laws, 84
Anti-unionism, 136
Arcadian Consolidated Copper Company, 71, 87, 125
Arizona, competitors, 51; copper production, 52, 83; freight costs, 63; mines, 77, 81; inferiority over Michigan copper, 91; new fields, 119; interest in tariff protection, 151
Arizona Tariff Commission, 53
Armed forces, labor needs, 135–136; release of miners, 174
Arnold, H. Tracy, 41
Assessment system, in issuing of stock, 10, 31, 33–35
Atlantic Mining Company, 42, 56, 57, 66, 71, 74, 75, 110, 114, 124
Australia, imports from, 7, 82

"Bal surgeons," 104
Baltic (or South Range) lode, 65, 72, 75; discovery and yield, 90
Baltic Mining Company, 72, 74; control, 72; strikes, 114; acquisition by Copper Range, 124; haulage improvements, 126
Baltimore, smelters, 28, 48; electrolytic plants, 52
Benedict, C. H., 127
Bessemer process, 92, 189
Bigelow, Albert S., 71
Bigelow, Horatio, 34
Bigelow interests, 70, 73, 122; merger of properties, 121; anti-trust activities, 122–123
Bigelow-Lewisohn group, 72, 86, 87
Bingham, Utah, 89
Bisbee, Arizona, 89

INDEX

Blasting, early, 4; improvements, 24, 58
Board of Mediation, 134-135
Boston, mineral shipments to, 3; smelting, 28; chief early market, 35
Boston and Montana Mine, 71, 83, 90
Boston Stock Exchange, 32
Brussels, cartel headquarters, 148, 149
Buffalo, mineral shipments to, 3; freight rates, 62; smelting, 73
Butte, freight rates, 63; effectiveness of miners, 128; wage attractions, 130; labor troubles, 136
Butte and Boston Mine, 71, 83
By-products, of western copper mining, 92; importance, 147

California copper industry, 18, 46
California gold boom, 95
Calumet and Hecla, technological developments of, 27, 57, 59, 61, 67, 68, 125-127, 153, 162; properties, 40-41, 69-70, 73, 85-89, 123, 184; information and financing, 42, 43-45, 71, 119, 145-146, 151-152, 165; production, 45, 66, 83, 90, 116-117, 150, 160, 171, 178, 180; pool activities, 48-51, 79; depths and reserves, 56-57, 89, 183; employment and labor relations problems, 60, 109-115, 130-135, 155, 162, 171, 186; fires, 75, 114, 192; price-fixing activity, 77, 78; use of "C. & H." brand name, 81; association activity, 81-84, 149; failure to invest in western properties, 90, 91; integration problems, 121-124; cost studies, 141-142; signs of maturity, 143; prospecting exploration, 144, 165; attitude on tariff, 151; formation of Calumet and Hecla Consolidated Copper Company, 152; on vertical integration, 156; NRA relations, 161; selective mining, 163; scrap metal enterprises, 170, 178, 184; Premium Price Plan operations, 177, 182; new enterprises, 184-185
Calumet and Hecla Consolidated Copper Company, 152-192 *passim*. See also Calumet and Hecla
Calumet and Hecla Mining Company, 27-152 *passim*. See also Calumet and Hecla
Calumet conglomerate lode, 12-13, 34, 40, 55, 66, 119; copper content, 57; decline of production, 90
Calumet, Michigan, compared with Detroit wages, 137
Calumet township, 110, 112
Canada, low-cost production, 150-151; discovery of new copper deposits, 157
Canal, development, 19, 60
Capital, disinvestment, 119; unavailability, 147; reallocation, 155-156; easy supply, 189; heavy need, 191
Capital rationing, growth, 38, 69
Capital shift, beginning of, 164-165
Cartel, 148-149, 159, 160. See also Pool
Ceilings (price), raised, 181
Central Mine, 22-23; depths, 24; smelting, 28; dividends, 44; production, 56; control, 71
Champion Copper Company, 72, 152, 161; production, 117; acquisition by Copper Range, 162; selective mining, 163; declining yield, 180
Chicago and Northwestern Railroad, 62
Chicago, Milwaukee, and St. Paul Railroad, 72
Chicago, shipping to, 22, 35, 62
Chile, imports from, 3, 7, 10, 148, 151, 175
Chile bar contracts, 51, 52, 76
Churches, 104, 110, 111
Citizens' Alliance, 134, 136

Civil War, 8, 10, 13, 15, 27; transportation improvements during, 19, 20; technological changes after, 30; financial ethics during, 37; effect on prices, 39; labor shortage, 97, 98; effect on wages, 100; effect on community life, 105
Clapp, Channing, 64, 76, 77, 78, 81
Clark, Joseph W., 71
Cleveland, shipping monopoly, 19, 20, 62; smelting, 28, 29, 43
Cliff Mine, 11, 12, 34, 35; production, 14, 16; freight costs, 23; depths, 24; technology, 25, 28, 30; assessments, 33; first C.O.D. sales, 36; bad management, 37; decline, 43, 56; labor problems, 97; silver finds, 100
Clifton district, New Mexico, 63
Coal, use for fuel, 27–28; delivery and cost of, 28, 29, 151; pulverizing, 152
Code, NRA, 159
Collapse (1929), 157
Collective action, repression, 113
Commission selling, 36
Commission smelting, 35
Communities, 103–104, 189
Community life, 103–104; pattern, 109–112; company policies, 131; influence of depression, 166–169
Company unions, 114, 171
Competition, 91–92, 120
Concentration of control, 121–125
Confederate privateers, 15
Conglomerate rock, 8, 90
Congress. See U. S. Congress
Congress of Industrial Organization, 171–172
Connecticut influence, 7, 72
Conservation, 182–183
Conservatism, in operations, 69, 189
Consolidation of properties, 41–42, 70–71; lack of, 120; effect, 144; progress, 162
Construction expenditures, 119

Consumption, increases, 76
Contract wage system, 98–99; effects, 131; change, 153
Controls, Michigan stake in, 149–151; intensification of, 157–159; Michigan benefits from, 159–161; system of, 160
Conversion to other enterprises, 184–185
Copper and Brass Research Association, 150
Copper content of ore, 146
Copper Country, exploration and early surveys, 1–3; description of, 1, 8, 9
Copper deposits, location, discovery and nature, 1, 12–13, 65, 117, 122, 144, 188, 190
Copper Exporters Association, Inc., 148–149, 151
Copper Exporters, Inc., 149; international cartel formed, 151; price maintenance, 157; collapse, 158
Copper Falls Mining Co., 9, 34, 41, 57
Copper Handbook for 1911, 108
Copper Institute, 149
Copper mineral, 5
Copper Miners, Association of, 85
Copper mines, Maine and Vermont, 95
Copper Price Commission, 172
Copper Producers' Committee, 138
Copper Queen Mine, 83
Copper Range Consolidated Company, 72; acquisition of other properties, 124, 152, 162, 165; strikebreaking activities, 133; production, 150, 161, 171; 1923 Annual Report, 151; improvements, 162; labor elections, 171; Metals Reserve Company purchases, 172; special contracts, 177; exhaustion of Champion Mine, 180; closing, 180; White Pine property in Ontonagon County, 183–184; continual land purchase, 184; fabri-

cation plant and electric power development, 185
Copper Range Railroad Company, 72
Copper tariff of 1869, 53
Cornwall mines, 4–5, 7
Cornish labor, 95
Corporations, use and development, 9, 31–32
Cost of living, western, 94
Cost-plus technique, 142, 179
Cost-price plateau, adjustment to, 151–155
Cost reduction, need of, 30; studies in, 120–128, 139
Costs, rapid rise, 179
Crisis of 1907, 118
Cuba, ore from, 4
Currency, little use at mines, 101
Curtailment of production, national and international attempts, 143, 148

Daly, Marcus, of Anaconda, 86
Darrow, Clarence, 133
Death benefits, 109
Depletion reserves, 119
Depression, impact of, 143, 146, 157–169
Depths of mines, 24–25, 56–57, 66, 89–90, 146, 191
Detroit, shipping monopoly of, 19, 20, 62; smelting, 28, 29, 43; labor competition, 129, 135, 136, 137, 155
Detroit and Lake Superior Copper Company, 43, 72, 73
Detroit and Waterbury Copper Smelting Works, 28
Disability benefits, 109
Discoveries. *See* Copper deposits
Diversification, drive for, 169
Dividends, early record of, 10; during Civil War, 15; fluctuations of, 33, 65; development of, 75, 80; peak, 116–118; decline, 145–146; contribution to capital shift, 165; World War II, 171
Draft, effect on labor, 97–98
Drilling, developments, 4, 24, 57–58, 125–126, 152
Dumping abroad, efficacy of, 47
Duties, import, 158

East, producers in, 7
Eastern Exploration Company, 165
Economic survey of copper area, 185
Electric industry, expansion, 76, 118
Electrolytic copper, price, 88; comparison with lake copper, 91; rise of, 123; refining, 52, 73, 92, 189
Ely, Nevada, 89
Emigration, to Canada, 97; beginnings, 129; rise, 136, 166, 171, 186; effects of, 167, 179
Employees' Aid Fund, 109
Employment, summary of, vii; growth, 96–98, 105–106, 116; categories, 102; diversification, 110; insecurity, 113; decline, 145, 155, 160, 171; poor prospects for, 185–186. *See also* Labor
Engineering and Mining Journal, quoted, 49, 63, 106
England, labor from, 95
European Producers Association, 83
Excess profits taxes, 176
Exhaust steam, use of, 127, 152–153
Exhaustion of mines, 146, 160
Expansion costs, 69
Exploitation, 69, 184, 189
Exploration. *See* Copper Country
Exploratory work, 165, 183, 185
Explosions, 103
Explosives, 57–58
Exports, early data on, 9–10; balance of, 45, 150, 173; increase in, 47, 158; quotas, 50, 148

Fabrication, shift to, 156, 165, 170

INDEX

Financial interest groups, 71–72
Financial operations, early difficulty, 10–11, 32–35
Finnish immigrants, 93, 113, 130
Fires, mine, 75, 78, 90
Flotation plants, installment, 127, 153
Food products industry, 186
Foreign-born, decline of, 128
Foreign sales, negotiations for, 49
France, 50, 95
Franklin Mine, opening, 14; technological improvements at, 26, 57; control and operation, 33, 35, 37, 40–41, 125; increases in production, 66; concentration of labor, 110
Freight costs, 23, 61–63, 93, 151
Froebel system of kindergartens, 112
Frontier conditions, elimination of, 107
Fuel, 27–28, 152. *See also* Coal

Garment manufacturing, prospects in mining country for, 186
Geologists, employment of, 91
Geology, knowledge of, 24, 42, 190
Germans, as laborers, 93, 95
"Giant powder," 58
Gold, as by-product, 92
Gold mining, 165, 174
Goldfield Mining Company, Nevada, 165
Government. *See* U. S. Government
Great Lakes waterway, 9, 61
Greeley, Horace, on hours of labor, 102
Green Bay, Wisconsin, 21
Grievances, 113, 132. *See also* Labor
"Gutting," 40

Haggin, James B., President of Anaconda, 80; pool activities of, 81–85, 91
Hancock, roads to, 21; smelting at, 28, 43, 61; shipping at, 61
Harbor improvements, 20, 61

Harshaw Chemical Company of Cleveland, 184
Haulage, 67, 126
Health insurance, 104, 111
Hecla and Torch Lake Railroad, 61
Henry, Alexander, 1
Higginson, Henry Lee, 44
Hoisting, 24–25, 59, 68
Holmes and Lissberger, bankruptcy, 48
Hopkins, Harry, 167
Hospitals, 104, 111
Houghton, Douglass, 2
Houghton, Michigan, 21, 61
Houghton County, 1; discoveries in, 12; smelting for, 43; concentration of mining, 56; employment and population conditions, 106, 164, 167, 186–187; Board of Supervisors, 111, 132, 168
Hours of work, 101–103, 107. *See also* Labor
Housing, 103–104, 110
Howe, Thomas M., 34
Hulbert, Edwin J., 13
Huron Mine, 27, 34, 41
Hussey, Dr. C. G., 28, 29, 34, 37
Hussey, C. G., Company, 165
Hussey-Howe group, 34, 43
Hydroelectric plant at Victoria, Michigan, 162

Immigration, importance of, 9, 94, 96; rate of, 106–107; encouragement of, 107; cause of labor troubles, 113–114; peak of, 128; value of, 189. *See also* Labor
Immigration laws, effect on labor costs, 156
Imports, effect on prices, 39; increase of, 174; deficit, 181
Incentive wages, 9, 94, 99
Incorporation, regulations, 31
India, scrap from, 80
Indians, discovery of copper, 1–2

Industrial relations, 134
Industry, diversification, 167
Inflation, effect on labor, 98, 105
Information, exchange, 159
Innovations in processes, 191
Integration, need of, 124, 151, 153
Interior, Department of the, on subsidy, 183
Interlocking directorates, 33
International agreement, 158
International Union of Mine, Mill, and Smelter Workers, C. I. O., 171–172, 182
International Workers of the World, 130, 136, 138
Inventions, 191
Irish laborers, 93, 95
Iron Age, 54, 135
Iron country, Upper Superior, 61, 107, 115, 129, 156
Iron miners, 101, 109
Ishpeming Gold Mining Company, 165
Isle Royale Copper Company, 24, 41, 57; establishment, 66, 70; Bigelow control, 73; success, 71; production, 117, 171; Calumet and Hecla holdings, 123; difficulties, 144; Metals Reserve Company purchases, 172; special contracts, 177; average daily wages, 179

Johnson, President Andrew, 39, 46
Joint management, savings from, 74

Kearsarge amygdaloid lode, 65
Kearsage Mine, control of, 70, 71; production, 83
Kennecott Copper Company, 150; reductions, 157, 158; exports curtailed, 159; control of reserves, 182
Keweenaw County, 1, 3; discoveries, 12, 13; roads to, 21; dams, 26; smelting for, 43; Mohawk Mine, 65; population trends, 167

Keweenaw Peninsula, 1, 61
Knights of Labor, 114

Labor, shortages, 9, 16–17, 75, 113, 128, 129, 179; sources and supply, 9, 94–96, 164–165, 174, 189; costs, 23, 29, 92, 127–128, 151, 179; productivity, 67, 163; mobility, 96, 98, 156; hours, 101–102; categories, 102; organization and repression, 112–115, 116, 130–132, 135, 171–172; reallocation, 141, 155–156; layoffs, 162–163; freezing of, 174; problems, 179–180. See also Emigration, Employment, Immigration, Living Conditions, Strikes, Unionism, Wages, Working conditions
Labor relations, 115
Labor saboteurs, 114
Labor saving, progress, 30, 135
Lac la Belle, 29, 61
Ladders, use of, 25, 58, 103
Lake agreements, 46–54
Lake Chemical Company, 184
Lake copper, 88, 91
Lake Superior, transportation on, 18–19
Lake Superior Copper Company, 95
Lake Superior Smelting Company, 73
Land, rental, 184, 186
Land laws, development, 6
Land purchases, 70–71, 111, 184
Language barriers, 107, 115
Law enforcement, company control, 104
Laws, general mining, 31. See also Land laws; Michigan, State of; U. S. Congress
Lawson, Thomas, 85–89
Lead lands, leasing, 3
Lead mines, Wisconsin, 3, 94–95; Maine and Vermont, 95
Leases, War Department, 3, 6
Lee-Higginson Company, 44

INDEX

Leighton, John, 41
Lewis, John L., 133
Lewisohn, Leonard, 71, 77, 78, 80, 81, 84, 86-89, 161
Lighting, electricity for, 68
Liquor, in frontier camps, 104
Livermore, Colonel Thomas L., 81, 82, 85-89, 91
Living conditions, 103
Living costs, 110
Loading, mechanical devices, 152
Locomotives, use of, 26, 67, 126
London, market, 8, 39, 51, 52; metal exchange, 148
Lumber industry, Michigan, 185
Lumber operations, growth, 168

Mabbs, John, 58
Machinery, early repairs, 28
Mackinac, Straits of, 63
MacNaughton, James, 156
Mails, early service, 21
Maine, shipbuilders, 46; copper and lead mines, 95
Management, conservatism, 189. *See also* Administration, Corporations
Man-engines, 5, 25, 58
Manpower shortage, 98, 176
Manufacturing plants, dearth of, 168-169, 186
Market values, of copper, 145-146
Markets, early, 35. *See also* Cartel, Pool, Sales
Marquette, Houghton, and Ontonagon Railroad, 62-63
Marquette Iron Country, 22
Maryland, producers, 7
Mason, Thomas F., 34
Mason-Perkins group, 34
Mass copper, 5, 14
Mass Mine, 66, 70
Mass production methods, 60, 111
Maturity, signs, 89, 90, 116, 192
Mechanization of mines, 60

Mellen Ward and Company, 41
Mesabi iron range, Minnesota, 136
Metallurgy, 92, 154
Metals Reserve Company, purchases, 172; special contracts, 177, 179, 180; aid to Quincy reclamation plant, 178
Michigan Act, 84
Michigan College of Mining, 162
Michigan copper, output and statistics, 89; comparison with Western, 91-92
Michigan iron country, 94
Michigan Mine, 66, 70, 71
Michigan Smelting Company, 72-73
Michigan, Legislature, acts affecting copper, 2, 20, 21, 31-32, 34, 41, 42, 45, 50, 63, 131-135, 161
Michigan, State of, survey by, 3; poor road building, 20; census of 1894, 109-110; governor, 122, 172; attempts to settle strike, 133
Michigan, State Social Welfare Commission, 168
Middle West, consumption of copper, 150-151
Middle West Utilities Company, 162
Mill recovery, slow progress, 27
Milling, cost, 23
Milling technology, progress, 68, 125-127
Mine Emigrant Society, 97
Mine managers, attitudes of, 132-133
Mines and Minerals, House Committee on, 21
Mineral Agency, 3
Mineral Range Railroad, 43, 61
Miners, behavior and description, 98
Minesota lode, discovery, 12
Minesota Mine, production, 14, 16; freight costs, 23; depths, 24; technological improvement, 25, 27; use of assessment system, 33; management, 35, 37; decline, 56; Germans at, 95; wages, 100
Minimum wage, 132, 161, 165

Mining, early methods, 4-5
Mining Magazine, 98
Minnesota iron fields, wage increases, 129; labor shortage, 134-135
Mismanagement, mine, 37
Mitchell, John, 133
Mohawk Mine, 65, 71; security prices of, 119; production, 150; exhaustion, 160; Copper Range control, 162
Monopoly, 45, 122, 176. *See also* Cartel, Pool
Montana, copper, 50, 52, 91; mines, 81, 88
Moyer, Charles, 134
Murdoch, Angus, 88, 93, 94, 111-112, 115

National Guard, strike duty, 132
NLRB elections, 171-172
National Mine, 34, 36, 56, 97, 100
NRA, legalized combinations under, 158, 160, 161, 165
National Resources Development Bill, 182
Nationality barriers, 115
Nativity, of laborers, 94-96
Navigation, difficulties, 4
Navy Department, contract with Pewabic, 35
Nevada, new fields, 119
New Deal, controls, 182
New Mexico, new fields, 119
New York, market for copper, 35; pool meeting at, 46; freight cost to, 62, 63
Nickel mining, copper content, 157
Nitroglycerin, 24, 58
Nobel, Alfred, 24
Noetzel, B. D., 182-183
North American Mine, 25
Northwestern Mining Company, 35

Obsolescence, high rate, 67

OPA, 173, 181
Oil flotation process, 189
Old Dominion Mine (Globe, Arizona), 71
Old-age retirement plans, 111
Ontonagon, port, 19; roads to, 20, 21; dams, 26; smelting, 29; harbor improvements, 61
Ontonagon County, 1, 12, 13; decline of mines, 43; labor problems during Civil War, 97
Operations, integration of, 121-125
Osceola Consolidated Copper Company, 44, 51, 56, 61, 74; dividends, 44; organization, 55; depths, 56; technological improvements, 58; production, 66, 83, 116-117; acquisition of properties, 70, 121; control by Bigelow interests, 71, 73; expenditures, 75; attitude on Syndicate, 79; Calumet and Hecla acquisitions, 122-123, 152
Overexpansion, 146
Overproduction, problems, 147-149, 157-159
Overvaluation of properties, 119
Oxidation in smelting, 29

Paine, William A., 71-72
Paine-Stanton group, 72
Paine-Webber Company, 71
Paris, meeting after collapse of Syndicate, 80
Paternalism, 94, 109, 115, 189-190; benefits, 131; evils, 134; impact on labor costs, 190
Perkins, T. Henry, 34
Permits, early mining, 3, 6
Peru, imports from, 7
Pewabic amygdaloid lode, 12, 14
Pewabic Mine, depths, 24, 56; technological improvements, 25, 57; control and operation, 35, 40-41, 42, 70, 90

Phelps-Dodge Copper Co., 150, 157, 161, 182
Phoenix Mine, 34, 61, 66, 70, 71
Pioneer miners, 96
Pittsburgh, smelting, 29, 36, 43
Plant expansion, 65
Pool, formation and operation, 46–54; breakup, 76; formed by Syndicate, 79
Pool-tariff-dumping arrangement, 52–53
Population, growth, 96–98; 105–106, 167; decline, 166–167; present trends, 186–187
Porphyry mines, western, 120, 127
Portage Lake, 12, 61
Portage Lake amygdaloids, 13
Portage Lake and Lake Superior Ship Canal, 61–62
Portage Lake Mining Gazette, 20, 21, 24, 27, 35, 40, 58, 62, 97, 102, 103, 105, 113
Portage Lake Smelting Works, 28, 29, 43, 97
Positive lag relationship, 191
Precious metals, as a by-product, 147, 154
Premium Price Plan, 173–177, 180–182
President of the U. S., 1, 6; signed tariff suspension, 181; veto of subsidy bill, 183
Price control, by companies, 109; by government, 136, 138, 139, 140–141, 143, 173, 174, 181
Price differential, 47
Price Fixing Committee, 139, 141
Price movements, 15, 16, 39–40, 54–55, 65, 74–76, 91, 138, 181, 182
Price war, western fields, 48
Prices, effect of, 118, 146, 191–192
Priorities, 176
Producers' associations, 42, 81–85
Production, world, vii, 64, 79, 118; rate of, 9–10, 13–14, 16, 18, 39–40, 53, 60, 64, 65–66, 75, 116–117, 143–145, 171, 182; taxes, 32; restriction, 53, 82, 147–149, 182; exchange of data, 83–84; encouragement by Premium Price Plan, 173; war economy, 177–179
Production-price relationships, 14
Productivity of labor, 56. *See also* Labor
Profits, 140, 141, 174, 176. *See also* Dividends
Property development, 55–56
Prospecting, 4, 140, 144. *See also* Copper Country
Protective tariff, 8, 28, 41–42, 45–46, 150, 151, 160, 161, 181
Public assistance, Houghton County, 164

Quincy Mine, 14, 15, 34, 108; technological developments, 25, 26, 57, 59, 67, 69, 73, 75, 126; financial affairs, 33, 35, 37, 44, 51; court victory over pool, 51–52; depths, 56, 89; production, 66, 72, 83, 116–117, 150, 171; acquisition of properties, 70, 125; independence, 71; labor relations, 109, 114, 133, 171; difficulties, 144; Metals Reserve Company, 172, 178, 180; special contracts, 177; closing, 180
Quotas, NRA, 159; Premium Price Plan, 173; method questioned, 175; revisions, 176

Radicalism, fear of, 131, 136
Railroads, development, 19, 21–22; extension, 53–54, 60–63, 153; ownership, 73
Rand air compressor, 58
Reassessment of properties, 119
Recession (1949), 186
Reciprocal trade agreements, 182

Reclamation, development, 126–127, 145, 154, 160, 162
Red Jacket shaft, 67, 89
Regulation of mining, 31–32
Reimportation, 48–49, 77
Relief, heavy burden of, 162, 167
Rent of housing, 110, 111
Reports, annual, 22, 50
Republic Steel Company, 185
Reserves, known, 182, 184–185
Resources, national, 182–183
Retrenchments, mine, 40
Rhodesia, new deposits, 157
Rio Tinto Company, 81, 85, 88
Rioting, 132
Roads, need and development, 20–21
Rock cars, 26
Rock sorting, underground, 153
Rockefeller, William, 85, 86, 87
Rogers, Henry H., 85–88
Rothschilds, London, 84, 88; Paris, 79–80
Russell, H. S., 44
Russia, scrap from, 80
Russo-Japanese War, 118

Safety records, 103
St. Mary's Mineral Land Company, 152, 162
Sales, handling, 36, 124; quotas, 148; to consumers only, 159
Sands, retreatment, 127
Sandstone beds, 8
Sault Ste. Marie, 3, 18
Savings, operating, 123–124
Sawmills, investments, 73
Scandinavians, immigration, 97
Schoolcraft, Henry R., 2
Schools, 104, 110, 111
Schooners, early use, 3
Scrap copper, increase in, 8; foreign imports, 79–80; recovery, 146–147, 157, 170, 178, 184
Secretan Syndicate, 78–81

Security prices, decline, 119–120
Selective mining, 145, 153, 155, 163
Selective Pricing, 141, 172
Sellers' market, 118
Shaw, Quincy A., 41, 44, 91
Sheathing, falling demand, 8
Sheet copper, fabrication, 165
Shell and cartridge requirements, 118
Sherman Anti-Trust Act, 82, 122
Shipbuilding, domestic, 7
Shipping monopoly, decline, 20
Shullsburg, Wisconsin, 185
Sick benefits, 109
Sight drafts, 101–102
Silver, presence of, 13, 50, 73, 92, 100
Silver mines, Maine and Vermont, 95
"Silver waifs," 13
Single men, predominance, 103
Skelton, Alex, 143, 151
Skips, use of, 25, 30, 58, 68
Slag, 29
Slimes, 127, 153
Smelting, 28–30, 46, 35; costs, 23; Michigan copper, 29; integration with manufacturing, 72–74; improvements, 153
Smith, Hoval A., tariff study by, 53
Social pattern, 112
Socialism, among Finnish laborers, 130
Société Industrielle et Commerciale des Métaux, 78
South American labor, 46
South Pewabic property, 42
South Range, lode discovered, 65
Spain, imports from, 7
Special census of 1902, 91
"Special contracts," 177, 179, 180
Speculation, 4, 6, 9, 30–38, 119
Springfield (Ohio) *News*, 37
Stabilization, production, 172, 178
Stairs, use at mines, 58
Stamping, progress, 5, 25–26, 59
Standard Oil Company, interest in copper mines, 76, 85–89, 122

INDEX

Stanton, John, 71, 72
Stanton-Gay interests, 71
State legislature. *See* Michigan Legislature
State roads, development, 21
Steam power, application and development, 7, 25, 26, 30, 57, 68, 127
Stevens, Horace, 74, 111
Stock exchanges, eastern, 9
Stockholders, liability, 31
Stock market, collapse, 149
Stocks, issue and fluctuations, 32–35
Street railway system, mine opposition, 115
Strikebreaking, 113–115, 132, 133
Strikes, growth and repression, 113–115; Calumet and Hecla (1913–1914), 119, 126, 130–135; post war, 181
Subsidy, result of pool, 52; program, 52, 174, 178, 180, 183
Sulphide ores, 92
Sulphur, lack of, 9
Superintendents, mine, 36
Superior, Michigan, 13
Surface workers, wages, 99
Surpluses, sales abroad, 53
Surveys, early, 3
Swansea, smelting, 50
Swedish immigrants, strikes of, 113
Swineford, Alfred, 13, 15, 98
Switzerland, labor from, 95
Syndicate, establishment of, 78–81

Tailings, reworking of, 127, 144, 162, 170
Tamarack Junior Mine, purchase and control by Osceola, 70, 71
Tamarack Mining Company, 55, 66, 74; vertical shafts, 67; electricity for lighting, 68; control and financing, 71, 73, 79, 123–124; production, 83, 90, 117; depths, 89

Tariff, iron and steel, 45
Tariff action, U. S. Congress, 158, 182. *See also* Protective tariff
Taussig, Frank William, 1, 53
Tax policy, for rectifying profits, 142
Taxes, state, 21, 32
Teaming, 23, 99
Technology, innovations and developments, 22, 30, 56–60, 67, 125–127, 152–153, 191; difficulties, 190–191. *See also* Blasting, Drilling, Haulage, Hoisting, Loading, Reclamation, Smelting, Stamping, Tramming, Washing
Telegraph lines, 22
"Ten cent copper," 76–78
Tennessee copper producers, 46
Thomas-May Stock Piling Act, 182
Timber lands, investments, 73
Timber sales, 184
Timbering, use in depth mining, 24
Tolls, collection of, 19
Torch Lake, 61, 127
Tourist industry, 168, 184, 186
Trades, increase in mining area, 110
Trammers, 115, 136
Tramming, progress in, 24, 126
Transportation, monopolistic prices, 18–19
Transportation system, need and development, 9, 18, 20, 60–63. *See also* Canal, Freight costs, Railroads, Roads, Shipping, Water transportation
Treasury Department, custody of mineral lands by, 6
Tribute, for waste sands, 27, 40–41
Trimountain Mining Company, 72, 124–125, 152
Trust problem, 82–84
Turbine, low-pressure, 127

Underground expenditures, 23; workers' wages, 99

Unemployment, 155, 171, 186
Union contracts, 171
Union demands, 132
Unionism, 94, 107, 115; repression of, 113–115
United Kingdom, 7
United Metals Selling Company, 85–89, 138
United States consumption of copper, decline, 147
U. S. Bureau of Labor Statistics, 156
U. S. Bureau of Mines, 153
U. S. Census (1910), 128
U. S. Census (1940), 186–187
U. S. Congress, 1, 2, 6, 82; grants for canal, 19; House Committee on Mines and Minerals, 21; joint resolution of Michigan Legislature to, 45; pressure for strike settlement, 133; tariff action, 158, 161, 181; failure to pass new subsidy bill, 183
U. S. Federal Circuit Court, Michigan, 122
U. S. Federal Trade Commission, 138–140, 141, 182, 183
U. S. Geological Survey, 6, 120, 139, 141
U. S. Government, 2; orders and contracts, 15, 35; physical improvements by, 20, 21, 62, 190; disposal of scrap, 40; attempts to settle strike by, 133; ownership discussed, 140; controls, 173–174; reserve stocks exhausted, 181
U. S. Mining Census (1902), 93
U. S. Tariff Commission, 154, 172
Unmanufactured copper, foreign trade in, 47
Uren, Richard, 58
Utah, new fields, 119

Vandenberg, Senator Arthur, 161

Ventilation, 59, 103
Vermont, producers in, 7; copper and lead mines, 95
Vertical integration, 156
Vertical shafts, introduction of, 67
Vessels, ownership, 73
Victoria, Michigan, 162
V-J Day, 181
Violence, in strike, 133
Vitality, mining lack of, 170–171
Volunteering (Civil War), 97

Wadell-Mahon, New York strikebreakers, 133
Wages, differentials, 93, 107, 130–131, 156, 164, 179; rates, in mines, 92, 93, 94, 98–101, 107, 109, 155, 171, 177; problems, 179–180
"War-babies," 17
War Department, 3, 6
War Industries Board, 138, 139
War Labor Board, 177
War Manpower Commission, 174
WPA, 165, 168
WPB, 173
Wartime, prosperity, 117–118, 134; labor shortages, 128–129, 134–138; controls, 138–140, 174, 182; profits, 141–142, 180; surplus stocks, 146; production, 172, 177–179
Washing, new techniques, 26, 27, 59, 68–69
Waste sands, disposal, 26, 27; copper content, 59
Water, milling necessity for, 25–26
Water transportation, system, 11, 18; rates, 19, 23
Waterbury and Detroit Copper Company, 42–43
Webb-Pomerene Act, 148, 149
Western copper mines, advantages, 18, 91–92; speculation, 37; collapse of boom in, 46; Lake Agreements activities of, 51; dominance of, 63, 64;

INDEX

unionization, 115; importance to Michigan, 188
Western Federation of Miners, activities of, 129, 130-134, 136; demands of, 132
Western manufacturers, sales to, 35
Wheat country, Upper Superior, 61
Wholesale Prices, Wages and Transportation, Aldrich Report on, 101
Wilfley concentrators, 68
Winchester drill, 57
Winding engines, introduction of, 25
Winter shipping, 62
Wolverine Copper Company, 66, 71, 162

Wolverine Tube Company, of Detroit, 184
Women, needs for employment of, 186
Wood, for fuel, 27
Working conditions, 103, 109
Workmen's compensation, 131
World production, importance to Michigan mines, 188
World War I, effects on copper mining, 138, 176

Yields, mine, 90

Zinc, mining, 173